HYPNOSIS AT ITS BICENTENNIAL

Selected Papers

Papers chosen from those presented at the Seventh
International Congress of Hypnosis and Psychosomatic Medicine,
Philadelphia, Pennsylvania, July, 1976

HYPNOSIS AT ITS BICENTENNIAL

Selected Papers

Edited by

Fred H. Frankel, M.B.Ch.B., D.P.M.

Department of Psychiatry
Beth Israel Hospital
Harvard Medical School
Boston, Massachusetts

and

Harold S. Zamansky, Ph.D.

Department of Psychology
Northeastern University
Boston, Massachusetts

PLENUM PRESS · NEW YORK AND LONDON

Library of Congress Cataloging in Publication Data

International Congress for Hypnosis and Psychosomatic Medicine, 7th, Philadelphia, 1976.
Hypnosis at its bicentennial.

Includes index.
1. Hypnotism – Therapeutic use – Congresses. 2. Hypnotism – Congresses. I. Frankel, Fred H. II. Zamansky, Harold S. [DNLM: 1. Hypnosis – Congresses. 2. Psychosomatic medicine – Congresses. W3 IN415 7th 1976h / WM415 I612 1976h]
RC490.I5 1976 615'.8512 78-16605

ISBN-13: 978-1-4613-2861-2 e-ISBN-13: 978-1-4613-2859-9
DOI: 10. 1007/978-1-4613-2859-9

Softcover reprint of the hardcover 1st edition 1978

A Division of Plenum Publishing Corporation
227 West 17th Street, New York, N.Y. 10011

To **Ernest R. Hilgard**, Professor of Psychology at Stanford University, distinguished scientist and scholar, whose contributions to the understanding of hypnosis have gone far toward integrating the field into the mainstream of psychology. He has helped to bring together many colleagues with diverse points of view into a strong international society.

Foreword

Since the first International Congress for Experimental and Therapeutic Hypnotism in Paris in 1889, there have been several periods of widespread interest in hypnosis among the professions as well as the lay public, followed by periods of profound neglect. Since the end of World War II, however, we have witnessed not only a strong resurgence of interest in hypnosis throughout the world but also the gradual development of the kind of infrastructure which a field requires to survive and prosper. The burgeoning clinical literature has been matched by a dramatic increase in the amount of systematic research carried out in a wide range of institutions throughout the world. A tradition of triennial major world congresses has been established, beginning with the 3rd International Congress for Hypnosis and Psychosomatic Medicine in Paris in 1965. These meetings, encouraged and sponsored by the International Society of Hypnosis and its predecessor, the International Society of Clinical and Experimental Hypnosis, are sponsored by universities and provide a forum for the exchange of ideas among scientists and clinicians throughout the world.

The recent scientific meetings have been of sufficient import that instead of publishing Proceedings, they have inspired edited volumes based on the most exciting material reported. This volume evolved from the 7th International Congress which met in Philadelphia in 1976. The editors of the volume deserve our thanks not only for selecting outstanding manuscripts but also for helping authors put their material into a format familiar to clinicians and investigators alike. These papers represent the thinking of leaders in the field and reflect a far broader range of ideas toward the understanding of hypnosis and its application to clinical problems than is usually available in any single volume. It is this diversity of views which characterizes meaningful exchange across national boundaries. This, like the volumes inspired by earlier meetings, is a unique collection of manuscripts which makes a permanent contribution to our understanding of hypnosis.

The Philadelphia International Congress of Hypnosis and Psychosomatic Medicine could not have taken place without the concerted effort of a great many colleagues too numerous to acknowledge individually. Special thanks are due to the active cooperation of the two American constituent societies, the American Society of Clinical Hypnosis and the Society for Clinical and Experimental Hypnosis, who made possible the joint meetings. The officers and staff of these societies helped solve the many complex problems which are involved in such a joint meeting. The sponsorship of the University of Pennsylvania and The Institute of Pennsylvania Hospital helped to assure the high quality of the meetings. We are most grateful, however, to the more than 600 colleagues from 19 countries who came to the meetings to share ideas. This volume should provide a permanent record for those of us who were fortunate enough to participate in the meetings and give some feeling of the excitement, novelty, and diversity of the ideas expressed to those who could not be there.

Martin T. Orne M.D., Ph.D.
President,
International Society of Hypnosis

Preface

In the mid 1770's Franz Anton Mesmer introduced his notions regarding animal magnetism to the scientific community. In the ensuing two hundred years the conceptualization of hypnotism, the successor to animal magnetism, has undergone extensive transformation as a result, in part, of increasing experimental and clinical sophistication. The papers in the present volume provide a sampling of several aspects of the theory, research, and practice of hypnosis at the time of its bicentennial.

We have selected papers from among those presented at the 7th International Congress in Philadelphia that reflect differences in interest, methodology, and technique in countries throughout the world. In editing the papers we have tried, where possible, to retain the stylistic characteristics of the individual authors.

The papers are assembled in four categories. In the Historical and Theoretical section are included two papers that deal with the neodissociation view of hypnosis - the most recent and compelling conceptualization of the phenomenon. The paper by Ernest Hilgard was presented at the Congress as the Presidential Address. Also included in this section are two papers that increase our appreciation of two important figures in the history of hypnosis.

The Experimental section surveys the wide variety of experimental interests and methods throughout the world, and includes papers that examine the relationship between hypnosis and such variables as hemispheric asymmetry, primary process functioning, and electrical potentials of the brain. Also included are papers that provide new perspectives on animal hypnosis and self-hypnosis.

The section on Clinical Perspectives and Reports, in addition to reviewing several different clinical orientations, emphasizes some of the similarities between behavioral methods and those of clinical hypnosis. Several papers also underscore the strong impact of these two systems upon each other in contemporary clinical practice.

The last section, Clinical Studies, presents a series of papers on the efficacy of hypnosis in the treatment of a variety of conditions such as migraine, asthma, sexual dysfunction, pain, and anxiety.

F.H.F. and H.S.Z.
Newton, Massachusetts
Spring, 1978

Contents

I: Historical and Theoretical

LISTENING WITH THE THIRD EAR: ON PAYING INATTENTION EFFECTIVELY

Kenneth S. Bowers

University of Waterloo, Canada

Abstract: Dissociation involves the registration of information at a relatively low level of analysis that can influence cognition, affect, or behavior without the information itself being noticed at a higher, conscious level. In psychotherapy, dissociated information may take the form of subtle therapeutic maneuvers that favorably influence a patient without his/her awareness. Milton Erickson is a noteworthy practitioner of such subtle control. In the domain of hypnosis, the talented hypnotic subject's ability to dissociate information tempers and qualifies the recent claims for an absorptive account of hypnosis. It is argued that the high hypnotizable subject's ability to respond to peripheral information in a dissociated manner permits absorption in a focal or primary involvement. Historical and contemporary illustrations are marshalled to support the claims for the importance of dissociation in psychotherapy and hypnosis.

Freud (1959) once told of a patient who was walking down a street and suddenly, inexplicably, broke into tears. Being psychologically-minded, the woman quickly reflected back on her state of mind just prior to the crying jag. Although she had not noticed it at the time of its occurrence, the woman now recalled having been preoccupied with a highly organized and morose daydream in which she had been first seduced, then impregnated, and finally abandoned by a local pianist who in reality did not know her at all. Similarly, Morton Prince (1915) describes various patients who had undergone phobic or hysterical attacks with no conscious memory of their cause. Nevertheless, when his patients were able to suspend willful directed thinking and to achieve what Prince called a state of abstraction about the dysphoric episode, they were often able to retrieve the thoughts and fantasies which immediately preceded their attack. According to Prince, "The recovery of these memories has been always a surprise to the patient who, a moment before, had been utterly unable to recall them, and had declared the attack had developed without cause..." Frequently, the offending ideas were "suggested by a causal and apparently insignificant word in a sentence occurring in a conversation on indifferent matters, or by a dimly conscious perception of (some feature) of the environment (p. 29-30)." Nevertheless, these environmental pebbles, falling on the senses of the unwitting victim, triggered a cognitive avalanche of associated thoughts and images, which remained largely unconscious, mobilizing a great deal of unexplained affect in the process. (See also Janet, 1965, p. 97).

These examples imply several interesting points that should be made explicit. First of all, there seems to be a flow of thoughts, images, and fantasies that can remain unnoticed or unconscious at the time they are occurring, but which can be retrieved under special circumstances. Second, this flow of what Prince (1915) calls coconscious ideation can have a pronounced if inexplicable impact on one's conscious thought, perception, and behavior. Third, this coconscious flow of thoughts and images can be stimulated and modified by environmental features that are not themselves represented in focal consciousness. These notions are of course not new, but I think they have some unrecognized implications for hypnosis and psychotherapy that deserve elucidation.

Before going on to these implications, however, it is important to note that the clinical examples from the writings of Freud and Prince are in no way anomalous or misleading. The clinical literature is replete with such examples, although a great deal of it is buried in the prebehavioristic era recently reviewed so elegantly by Ellenberger (1970). What is new is the extent to which recent experimental literature is beginning to fathom the importance of unconscious determinants of behavior. Let me take a moment and juxtapose the old and the new. Boris Sidis, in 1902, reported on a hysterical lady whom he hypnotized and gave suggestions for anesthesia of the right arm and hand. Predictably, her arm became totally insensitive to pin pricks, and somewhat dysfunctional as well. However, when told to think of a number and pricked with a pin several times in her anesthetized arm, the patient "invariably thought of a number corresponding to the number of pricks made (p. 46)." It was as if the pin pricks qua pain were registered and processed out of conscious awareness; however, their occurrence nevertheless influenced her conscious thoughts in a clear and consistent manner.

Consider now a modern experiment reported by Donald MacKay in 1973. Employing a dichotic listening paradigm, MacKay presented tape-recorded sentences to one ear of a subject. Each sentence included an ambiguous word that could be interpreted in one of two ways. Consider, for example, the sentence, "They threw stones toward the bank yesterday." The word "bank" could mean either a place to keep money, or it could be a river bank. As the sentence was presented, the subject was to repeat it out loud and word for word - a process called shadowing. Shadowing forces the subject to focus all his attention on the ambiguous sentence, which in turns means that the subject can pay very little attention to a separate auditory input delivered to the other ear. On this unattended channel, a disambiguating word appeared simultaneously with the presentation of the ambiguous word on the attended channel. For example, when the word "bank" appeared on the attended channel, the word "river" or the word "money" would be administered to the unattended channel. Although subjects remained unaware of the disambiguating words presented to the unattended channel, these words nevertheless had a significant effect on the subjects' interpretations of the ambiguous sentences they had shadowed. Thus, the subjects receiving the word "money" on the unattended channel more often than not interpreted the ambiguous sentence to mean a bank where money is kept. Conversely, subjects who were presented the word "river" on the unattended channel generally understood the sentence to mean that people threw stones at the river bank. In effect, the unattended, disambiguating word, though itself processed to a less than conscious level, had a measurable impact on what the subject <u>did</u> consciously perceive - namely, the meaning of the ambiguous sentence. Despite their differences in other respects, both the Sidis and MacKay studies demonstrate that an event not represented in consciousness can nevertheless have a pronounced impact on a person's conscious perceptions.

As the earlier examples from Freud and Prince suggest, information processed to a less than conscious level can have more of an affective than a perceptual impact. A particularly dramatic example of this effect was reported by Levinson (1967). Upon emerging from pentathol-induced general anesthesia, a surgical patient became inexplicably weepy and depressed. When this emotional state persisted, the patient was hypnotically age regressed back to the time of the operation, whereupon she blurted out that the surgeon was saying that she might have cancer - repeating almost word for word what the physician had actually stated during the course of the operation. One is reminded by this example of Breuer's (Freud & Breuer, 1974) original claim that many hysterical disorders originated by virtue of the patient receiving traumatic information in an altered state of consciousness, or what Breuer termed a hypnoid state. Parenthetically, Freud later abandoned Breuer's dissociative or state specific hypothesis of hysteria in favor of what he termed defence hysteria. In view of Freud's growing influence and prestige, this latter interpretation helped to move psychiatry away from both the concept of dissociation and the use of hypnosis. And indeed, it is by no means necessary for a person to be in a dissociated or hypnoid state to be adversely affectd by ideas or thoughts that remain, for the most part, outside of consciousness. Donald Meichenbaum, for example, has developed a therapeutic strategy that begins by having patients eavesdrop on their own internal fantasies and dialogues, which are almost invariably self-deprecating and demeaning (Meichenbaum, 1975). Patients are often surprised at the dysphoric nature of their "unconscious" ideation and only when they become aware of what they are doing can they combat the tendency to denigrate themselves. Although the negative self-statements unearthed in Meichenbaum's patients originate inside the patient, the internal source of these statements may not be essential to their impact.

For example, in an unpublished study conducted in my laboratory, Heather Brenneman (1975) employed the dichotic listening paradigm to study the impact of unattended, dysphoric information on the subject's mood. Subjects were asked to listen to a prose passage administered to their right ears and to detect numerous errors contained therein. Such error detection was accomplished by having subjects simultaneously read an error-free typescript version of the prose passage and to indicate on it any errors of omission or commission made in the auditory version. While engaged in this editing task, subjects were to ignore material delivered to their left ears. On this left, unattended channel, subjects were presented a sort of stream of consciousness monologue, spoken in first person, that berated the mindlessness and stupidity of the experiment, and indulged in self-castigation for not having the guts to tell the experimenter off. After this ten-minute experimental intervention, subjects receiving the dysphoric information on the unattended channel were significantly more depressed and emotionally upset generally than normal controls who had received emotionally neutral information on the unattended channel. Thus, unattended dysphoric information, whether internal or external in origin, can evidently have an adverse impact on a normal, waking person's emotional state.

Notice that in Brenneman's research, subjects were preoccupied with editing a prose passage and were therefore inattentive to, though influenced by, the dysphoric stream of consciousness message. The experimental format is remarkably similar to a favorite procedure of Pierre Janet's, called "the method of distraction." This method involved occupying a patient's conscious awareness with some task - reading a book, conversing with a third person - and then whispering hypnotic-like suggestions to the patient so occupied (Janet, 1901, p. 252; Sidis, 1898, p. 97). Consider the following example taken from Janet (1901). One of his patients,

> Leonine --- (is not) suggestible in the waking state. If we speak to her directly and command a movement, she wonders, questions, and does not obey; but when she is speaking to other persons, we may succeed in whispering our command behind her, without attracting her attention. She thus no longer hears us and tries no longer to resist; it is then that all suggestions are executed and that we may modify her mind as we wish (pp. 257-258).

Or another example: A woman of 30, suffering for years from hysterical paralysis from the waist down, was seated in a chair, totally engaged in conversation with another doctor. While standing behind her Janet "told (the patient) in a low tone to get up and walk. To her amazement, she did as she was told, and was cured from that time (Janet, 1925, p. 213)."

In commenting on Janet's method of distraction, Morton Prince argued that "The whisper undoubtedly acts as a suggestion that the subject will not consciously hear what is whispered. The whispered word-images are accordingly dissociated, but are perceived unconsciously, and whatever unconsciousness exists can be in this way surreptitiously communicated with and responses attained without the knowledge of the personal consciousness (Prince, 1915, p. 317)."

I have rather promiscuously cited literature, both old and new, which converges on a simple point, namely, that information of either internal or external origins can remain largely unnoticed and unappreciated at the level of conscious experience, yet be processed at a lower level of analysis, and in a way that influences conscious thoughts, overt behaviors, and feelings. Moreover, unnoticed information of this sort can be initially received in a normal waking state, an altered hypnotic-like state, or an unconscious state. Finally, special techniques for recalling the originally unattended and unnoticed information may occasionally be successful.

The fact that information can be processed at a lower level of analysis without being experienced at a higher, conscious level, has considerable importance for both psychotherapy and for hypnosis. In psychotherapy, patients frequently offer considerable resistance to various therapeutic maneuvers. The process of changing can often be as threatening as the prospect of continued suffering. My hunch is that resistance is more apt to counter treatment efforts the more salient and obvious the therapeutic strategy is (Bowers, 1975). For example, a therapist's explicit demand to free associate can be met with the most cunning subversion by the patient. On the other hand, if the treatment maneuvers are oblique and subtle, they are more difficult for the patient to notice and counteract. Milton Erickson is, of course, a veritable Master of the Oblique. Let me give just one example of how he helped a patient without the patient even realizing that she was being treated. In his paper on interspersal techniques, Erickson (1966) tells of a newly-hired secretary who regularly suffered "migrainous" headaches lasting from three to four hours, which she would typically sleep off in the lounge. Since she strongly objected to being hypnotized, Erickson resorted to a rather unusual device. When she showed up with a headache one day, he refused to excuse her and instead required her to take dictation from him of some incoherent verbalizations of a psychotic patient. Within 10 minutes, her headache was gone. Subsequent similar efforts were sometimes successful, but sometimes not. Unbeknownst to the patient, what had actually happened was this: Erickson had interspersed into some of the dictated psychotic ramblings certain well camouflaged therapeutic suggestions aimed at eliminating the secretary's headaches; doctored passages were effective and undoctored passages were ineffective in this regard. The secretary had no conscious idea of why or how her headaches were removed, although she vaguely associated her cure with taking dictation from Erickson, since typescripts of the doctored material, dictated by someone else who did not properly intonate the implicit suggestions, had no therapeutic effect whatsoever. In effect, Erickson had successfully circumvented the patient's resistance by a simple but subtle appeal to the patient's "third ear" - the ear that heard the therapeutic ideas without consciously noticing them for what they were. The lack of conscious awareness of these suggestions may well have been critical to their success, since the patient could not resist what she did not clearly notice. Certainly Janet (1901, 1925, 1965), Sidis (1898, 1902) and other early psychologists argue that hysterical patients frequently resisted direct and obvious suggestions, whereas these same suggestions were effective when whispered to and unnoticed by the otherwise distracted subject.

Lest I leave the impression that Erickson is uniquely capable of subtly maneuvering his patients, let me provide another example, this one from politics. Former U.S. President Lyndon Johnson's press secretary, George Reedy, has actively argued against an official devil's advocate in the realm of foreign policy and for a very interesting reason. It was Reedy's observation that whenever George Ball, a sort of self-appointed devil's advocate, attempted to argue against further Viet Nam involvement, Dean Rusk, Robert McNamara, McGeorge Bundy, Lyndon Johnson and other cabinet members would listen patiently,

> automatically discounting whatever he said. This strengthened them in their own convictions because the Cabinet members could quite correctly say: 'We heard both sides of the issue discussed'....I think the moment you appoint an official devil's advocate you solidify the position he is arguing against.

> In contrast, I saw Clark Clifford change President Johnson's mind and not once dissent in the process. I think I was one of the few people in the room who caught on to what Clifford was doing. In fact, Clifford did not draw any conclusions. He would get up at cabinet meetings and go on with long, rambling, apparently aimless briefings in which he would merely sum up the world situation and leave it at that. But what he was doing was subtly planting in the minds of the people around the table and in the mind of the President a set of facts and a series of predicates upon which one could come to only one conclusion. When President Johnson said that Clark Clifford had not changed his mind on Viet Nam, I think Mr. Johnson was being honest. I don't think he knew Clifford was changing his mind (Reedy, 1971, p. 13).

Here we have a telling example of how the whole issue of resistance to a new view was circumvented. Johnson did not resist Clifford's subtle machinations, partly because he did not recognize them as such, and partly because he did not have to recognize consciously the change in his position on Viet Nam for what it was. This in contrast to Johnson's adverse reaction to George Ball's straightforward but ineffective dissent from the administration's position - an approach that was not only an obvious attempt to change Johnson's mind, but one which, if adopted, would have required an explicit abandonment of an official administration position - a very onerous thing to do both politically and personally.

There is one more lesson to be learned from this example. Viet Nam had to be one colossal headache for Johnson, a headache from which he devoutly wanted relief - but, and here's the rub - relief with honor. So, Johnson was as motivated to be rid of his Viet Nam headache as Erickson's secretary was to be cured of her psychosomatic one. But both Johnson and Erickson's patient resisted explicit, straightforward attempts to alter their respective conditions out of some unruly combination of pride, autonomy, and self-esteem. It is such factors as these that often make subtlety necessary, but it is the patient's desire for change that sensitizes his third ear, allowing him to hear influential messages which nevertheless remain unnoticed and, therefore, unresisted.

We have seen that as long as the patient is awake and conscious, his critical capacities <u>may</u> need to be circumvented by the use of indirect, camouflaged suggestion. However, if the patient is unconscious or hypnotized, with his reality testing powers in abeyance, more direct suggestions are in order. Boris Sidis (1898) long ago recognized this when he argued that, "<u>In the normal state a suggestion is more effective the more indirect it is</u> (p. 52)," whereas in hypnosis "<u>The more direct we make our suggestion the greater the</u>

chance of its success (p. 79)."

Some things that can be accomplished by direct suggestion in hypnosis and even in patients under general anesthesia are truly extraordinary. In a recent report by Clawson and Swade (1975), for example, Clawson was called upon to stop the bleeding of his own grandson undergoing emergency surgery. While the patient was under deep general anesthesia, Clawson said, "Jac, your subconscious mind has the ability to stop bleeding. Now I want you to stop this bleeding." According to Clawson, "The bleeding stopped immediately, and the operation was completed (p. 162)." Do not ask me how these simple suggestions delivered to an unconscious person can have such a profound effect on such a primitive function as bleeding, but it is worth noticing that such reports are becoming more frequent in the literature.

So far, we have focussed on the implications for psychotherapy of information processed by the third ear - i.e., information effectively processed to less than conscious levels. However, this formulation also helps us to broaden our understanding of hypnosis. In this regard, I would like to make two points. First of all, critics have often pointed to certain paradoxical features of hypnotic phenomena which seem to discredit their genuineness or authenticity. It does seem curious, for example, that a person who is presumably hypnotically deaf can nevertheless be responsive to verbal suggestions that his hearing will be fully restored. Such a verbal restoration of hearing seems to argue against the notion that the person had previously been unable to hear - despite his claim that he heard nothing during the period of suggested deafness. What I would like to argue is that such a person is in fact not deaf, if the standard of deafness is organic loss of hearing (Malmo, Boag, & Raginsky, 1954). However, it seems not only possible, but likely, that hypnotic suggestions for deafness can leave the process of hearing intact while eliminating the consciousness of what is heard. In other words, the hypnotically deaf person registers sound and speech at a lower level of analysis that he does not notice at a higher, conscious level; he hears unconsciously, as it were. Moreover, what is heard unconsciously can have a profound impact on how a person reacts. Recall for example the unwitting compliance of Janet's hysterical patients to whispered suggestions they did not consciously notice, since they were otherwise distracted and preoccupied. Similarly, the hypnotically deaf subject can comply with suggestions heard unconsciously - even when the suggestions are aimed at the restoration of hearing. In effect, such restorative suggestions are heard without being noticed, but effectively return to the subject the capacity of noticing what he hears.

I have chosen hypnotically-induced deafness as an example of how information registered at one level need not be noticed at a higher, conscious level. However, it is Ernest Hilgard's (1973; Knox, Morgan, & Hilgard, 1974) elegant work with hypnotically-induced pain analgesia which is currently the most persuasive experimental grounds for the distinction between registering information on one hand, and consciously noticing it on the other. In effect, Hilgard and his associates have shown that the usual denial of ordinarily painful stimuli by the hypnotically analgesic subject is only half the picture. If special report techniques like automatic writing are employed, such subjects report a painful state of affairs commensurate with intensity of the stimulus. Somehow, hypnotic analgesia operates to eliminate conscious appreciation of the pain that is in fact registered and even accessible via certain automatized report techniques.

It was precisely specialized techniques of communication, such as automatic writing, that were devised and exploited by Janet, Prince, and other early workers who wished to deal with non-conscious aspects of patients' functioning and experience. The more things change, the more they stay the same.

The "third ear" processing of unnoticed information has a second implication for hypnosis. As Spanos and Barber (1974) have recently noted, there seems to be a convergence in the hypnosis literature on the notion of subjects' involvement in suggestion-related imaginings. Sarbin's notion of role involvement (Sarbin & Coe, 1972), Shor's (1962) hypnotic role-taking involvement, Josephine Hilgard's (1970) imaginative involvement, Spanos and Barber's goal-directed strivings (1974) and Tellegen's notion of absorption (Tellegen & Atkinson, 1974) all seem to recognize the importance of total cognitive immersion in a narrow range of input as an important dimension of hypnotic and hypnotic-like states.

I agree with this convergent view, but I think it important to recognize its limitations. For example, the notion of role involvement or absorption does not explain, at least to my satisfaction, why highly hypnotizable subjects are so much more responsive to sleep-administered suggestions than their low hypnotizable counterparts. Evans (1972) and his colleagues have demonstrated rather persuasively, I think, that there is indeed a sizeable correlation between hypnotic susceptibility and the ability to respond to simple motor suggestions administered in alpha-free, Stage I sleep. It simply presses credibility too far to assume that subjects, however hypnotizable, become imaginatively absorbed in suggestions administered to them while they are sleeping. Something else is necessary to account for this phenomenon, and this "something" seems to involve the hypnotizable person's heightened ability to register and effectively process information that is not fully represented in ordinary waking consciousness. This ability has historically been referred to as the hypnotizable person's capacity for dissociation, and Hilgard (1973) in his neo-dissociation view of hypnosis has recently been calling our attention to this all but forgotten dimension of hypnotic phenomena.

In a recently published book (Bowers, 1976), I have argued for an intimate connection between the high hypnotizable's absorptive and dissociative capabilities. In effect, I think the effortless absorption in dramatic productions, novels, and hypnotic suggestions, so characteristic of high hypnotizable persons, is permitted and preserved by their dissociative capabilities. To put my point as succinctly as possible, highly hypnotizable subjects are not easily distracted from their absorptive involvements precisely because they can process and appraise potential distractions at a less than conscious level. Low susceptibles on the other hand are constantly peeking at these peripheral stimuli in order to appraise their significance, but in so doing, lose the thread of their primary involvement. In the Evans' studies on sleep suggestibility, for example, low susceptibles tended to awaken when suggestions were administered, rather than responding in accordance with them. In another investigation by Van Nuys (1973), high susceptibles were much less distracted by irrelevant thoughts than low susceptibles.

Whether or not this proposed connection between dissociation and absorption holds up is a matter for future research to decide. However, I, at least, am convinced that no theory of hypnosis should long endure that does not treat its dissociative features sympathetically. The historical and clinical evidence for their importance is simply overwhelming. Moreover, as I have tried to indicate in earlier parts of this paper, the general statement of dissociation, i.e., of registering information at a lower level of analysis that is not noticed at a higher, conscious level, is an extremely fertile one, not just for a theory of hypnosis, but for theories of psychopathology and psychotherapy as well.

REFERENCES

Bowers, K.S. The psychology of subtle control: An attributional analysis of behavioral persistence. Canadian Journal of Behavioral Science, 1975, 7, 78-95.

Bowers, K.S. Hypnosis for the seriously curious. Monterey, California: Brooks-Cole, 1976.

Brenneman, H.A. The effect of unattended information on mood by persons high and low in hypnotic susceptibility. Unpublished Honors thesis, University of Waterloo, 1975.

Clawson, T.A., & Swade, K.H. The hypnotic control of blood flow and pain: The cure of warts and the potential use of hypnosis in the treatment of cancer. American Journal of Clinical Hypnosis, 1975, 17, 160-169.

Ellenberger, H.F. Discovery of the unconscious: The history and evaluation of dynamic psychiatry. New York: Basic Books, 1970.

Erickson, M.H. The interspersal hypnotic technique for symptom correction and pain control. American Journal of Clinical Hypnosis, 1966, 8, 198-209.

Evans, F.J. Hypnosis and sleep: Techniques for cognitive activity during sleep. In E. Fromm and R.E. Shor (editors), Hypnosis: Research developments and perspectives. Chicago: Aldine Atherton, 1972.

Freud, S. Hysterical phantasies and their relation to bisexuality. In S. Freud, Collected papers, Vol. 2. New York: Basic Books, 1959. (Originally published in 1908).

Freud, S., & Breuer, J. Studies on hysteria. Hamondsworth, England: Pelican, 1974. (Originally published in English in 1955).

Hilgard, E.R. A neo-dissociation theory of pain induction in hypnosis. Psychological Review, 1973, 80, 396-411.

Hilgard, J.R. Personality and hypnosis: A study of imaginative involvement. Chicago: University of Chicago Press, 1970.

Janet, P. The mental state of hystericals. New York: G.P. Putnam, 1901.

Janet, P. Psychological healing: A historical and clinical study. London: George Allen and Unwin, 1925.

Janet, P. Major symptoms of hysteria. New York: Hafner, 1965. (facsimilie of 1929 second edition).

Knox, V.J., Morgan, A.H., & Hilgard, E.R. Pain and suffering in ischemia. Archives of General Psychiatry, 1974, 30, 840-847.

Levinson, B.W. States of awareness during general anesthesia. In J. Lassner (editor), Hypnosis and psychosomatic medicine. New York: Springer Verlag, 1967.

MacKay, D.G. Aspects of the theory of comprehension, memory and attention. Quarterly Journal of Experimental Psychology, 1973, 25, 22-40.

Malmo, B., Boag, T.J., & Raginsky, B.B. Electromyographic study of hypnotic deafness. Journal of Clinical and Experimental Hypnosis, 1954, 2, 305-317.

Meichenbaum, D. Toward a cognitive theory of self control. In G. Schwartz and P. Shapiro (editors), Consciousness and self-regulation: Advances in research. New York: Plenum, 1975.

Prince, M. The unconscious. New York: Macmillan, 1915.

Reedy, G. Discussion of "Powers of the presidency." Center Magazine, 1971, 4, 7-18.

Sarbin, T.R., & Coe, W. Hypnosis: A social psychological analysis of influence communication. New York: Holt, Rinehart and Winston, 1972.

Shor, R.E. Three dimensions of hypnotic depth. International Journal of Clinical and Experimental Hypnosis, 1962, 10, 23-38.

Sidis, B. The psychology of suggestion. New York: D. Appelton and Co., 1898.

Sidis, B. Psychopathological researches in mental dissociation. New York: G.E. Steckert, 1902.

Spanos, N.P., & Barber, T.X. Toward a convergence in hypnosis research. American Psychologist, 1974, 29, 500-511.

Tellegen, M., & Atkinson, G. Openness to experience and self altering experiences ("absorption"), a trait related to hypnotic susceptibility. Journal of Abnormal Psychology, 1974, 83, 268-277.

Van Nuys, D. Meditation, attention, and hypnotic susceptibility: A correlational study. International Journal of Clinical and Experimental Hypnosis, 1973, 21, 59-69.

STATES OF CONSCIOUSNESS IN HYPNOSIS: DIVISIONS OR LEVELS?

Ernest R. Hilgard

Stanford University, U.S.A.

Abstract: The metaphor of depth has long been used in psychology to indicate more profound layers of the mind, and is familiar in the writings of Freud and Jung. A different line of development, contemporary with theirs, was developed by Janet, whose concept of dissociation described splits in personality, often in the context of multiple personalities. The secondary personalities exhibited few of the characteristics of the unconscious of Freud or Jung. Recent work has shown that a modern version of dissociation may be desirable. In hypnotic analgesia there may be no pain felt at the level of conscious report in the hypnotized condition, although by special techniques some experience of pain is reported at a covert or subconscious level. These observations have given rise to the concept or metaphor of a "hidden observer," as one of the divisions of consciousness. The hidden part represents data that are processed and not consciously perceived, yet may become available to consciousness. The observations are not limited to pain, and one illustration is given of creative story telling, in which comparable splits may be detected. It is important not to limit considerations of consciousness to the passive-receptive mode, for the active and controlling mode is equally important, and is, indeed, the one most commonly studied in hypnotic behavior. The modern form of dissociation theory - called neodissociation - proposes that there are numerous cognitive and motor control systems that are not highly integrated, and may become more completely separated through hypnotic procedures. Their explanation remains a task for the future, although some neurological leads are promising.

The mind is a complex object, and there are different ways of looking at it. It can be viewed as a tree, with the conscious part, like the trunk and leaves, visible above the ground, while there are roots that go deep, and draw nourishment from sources that are invisible beneath the surface. This is a crude analogy to depth psychologies that view the mind according to its layers or levels. Alternatively, the mind can be viewed as divided into parts, like a garden apartment, in which there is some unity to the whole, but your acquaintance with the mind is always partial, just as you will see different apartments in the house depending on the door through which you enter. This analogy may serve for those views of the mind that were prominent in dissociation theories that saw its different parts as unlike, but perhaps side-by-side and not according to which is higher or lower.

DEPTH PSYCHOLOGIES

The metaphor of depth that characterizes the psychology of levels has been used from time immemorial. It has the root meaning of profound - pro fundus in Latin, meaning near the bottom, that is, close to the greatest depth. A fragment from Heraclitus, the Greek philosopher who lived in 500 B.C. reflects the depth concept of many centuries ago: "You could not discover the depths of the psyche, even if you traveled every road to do so, such is the depth of its meaning."

I wish to begin with a consideration of some of the ideas that became current with the depth psychologies of Freud and Jung. I shall pass over their antecedents, in which hypnosis played a role.

Both Freud and Jung began with an essential duality of the mind, that between the conscious and the unconscious. As their theories evolved, matters became more complex, but for our purposes we can hold to this major duality. In his remarkable book on the discovery of the unconscious, Ellenberger (1970) distinuished between the closed and the open view of the hidden part of the mind.

The closed view was represented by Freud, at least in his earlier formulations. That is, the unconscious was limited to the experiences of the individual as represented by his own repressed memories and tendencies. To be sure there are powerful impulses and drives that are inherited, particularly sex and aggression, but that is true of high functions as well. We could not have stereoscopic vision if evolution had not provided us with two eyes and the brain to use them. But the contents of both the conscious and the unconscious depend primarily on individual experience.

The open view of the unconscious was represented by Jung, in that the memory tape (if we may think of the memory in that way) has been somewhat pre-recorded by the experiences of the race, and is subject to inputs from universal sources outside the individual during the individual's lifetime. That is, a person's unconscious is subject to influences beyond those of his immediate interactions with the environment of things and of other people. I am of course talking about Jung's collective unconscious, the unconscious of the archetypes. Both Freud and Jung evolved more complex systems for describing the personality but this flavor of difference has been preserved in the views of their followers.

Freud's unconscious, based on the repression of unacceptable or forbidden sexual wishes in childhood, led in the extreme to the conception of the unconscious as a seething cauldron of very primitive impulses. Ultimately the id became the repository for this picture of irrationality and impulsivity. Lest I seem to be exaggerating, because much of contemporary psychoanalysis is presented in blander terms, recall the psychoanalytic description of schizophrenic ideation, the disturbing hallucinated voices, the regressive behavior, as "the return of the repressed." What psychoanalytic therapy attempts to do is to rid the unconscious of its antisocial power, and its control over ordinary behavior, expressed in Freud's brief statement: "Where id was there must ego be."

It is somewhat more difficult to pin Jung down on the precise roles of the personal unconscious and the universal or collective unconscious. As with Freud, much of the evidence comes from the dream-life or undirected fantasy; these mental products, represented in consciousness, help to make inferences about the unconscious. Neither Freud nor Jung tries to make the unconscious conscious - both infer the unconscious from its conscious derivatives.

Whether one adopts a Freudian position or a Jungian one, the unconscious is seen to differ markedly in quality from the conscious. Conscious and unconscious differ not only in content but in kind, and there is some tension between them. To explore too deeply is dangerous; to learn from the experience of exploring the depths requires both strength of character and expert guidance.

So much for the historical depth psychologies.

DISSOCIATION PSYCHOLOGY

A somewhat different line of development from that of Freud and Jung began with Pierre Janet, a contemporary of theirs, who, for accidents of personality and leadership qualities, never had the following that they developed, although his views were echoed for a time in this country by Boris Sidis, Morton Prince, and others. The basic difference between Janet's position and that of the depth psychologies is that many of his observations were made on dual personalities, in which the hidden part differed from the usual conscious personality, but exhibited few of the characteristics of the unconscious of Freud or Jung. Both the open and the hidden personalities were actually revealed in behavior. At an empirical level, the inference to an unconscious, as required by Freud and Jung, was not needed: the dissociated personality occasionally manifested itself exactly as the normal one usually did. Some part of the personality was said to be dissociated from the primary personality but the split may be thought of as a division, rather than as a layering in which one part is deeper or more primitive than another. The barrier between the parts, in the Freudian theory, is a repressive barrier; the barrier in dissociation is commonly an amnesic one. I have illustrated this difference between the depth psychologies and dissociation in the diagram of Figure 1.

In recognition of this difference, Morton Prince preferred to refer to the parts of a multiple personality as coconscious rather than as subconscious or unconscious.

An early case of divided personality was published by Azam (1887) after many years of observation, and has since been referred to frequently as a kind of prototype of dual personality. His patient, Felida X, in her normal personality earned her living as a seamstress. She was described as sullen and taciturn, with many headaches and neuralgias that would today be called psychosomatic. After a crisis, however, she would awaken as a different person, gay, vivacious, and free of symptoms. This secondary person, more "healthful" than the "normal" one, knew all about the symptoms of the primary personality, but the primary person had no awareness of the secondary one, except as she was told about it by others.

Because of the picture of the unconscious that has come to us from psychoanalysis as primitive, impulsive, a residue of forbidden wishes, it is important to note that, as with Felida X, the secondary or hidden personality is frequently more "normal," better adjusted, healthier than the primary personality. It is the secondary personality that typically has the whole set of memories, and therapy is directed to bringing about an integration based on it rather than the typical personality that at first presents itself as the primary one (Mitchell, 1925). Of course this generalization is not universal, but it is found true sufficiently often to justify a distinction between dissociation and repression in the usual sense.

This has been a rather long introduction to set the stage for deciding how to view the hypnotic consciousness against a background of both depth and dissociation interpretations deriving from past theories.

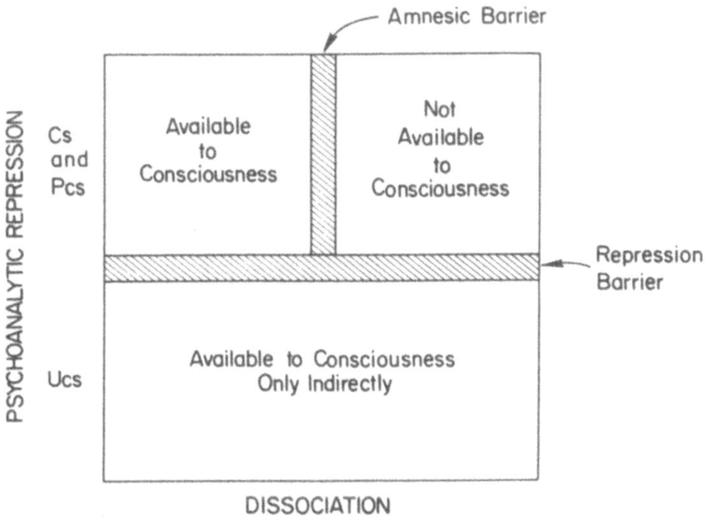

Fig. 1. A diagram representing the difference between amnesia in dissociation and repression in depth psychology. (From Hilgard, 1977b. Reprinted by permission of Plenum Press).

Let me say before going on that there need be nothing contradictory between a depth and a dissociation interpretation; both interpretations may be applicable at once, but either alone is then likely to prove to be a partial explanation of what is taking place.

Let me illustrate how dynamic and dissociation psychology may come together in explaining the results of an experiment on hypnotic amnesia that draws upon repression as well as amnesia. Clinical cases of amnesia often possess some properties in common. One point is that what is lost is ordinarily the personal memories, not the impersonal ones. That is, the person who turns up lost at the police station to try to find out who he is can speak the language perfectly well; he may have stubs from bus tickets that he bought, showing that he knows how to use money and make change. His memories are not gone, only those that pertain to his own experience. Upon examination, it is often found that his forgetting is related to some incident that aroused guilt in him; in the concealing of this event, related experiences that might serve as reminders of it are also forgotten. This, then, is a picture of motivated forgetting that follows very much the repression model. The fact that the amnesia may be relieved by hypnosis shows that this motivated forgetting does indeed have something in common with post-hypnotic amnesia, though nothing hypnotic need have been involved in producing the forgetting in the first place.

A doctoral dissertation in our laboratory, by Clemes (1964), produced a laboratory analogue through a study of selective forgetting. The hypothesis was that words loaded with troublesome emotion for the person would more readily become the targets of amnesia than neutral words treated in the same manner. Subjects first responded to a Kent-Rosanoff word association test in order to determine words that were "loaded," and words that were "neutral." This test has a long histroy, going back originally to Jung, and gave rise to the idea of "complex indicators" such as long reaction time in responding to emotionally charged words, bizarre responses, repeating the stimulus word, and so on. Having found for each subject a list of words associated with such evidences of conflict, lists were constructed with half the words critical ones and half neutral ones, the list tailored in each case to the individual. It was found that when these lists were learned under hypnosis there was no difference between the loaded words and the neutral ones, presumably because such rote learning of randomly organized lists is viewed as an exercise not personally relevant. After meeting the criterion of mastery, the hypnotized subject was told that he would forget half the words when roused from hypnosis and asked to recall them. The experiment was quite successful in this; subjects indeed found that they could recall some but not all of the words, and averaged about half the list. Because it has been shown by a number of investigators that forgetting after hypnosis is a mixture of ordinary forgetting and amnesia, a useful precaution is to score only those words that are forgotten in attempted recall while amnesia is present, but then recovered when amnesia is lifted (Nace, Orne, & Hammer, 1974). Clemes did this and found that his original hypothesis was supported, that is, that the emotionally loaded words were indeed the one most often forgotten in the partial amnesia, giving further evidence of some overlap between forgetting motivated by personal problems and post-hypnotic amnesia. I mention this to call attention to an interaction between what is learned from the depth psychologies and what is learned from hypnosis, as true in the laboratory as in the clinic.

Automatic Writing and Divided Attention

The distinction between a vertical division and a horizontal one - implying depth - is well illustrated by experiments on automatic writing. Here, too, the experiences outside the laboratory have some relation to those inside, although interpretations may differ.

The most famous case of automatic writing is that of Patience Worth. A St. Louis housewife, Mrs. Curran, began playing with the ouija board. Presently a spirit introduced herself as Patience Worth, and began dictating to her. Mrs. Curran's mother copied down the letters as the planchette pointed to them, soon almost as rapid as if typing. Five novels were published under the name of Patience Worth between the years 1917 and 1928; while they were not great they were not without literary merit and received favorable reviews at the time. Because Mrs. Curran was uneducated and had no pretense to being a writer, her productions caused a good deal of stir, recently reviewed in a book by Litvag (1972). The believers in spiritualism of course granted the reality of Patience Worth; those more naturalistically inclined saw this as evidence of a divided person, with a hidden creative part unknown to the normal personality. Whatever the interpretation, the production was a cognitive one, representing orderly discourse associated with secondary rather than primary process thinking, in the Freudian sense. In other words, this may be a subconscious product, but it is much more like a conscious one and better described as a split in the person rather than as something dredged up from more pimitive depths.

In our laboratory experiments we have found that it is not difficult to instruct a subject to permit a hand to perform simple mathermatical computations without the subject knowing that the hand is doing anything; at the same time the normal consciousness of the person may be occupied in naming the colors on a screen displayed before him. The whole experiment may be done posthypnotically, so that the subject, out of hypnosis, responds to the normal request to name the colors, and, at a signal that was earlier planted within hypnosis, begins also to do the computations. After it is all over the subject may have no awareness at all that the hand did anything. We have shown, as others have, that there is some interference between the conscious and the subconscious task, so that attention must somehow be divided between them. While this refutes an extreme interpretation of dissociation - that there should be no interference - it does not refute the fact that a cognitive operation can be performed without the person's knowing that he is doing it (Knox, Crutchfield, & Hilgard, 1975; Stevenson, 1976).

The tasks assigned in these laboratory studies are so impersonal that the division of consciousness is better described as a vertical split, rather than as one of depth. In other words, the mathematical computation and the color naming are equally impersonal; neither is so difficult as to cause any threat to the person on grounds of fear of failure.

DIVIDED CONSCIOUSNESS IN HYPNOSIS: THE HIDDEN OBSERVER

I have given two illustrations of dissociation within hypnosis, one of amnesia in which there was apparently an interaction with repression, the other of automatic writing which implies intact cognitive activity at the dissociated level. I wish now to take another step by pointing out how the covert or hidden experiences in hypnosis are described by the person when the covert experiences are made manifest in consciousness.

This all began, as I have pointed out elsewhere (Hilgard, 1973), when I was giving a class demonstration of hypnotic deafness, and rather by chance found that by using a special method of inquiry, similar to automatic writing, but using automatic talking instead, the subject was able to recount what he had heard while hypnotically deaf. We then turned to the studies of pain that had been going on in the laboratory to study the covert or hidden pain that was reported by subjects who were able to reduce their overt pain through hypnotic suggestion. We had used two types of pain, the pain of circulating ice water, known as cold pressor pain, and the pain of a tourniquet to the upper arm, followed by exercise, known as ischemic pain. Because the pain studies are reported in detail in the book that Josephine Hilgard and I have recently published (Hilgard & Hilgard, 1975), I shall limit my discussion here to some data from the cold pressor experiments, letting you take my word for it that the same general findings have been reported for the other pains as well, including those in surgery when hypnosis is the sole anesthetic. The major finding is that when pain overtly reported in hypnotic analgesia is greatly reduced, or even absent, at the hidden or covert level pain of considerable intensity may be reported, although it is rather common for the hidden pain to be somewhat less than normal pain, and for the person to report that even such pain as he felt at that level did not seem to bother him.

Some general results on pain reduction at the overt level and at the covert level are shown in Figure 2. These results differ slightly from those reported at the last Congress in Uppsala (Hilgard, 1975) because the experiments have been carried much further and only preliminary results were available then. Looking first at the cross-hatched columns, you see that pain as reported by the usual overt verbal statements is highest in the normal waking condition, reduced by waking suggestion, and further reduced by hypnotic suggestion. The scale adopted is a magnitude estimation scale, in which a number is assigned to the intensity of the pain, with 10 designated as an anchoring or critical value at which the subject would very much like to terminate the experiment but is willing to go on for a few seconds more, counting above 10 as the pain mounts. The mean in waking was above this critical value, as shown, while all other pains, on the average remained below it.

Now turn to the other columns, labeled covert pain. These reports were obtained by the method of automatic talking, in which the subject, while hypnotized, is told that at a signal the experimenter will be able to talk to a hidden part of him, and he will not know that he talked or what he said. The signal is commonly a hand placed on the subject's shoulder, and when the hand is removed he is amnesic for the experience, until the amnesia is later released.

In the case of waking suggestion, the subject had to be hypnotized after the experiment in order to use the method. The pain that he recalled after waking suggestion was essentially the same as that reported before; that is, overt and covert pain were essentially alike. In hypnotic analgesia, the results were quite different: the covert pain was substantially higher than the overtly reported pain, and about equal to the pain as reduced by waking suggestion.

One possible interpretation is that waking suggestion works by a diversion of attention away from the pain, and achieves some relief in that way. Hypnotic suggestion perhaps makes use of some additional dissociative process, related to amnesia, that permits a reduction beyond that by waking suggestion. However, when the hypnotic overlay is removed by the automatic technique, only the residual reduction remains that could have been produced by waking suggestion.

Lest it be argued that there is some falsification of memory involved, because the automatic questioning is done after the experiment is over, I wish to present Figure 3 showing what happens when the overt and covert reports are obtained simultaneously, the covert report by automatic key-pressing corresponding to automatic writing. Here the overt and covert reports are given simultaneously, the overt report given verbally, the covert one by automatic key-pressing. This has the advantage that the course of pain can be followed, with the final pain corresponding to that reported for hypnotic analgesia in the previous figure.

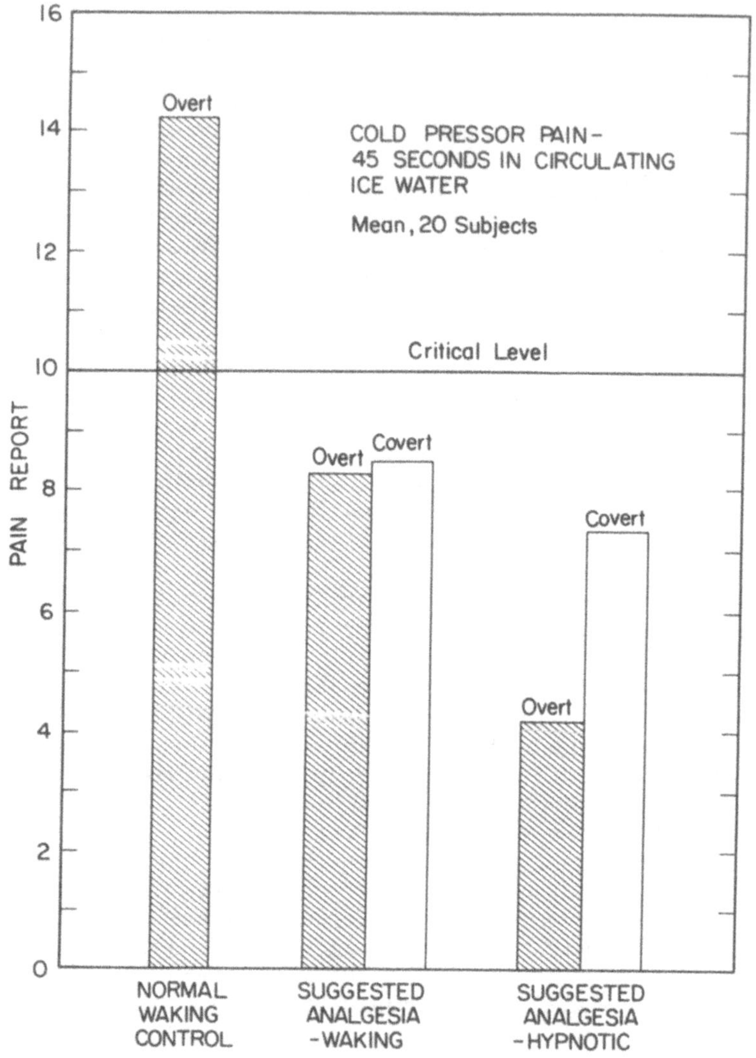

Fig. 2. Overt pain reduction through waking suggestion and hypnotic suggestion, and covert pain as revealed by automatic talking. (From data of Hilgard, Morgan, and Macdonald, 1975, as reproduced in Hilgard and Hilgard, 1975. Reprinted by permission).

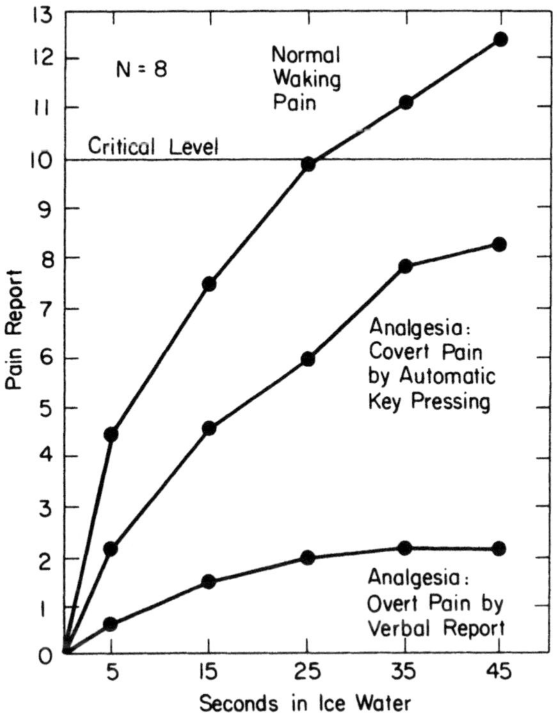

Fig. 3. Overt and covert pain in normal waking, waking analgesia, and hypnotic analgesia, with covert pain recorded by automatic key-pressing. (From data of Hilgard, Morgan, and Macdonald, 1975, as reproduced in Hilgard and Hilgard, 1975, page 172. Reprinted by permission).

I believe that these results on hidden pain, in the midst of hypnotically reduced pain, serve well to illustrate the kind of vertical split that is common in hypnosis between what the hypnotized part experiences and what some other part of the person knows. It is as though genuine parallel-processing has been going on, the same information being interpreted in two ways at once. This is essentially what the classical dissociation theory proposed, and I am now taking the position that we ought to reexamine dissociation and give it contemporary form. Because we need not be faithful to the classical theory, I am describing attempts in this new direction as a neodissociation theory.

Lest all of this be tied too closely to the study of pain, I wish to show how the same line of investigation can be turned to quite different subject matter, in this case the processes of creating a narrative when only the setting for the story is provided.

The subject of this informal experiment was a highly hypnotizable student whose story-telling was of a high order whether he was hypnotized or not. Although I am going to report a story told under hypnosis, he was quite capable of telling stories of essentially the same vividness when not hypnotized. He came to our attention because, with someone else, under hypnosis he had told a story of early 19th century England with such clarity and verisimilitude that he convinced those who heard him - himelf as well- that it must have been a case of regression to a prior experience. Only careful depth interviewing by Josephine Hilgard proved that he had forgotten memories sufficient to supply the details he had recounted so that the reincarnation concept was not necessary.

I gave him, under hypnosis, the following assignment.

"Just transport yourself to the scene I am about to describe. This is a place where you and some friends are exploring a newly discovered cave. You have already found the cave so you've come back to it with all the necessary equipment and you're prepared to explore it. Just describe what the scene is around you now."

The story took 17 minutes for him to tell; he reported his hypnotic depth as at 20 where 8 - 10 was sufficient for him to follow the usual suggestions in hypnosis of analgesia, hallucinations, amnesia and the rest. I shall quote a few passages and summarize the rest.

> Well, this cave we discovered is in Mexico, in the southern part of Mexico. The climate in this area is very lush. It's not tropical because the altitude is too high, but it's at a latitude that if it were at lower altitude it would be a tropical rain forest. But the combination of

> this latitude and altitude makes it a very lush green mountain area that doesn't ever get too hot. It keeps cool, around in the 70's or so, and it's really an ideal place for living as far as weather is concerned. It is still, however, rather moist and most afternoons for an hour or two it rains.
>
> The cave that several friends of mine and I are about to explore, we stumbled upon just a week ago when we were having a day off and taking a picnic. We just came to this spot that had been a favorite spot of one of my friends, we saw this huge rock, just a mammoth rock, several of them, sort of juxtaposed upon each other and covered with all sorts of vegetation. We climbed up and had our lunch. As we climbed down we realized that there was sort of a little tunnel that was formed by the series of rocks not quite touching each other. We climbed down about 15 feet which was as far as the light filtered into it, and we were afraid to go any further. We had no means of artificial light so we couldn't see. I yelled, however, down in the cavern and the echoing of my voice made us believe that this would be quite a large cavern.
>
> So we've come back......

Now he proceeded to tell in great detail how they used ropes to ease themselves into the cavern, flashlights to guide them, what they saw, stalactites, stalagmites, a reflecting lake - fanciful shapes and exciting colors.

One of the friends found another opening and they crawled through on hands and knees to discover a veritable Shangri-La.

> To our amazement we found ourselves in a beautiful small valley with vines growing down the sides and hills going sharply up in all directions, and in the back of the valley a waterfall falling down, cascading over rocks, forming a little river that went down along the base of the valley, formed one pool and trickled onward underneath the rocks. Flowers of every variety grew in abundance in this valley, so that one saw just as much yellows and reds and blues and all other types of colors as one saw the green vegetation. Again there was no sign of mankind having been there, although we were sure that we could not have been the only people to have ever enjoyed the beauty of this sight. Some of the flowers we see are huge flowers like none I have ever seen before. The blossoms would be as large as a basketball, thick with pollen, beautiful bright colors.

They remained for the afternoon, swam in the pool, lay in the sun, and found their way back deciding to keep their discovery to themselves in order to come back and enjoy it.

As I mentioned, I had him tell other stories while not hypnotized, such as the experiences of a coal miner in England during the early period of the industrial revolution, experiences with Indians on the western plains with a pioneer family, and the life of a stone-cutter in medieval Italy. He did each of these equally vividly so that my concern became the difference between telling a story under hypnosis and in the waking state.

> In hypnosis, once I create the pattern, I don't have to take any more initiative; the story just unfolds. In fact once I start talking I know the main outlines of what is happening.
>
> For instance, I knew ahead of time that there would be another room outside of the cavern, and I knew I would go outside but I didn't know what it would look like until I walked through and was describing it.
>
> In the waking state it seems more fabricated. I don't _see_ things that I describe in waking in the way I actually _see_ them in hypnosis. I really saw everything today that I described.

Inquiry by the hidden observer technique revealed that there was a part of him doing the planning, more like a stage director providing the promptings for the hypnotized part, the actor.

The hidden part knew, for example, that the cavern was to have a beautiful room, and that there would be a garden beyond. The hypnotized part did not know their _qualities_ until _seeing_ them. It is rather like the difference between the dream work producing a dream and the ultimate manifest dream. As he put it, "The two parts worked together to form a story." The hidden part also planned (and monitored) the length of the story.

The planning aspect appears to hold a much larger part of the story telling in the waking state.

Here we find an additional complexity, for we have a difference in the overt experiences while creating in hypnosis and creating in the waking state, but we have a concealed helper when the story is being created in hypnosis.

CONSCIOUSNESS AS SENSITIVE AND AS CONTROLLING

Now for a little theory.

Consciousness can be conceived in two major modes. The first of these is the mode of awareness, appreciation, esthetic sensitivity. The second mode is that of active agent, planner, and controller.

The characteristic mood of the 1960's led to a reevaluation of consciousness via drugs, Eastern religions, meditation, alpha training, ESP, and the numerous special cults that sprang up, characteristically laying great emphasis upon awareness, on the sense of pure being, on planes of experience that had their mystical or ecstatic components. Consciousness can indeed be viewed in this mode, but it is a partial view.

Consciousness can also be viewed in the active or executive mode, for it is only through consciousness that we can think ahead, having images of where we are going, and formulate plans for becoming the kind of person we would like to become or to accomplish the kinds of things we would like to accomplish.

These two modes of consciousness are not entirely separable, and even when they are differentiated, there may be some bridge between them. A St. Theresa may go to the mountain-top for her mystical experience and return to the valley to do her social services.

Let us now try to relate these two modes to the experience of hypnosis.

For the relationship of the hypnotic consciousness to experiences characterized according to the first mode, by sensitive awareness of inner states, selflessness, mystical experiences, or ecstasy, we need to have more exploration of deep and prolonged hypnosis. Actually most hypnosis is carried on at rather light levels, which is fortunate because these levels can be achieved by so many people. Erickson (1952) gave an account of deep hypnosis leading in some cases to a plenary trance, in which the subject becomes essentially inert or stuporous, but his discussions of this state were rather informal then and in later accounts (e.g., Erickson, 1962). The primary symptom that he noted was losing contact with the body, so that restoration may come as a shock, and Erickson warned that care should be taken to restore the normal condition slowly as a precaution against this. Although responses to the hypnotist came more slowly in the deep trance, the subject, according to Erickson, does not in fact lose contact.

A case of deep hypnosis has been reported by Charles Tart (1970). On a subjective scale of hypnotic depth he gave most of the expected responses to suggestion at a depth defined by him (with Tart's help) as a depth of 30, but continuing to go deeper he eventually reached a depth of 130. The usual phenomena of hypnosis were pretty much left behind at a depth of around 50 on his scale, when his own identity and that of the hypnotist began to change, the hypnotist becoming just a voice and his own identity changing from actuality to potentiality. Time became a meaningless concept. Much of his report reflects the kind of experiences that mystics have described. The particular young man giving these reports had served repeatedly as a subject in Tart's laboratory, where the vocabulary of unusual experience is part of the familiar conversation, and we do not know how general his experiences are. A similar unpublished study by Spencer Sherman (1971) at Stanford gave comparable results, and I have heard similar descriptions by those whom I have studied in prolonged hypnosis.

I do not wish to say very much about these experiences here because they are not typical of hypnosis as it is usually studied. For one thing, unless special precautions are taken, the subject loses contact with the hypnotist. At greater depths he no longer responds to suggestions. Only an implanted signal, such as touching his arm to bring him back, restores contact. Most of the subjects who participate willingly in these experiments have already had their expectations colored by meditation, drugs, Gestalt therapy, or other influences that make it hard to distinguish between what belongs to hypnosis and what belongs to something else. In any case, depth experiences as here described have been little studied with scientific controls. They are not the same as the exploration of the unconscious by free-association methods; their aim is not to solve problems but to have rich experiences of essentially passive sorts, of the kind described by mystics as noetic but ineffable, that is, giving a sense of having been enlightened, but finding nothing communicable from the knowledge gained.

Now for the other mode of consciousness - the active mode - as it is represented in hypnosis. At the levels at which hypnosis is most often studied, the active mode is the most familiar, in which control and loss of control are the essences of the experience. What one sees is that ordinary cognitive controls of behavior are changed in the midst of hypnosis. The hypnotized person may be unable to perform a familiar voluntary act, such as rising from a chair or speaking his name. On the other hand, he may gain voluntary control over normally involuntary processes, such as controlling blood flow, or no longer being sensitive to a painful burn. Most of the illustrations of hypnotic behavior and experience that are familiar represent either the enhancement or the inhibition of normal control processes. That being the case, the basic problem of hypnotic theory, as it bears on familiar hypnotic responsiveness, is to understand how these control processes are modified.

Normal control processes, outside hypnosis, are less unified, more fragmented, than we ordinarily believe. We are familiar with dreams that seem not to be our responsibility, although we must indeed be both the playwright and the stage manager of our dreams. Daydreams, too, often have an autonomous quality. If you introspect right now on your thoughts as you read this you will realize how many streams of self-talk go on at once. Even if you are quite attentive to the reading, you will find yourself carrying on several conversations with yourself: "Where will I eat lunch?" "I wonder who was present at that session?" You have short-range plans, long-range plans, accidental intrusions. Many of these are occasionally in awareness, occasionally set aside and ignored. Even Kurt Lewin, who, as a Gestalt psychologist would be expected to emphasize wholeness, was firm in his statement that personality is a weak Gestalt, not a strong one (Lewin, 1926).

While there are many diverse cognitive controls, they are not all active at once. They are arranged at any one time in a kind of hierarchy, so that some dominant control system has access to the expression of emotion and to overt behavior; other controls, if active, might express themselves differently in both feeling and action. If it were not for some sort of heirarchy, any triggered impulse might lead to a spasm of inchoate activity.

I have represented this in an oversimplified way in Figure 4. Ittindicates that there are many subsystems under some sort of dominant control by an executive system. The executive works under some constraints, so that everything is not all that orderly. The heirarchy is indicated crudely by the position in the chart of several subsystems. This is intended to represent the normal manner in which our thoughts activate what we do, what we experience consciously, and what we keep in abeyance.

What I now propose, as a general theory of the influence of hypnotic suggestion, is that the hierarchies of control become modified under hypnosis, according to the kinds of outcomes I have already described in the various specimens of hypnotic responsiveness.

A striking feature of these modifications, that leads me to refer to my theory as a <u>neodissociation theory</u> is that some cognitive systems, even though not represented in consciousness at the time, continue to register and process incoming information, and when such a system is released from inhibition it uses this information as though it had been conscious all along. This is the clinical picture that we find in multiple personality; it is the laboratory picture when the hidden observer is brought to light.

A more precise or molecular interpretation of what happens will require examining the roles of attention, amnesia and imagery more

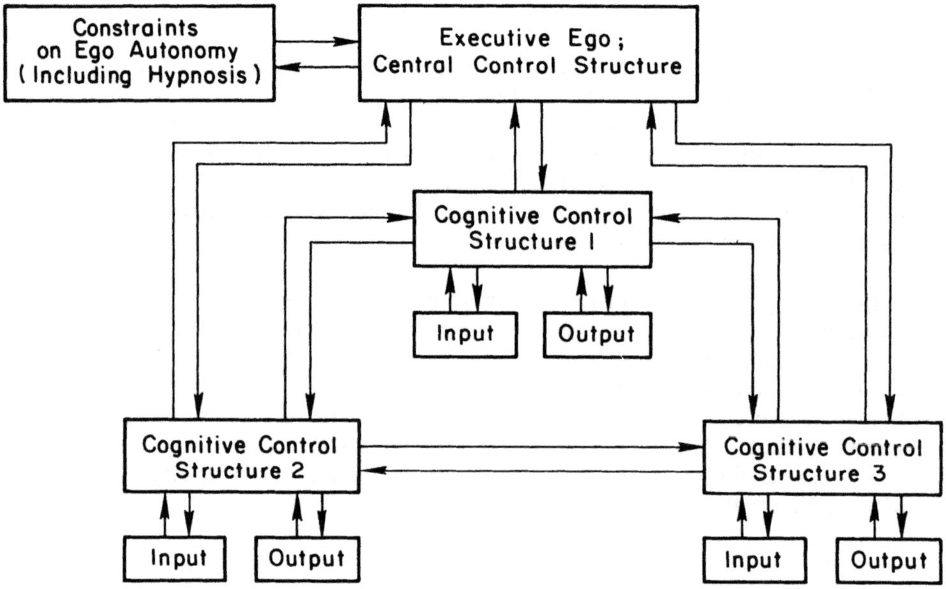

Fig. 4. A conceptualization of alternative cognitive control structures in hierarchical order. (From Hilgard, 1973. Copyright 1973 by the American Psychological Association. Reprinted by permission).

intimately, and to find appropriate neurophysiological bases for the parallel processing that occurs (Hilgard, 1977a).

NEUROPHYSIOLOGICAL LEADS

The advances in neurophysiology in the last decades have given us many leads for the study of dissociated activities and their integration. These are leads only, and a finished theory is something for the future. Let me cite only two as illustrative.

The clearest evidence of a dissociation of the vertical kind, in which cognitive processes are intact as far as they go, but separate, comes from the split-brain studies in which we find that the two hemispheres are quite specialized in some of their functions. In studies in our laboratory initiated by Paul Bakan (1969) and carried further by Raquel and Ruben Gur (1974) it has been shown quite clearly that hypnotic responsiveness is higher (in right-handed men especially) among those who, given an opporunity, prefer to use their right hemispheres. This is coherent with the findings of Josephine Hilgard (1965; 1970; 1974) that a high level of imaginative involvement is an important component of hypnotic responsiveness, and imagination, as we know, is a right-hemisphere activity. Because imaginative escape from harsh reality is one method by which hypnotic results come about, it is quite possible that the division between the hemispheres may eventually throw some light upon the dissociations that we study.

We may also have to deal with the horizontal division between the higher brain functions represented by cortical activity, and lower impulsive functions, as represented by the hypothalamus and the limbic system. I wish to close with one illustration of symptoms amenable to hypnotic treatment that have been characterized in this way.

The condition is that called anorexia nervosa, and is a fairly widespread disturbance, found especially among adolescent girls and young women. A thousand cases have recently been surveyed in England, as part of a student health survey (Zeeman, 1976).

The psychological interest in this case rests on the obvious imbalance of normal control systems, because food intake has become unrelated to bodily needs or to their usual expression in hunger and appetite.

The patient may describe the sudden changes as follows. She has been controlling her fasting, refusing food even though hungry. She may be hungry enough to enjoy the taste of food, even placing some in her mouth for the flavor, only to spit it out before swallowing. Suddenly, she says, she "lets go," and is helpless as she watches the "monster within her" devour food for several hours.

Eventually exhaustion, disgust and humiliation sweep over her, an experience that some anorexics speak of as a "knockout." She returns to fasting, but now with a somewhat different motivation - to rid herself of some sort of contamination.

We have here a kind of alternation between heirarchical control systems such as shown in Figure 4, with some of the characteristics of dual personality. In some respects it is more like a "possession state" because amnesia does not appear to be involved.

My reason for presenting the picture here is that there is a <u>third</u> state which can be used for the benefit of the patient. A British psychotherapist, J. Hevesi, has built upon this state, and apparently his patients were the only ones completely cured among a number surveyed.

This third state he calls <u>trance</u>. I do not find the word hypnosis used by him in connection with it, but hypnosis can be used, and has been used, to produce the state such as he describes. apparently it is sometimes found spontaneously, just as the patient awakens from a night of fitfull sleep. For a little while she is not preoccupied with food - neither thinking of the joy of eating nor scheming how to avoid eating. During that state she can reflect upon her condition, and achieve reassurance that she might become like other people.

Something psychologically similar is very frequent in multiple personality. The hidden part of the person, revealed only in a trance-like state, may represent the normal personality prior to something that led to the abnormal behavior, and this hidden normal personality can serve, under wise guidance, as the basis for integration. I mentioned this earlier in describing Felida X.

Note how this fits the pattern that I am proposing of alternative control systems, in some sort of hierarchy.

Zeeman, who is a student of the brain as well as of mathematics, proposes that the fasting stage is under cortical control, with the patient scheming very cleverly to avoid food; the goal is abnormal, but the mechanism is that of ordinary ego processes making plans and carrying them out against obstacles. At this stage, the limbic system, that usually controls these matters, is lower in the hierarchy. In the gorging stage, by contrast, the limbic system takes over without the usual inhibition by the cortex so that the balance turns the other way. The problem is to restore the appropriate balance by bringing in a more normal executive control that balances appetite, eating, and weight regulation.

Hypnosis, because it has access to control systems in its unique ways, can become a powerful force for integration. Our reason for an interest in dissociation is to bring the separate parts into an appropriate balance.

REFERENCES

Azam, E.E. Hypnotisme, double conscience et altération de la personalité. Préface de J.M. Charcot. Paris: Baillière, 1887.

Bakan, P. Hypnotizability, laterality of eye movements, and functional brain asymmetry. Perceptual and Motor Skills, 1969, 28, 927-932.

Clemes, S.R. Repression and hypnotic amnesia. Journal of Abnormal and Social Psychology, 1964, 69, 62-69.

Ellenberger, H.F. The discovery of the unconscious. New York: Basic Books, 1970.

Erickson, M.H. Deep hypnosis and its induction. In L.M. Le Cron (editor), Experimental hypnosis. New York: Macmillan, 1952. Pp. 70-112.

Erickson, M.H. Discussion of plenary trance. In G.H. Estabrooks (editor), Hypnosis: current problems. New York: Harper and Row, 1962. Pp. 255-260.

Gur, R.C., & Gur, R.E. Handedness, sex, and eyedness as moderating variables in the relation between hypnotic susceptibility and functional brain asymmetry. Journal of Abnormal Psychology, 1974, 83, 635-643.

Hilgard, E.R. A neodissociation interpretation of pain reduction in hypnosis. Psychological Review, 1973, 80, 396-411.

Hilgard, E.R. Neo-dissociation theory: multiple cognitive controls in hypnosis. In L.E. Uneståhl (editor), Hypnosis in the seventies. Örebro, Sweden: Veje Förlag, 1975. Pp. 7-14.

Hilgard, E.R. Divided consciousness: Multiple controls in human thought and action. New York: Wiley-Interscience, 1977a

Hilgard, E.R. Neodissociation theory of multiple cognitive control systems. In G.E. Schwartz and D. Shapiro (editors), Consciousness and self-regulation. Advances in research, Vol. I, New York: Plenum Press, 1977b.

Hilgard, E.R., & Hilgard, J.R. Hypnosis in the relief of pain. Los Altos, California: William Kaufmann, Inc., 1975.

Hilgard, E.R., Morgan, A.H., & Macdonald, H. Pain and dissociation in the cold pressor test: a study of hypnotic analgesia with "hidden reports" through automatic key-pressing and automatic talking. Journal of Abnormal Psychology, 1975, 85, 218-224.

Hilgard, J.R. Personality and hypnotizability: Inferences from case studies. In E.R. Hilgard, Hypnotic susceptibility. New York: Harcourt, Brace and Jovanovich, 1965. Pp. 343-374.

Hilgard, J.R. Personality and hypnosis: a study of imaginative involvement. Chicago: University of Chicago Press, 1970.

Hilgard, J.R. Imaginative involvement: some charactersitics of the highly hypnotizable and the nonhypnotizable. International Journal of Clinical and Experimental Hypnosis, 1974, 22, 138-156.

Knox, V.J., Crutchfield, L., & Hilgard, E.R. The nature of task interference in hypnotic dissociation. International Journal of Clinical and Experimental Hypnosis, 1975, 23, 305-323.

Lewin, K. Vorsatz, Wille, und Bedürfness. Psychologische Forschung, 1926, 7, 294-385.

Litvag, I. Singer in the shadows: The strange case of Patience Worth. New York: Macmillan, 1972.

Mitchell, T.W. Divisions of the self and coconsciousness. In C.M. Campbell, and others (editors), Problems of personality: Studies presented to Dr. Morton Prince. New York: Harcourt, Brace, 1925. Pp. 191-203.

Nace, E.P., Orne, M.T., & Hammer, A.G. Posthypnotic amnesia as an active psychic process: The reversibility of amnesia. Archives of General Psychiatry, 1974, 31, 257-260.

Sherman, S.E. Very deep hypnosis: An experiential and electro-encephalographic investigation. Unpublished Ph.D. dissertation, Stanford University, 1971.

Stevenson, J.H. The effect of posthypnotic dissociation on the performance of interfering tasks. Journal of Abnormal Psychology, 1976, 85, 398-407.

Tart, C.T. Self-report scales of hypnotic depth. International Journal of Clinical and Experimental Hypnosis, 1970, 18, 105-125.

Zeeman, E.C. Catastrophe theory. Scientific American, 1976, 234, 65-83.

THE ABBÉ FARIA: A NEGLECTED FIGURE IN THE HISTORY OF HYPNOSIS

Campbell Perry

Concordia University, Canada

Abstract: Virtually nothing is known of the Abbé Faria's life, except that he was born in Goa in either 1755 or 1756, and initiated public demonstrations of animal magnetism in Paris in 1813. He died in 1819, the year that his book On the Cause of Lucid Sleep was published. Most of his observations have subsequently been either ignored, or attributed to a contemporary, Alexandre Bertrand.

Faria's contributions were based upon a radical innovation in induction procedures. He replaced the elaborate rituals of the magnetic movement with simpler suggestive methods, by requesting the subject to close his eyes and focus his attention on sleep. After a short period he would instruct the subject with one word: "Sleep." With this procedure, based upon experience with 5,000 people, Faria laid the foundations of trait and skill theories of hypnosis by documenting individual differences in hypnotic response. Further, in contradiction to the magnetists, he believed that hypnotic phenomena depended almost entirely upon inherent abilities of the subject. In particular, he drew close parallels between the behavior of subjects capable of "lucid sleep" (his term for hypnosis) and the abilities of people who sleep walk and sleep talk. In this, he anticipated Braid's coining of the term hypnosis, from the Greek *hypnos* (to sleep).

Faria considered several plausible explanations of hypnotic phenomena and rejected them. He discounted the role of imagination (emphasized by the Benjamin

Franklin Commission of 1784) by a mistaken analogy to the phenomena of posthypnotic amnesia. He also gave little importance to the role of suggestion, believing that hypnotic phenomena were almost entirely the result of the hypnotized person's superior powers of concentration. Paradoxically, he was keenly aware of the role of suggestion in clinical settings.

Faria's contemporary effect was minimal, and the judgement of history has consistently underestimated his contribution. This is so, despite the fact that he anticipated much of what was later to be said by Bertrand, Braid, Liébeault, and Bernheim and laid the groundwork for several modern beliefs about the nature of hypnosis.

Very little is known about the life of the Abbé Faria. He was Portuguese, born in Goa in either 1755 or 1756. He said he was a Brahmin, but nothing is known about him until he came to Paris in 1813, at the age of either 57 or 58. He died six years later in 1819, the year in which his only writings were published - a book entitled <u>On the Cause of Lucid Sleep</u> (which was his term for hypnosis).

Initially, in Paris, he enjoyed a considerable vogue demonstrating hypnotic phenomena, including a very striking demonstration of taste hallucination. In this, he would suggest that the water that his hypnotized subjects were drinking was really wine, something that would have appealed to Parisians both for its theological implications and for its economic possibilities. However, public opinion quickly turned against him as the result of an incident in 1815, which had the effect of discrediting him completely. At one of his demonstrations, a subject simulated hypnosis, and in the middle of it, burst into laughter, and said, "Well, Monsieur l'Abbé, if you magnetize people the way you have magnetized me, you won't put many people to sleep. I have fooled you (Barracund, 1967, p. 70)."

From then on, he became a public joke, and this impression of him was encouraged by the animal magnetists, who very correctly perceived him as a threat to everything they stood for. Indeed, they regarded Faria as anathema to the extent of prohibiting all reference to his teachings from appearing in the magnetic journals. He has not done very much better since. All of the historians - Binet and Féré (1888), Bramwell (1906), Podmore (1964), Janet (1925), Hull (1933), and Ellenberger (1970) - say very little about him. Indeed Janet (1925) mistakenly attributed his major observations to a contemporary, Alexandre Bertrand. Bertrand espoused orthodox magnetic beliefs in his book of 1823 - four years after Faria's book. He changed his views under the influence of General Noizet

- one of Faria's good hypnotic subjects - and did not formally recant until a second book in 1826, in which he sided with the conclusions of the Benjamin Franklin Commission that magnetic phenomena depended upon the workings of the magnetized person's imagination. Janet's error was to date Faria's book as 1827 instead of 1819.

From then onwards, Faria's contributions fell into almost total neglect. In his book of 1843, Braid goes to considerable lengths to dismiss the accusation of "unacknowledged plagiarism" of Faria and Bertrand. Certainly, there are remarkable similarities in induction techniques and theorizing between Braid and Faria. What appears to have happened is that Braid read both Faria and Bertrand, assimilated their main positions, but came to different conclusions. Rather than being unacknowledged plagiarism, Braid's work seems to represent a few unacknowledged debts to the ideas of these earlier investigators.

Both Gilles de la Tourette, and Liébeault were influenced by Faria's writings, and the latter, in turn, passed on this influence to Bernheim. There was a small vogue for Faria at the turn of this century which led to his 1819 book being republished in France in 1903 with a long and laudatory introduction by D.G. Dalgado. Since collecting the material on which this paper is based, I have come across Barracund's History of Hypnosis in France, published in French in 1967. He is the first historian to have written extensively on Faria, and his evaluation of Faria's importance, made independently a decade ago, is very similar to my own.

To grasp fully the magnitude of Faria's contribution to the study of hypnosis, it is necessary to look at the views about hypnosis that were current at the time he lived. During the French Revolution, and subsequent Napoleonic Wars, there was little interest in animal magnetism. It began to revive in the first decade of the 1800's, and most of it was of the most unbelievable kind.

To begin with, there was de Jussieu who believed that the phenomena elicited by Mesmer could be explained in terms of animal heat. This was conceived of in terms equally as broad as the mesmeric notion of animal magnetism - as a principle underlying the universe. Likewise, there was Petetin, who believed that magnetic phenomena could be explained in terms of accumulations of animal electric fluid in the body. He had the notion that disease drove this vital fluid from the peripheries to the brain and nervous system. He supported this conclusion with a series of remarkable experiments on transposition of the senses in cataleptic patients. In the cataleptic state, these patients seemingly could not hear, but they could reply to questions addressed to the pit of the stomach, the finger-tips or the toes. Such patients were often "found" to be able to taste, smell or see exclusively in these regions.

Further, de Puységur, despite his permanent place in the history of hypnosis, also contributed to some of its less believable folklore. He came to believe that hypnosis was a form of mental transference from the magnetist to the subject, as opposed to the mesmeric belief in a magnetic or physical force. He also believed that magnetized subjects could diagnose their own ailments, could predict the course and date of their own cure, and prescribe appropriate treatment. However, it is fair to say that, given the state of medicine at the time, some of his magnetized patients were probably at least as successful as the doctors - which from all accounts would not have been difficult.

All these beliefs may seem rather odd given the findings of the Benjamin Franklin Commission of 1784 which had correctly shown that animal magnetism did not exist and that its phenomena could be more adequately explained in terms of touch, imagination, and imitation, of which the most important was the imagination of the magnetized person. The Benjamin Franklin Commission, however, made one major error of interpretation that was to haunt the history of hypnosis for the next hundred years. It concluded that because animal magnetism did not exist, it could not possibly have any curative effects. In the years between 1784 and the Revolution of 1789, there was intense pamphlet warfare on this issue, with the magnetists publishing a deluge of case histories to document the reality of their cures. This point has been discussed in greater detail elsewhere (Sheehan & Perry, 1976). It is sufficient to say that magnetism was successful for a considerable number of patients who had not obtained relief from conventional medicine. The flavor of the times can be seen from the testimony of one satisfied patient, whose case history was published in 1784:

> If it is to illusion to which I owe the health I believe I enjoy, I humbly entreat the experts who see so clearly not to destroy it; that they may enlighten the universe, that they leave me with my error and that they permit my simplicity, my frailty and my ignorance to make use of an invisible agent, which does not exist, but which cures me (Podmore, 1964, p. 65).

Not merely is this a rebuke to the doctors, scientists, and academics who made up the Benjamin Franklin Commission, it helps also to explain why the Commissions report had little effect on the practice of animal magnetism for the next 100 years. Whenever a technique can effect cures, it is not going to disturb most patients that the underlying theory and rationale are completely mistaken.

Given this historical context, it is not surprising that Faria's views on magnetism were highly unwelcome. To help this process along, his manner of expressing them was highly abrasive. The uncompromising quality of his views is expressed in quotations such as the following:

> I am not able to conceive how the human species can be so bizarre that it has to search out the cause of this phenomenon in a baquet, in some external force, in a magnetic fluid, in animal heat, and in a thousand other ridiculous extravagances of this nature, when this kind of sleep is common to all human nature by way of dreams, and to all individuals who get up, walk, and talk in their sleep (Faria, 1906, p. 33).

Faria's book is, at times, difficult to read, mainly because it is laced with heavy doses of the theology and the medical science of the early 19th Century. I am unqualified to comment on the theology; the medicine was dominated by notions of spirits and sympathies which were postulated in order to make up for the comparative lack of factual data on the nervous system and its disorders. Faria's most important contributions can be summarized as follows:

1) He developed a new terminology for hypnosis which emphasized internal psychological processes and which is remarkably similar to that of Braid. He referred to hypnosis as "lucid sleep"; subsequently Braid (1843) coined the term hypnosis from the Greek "hypnos: to sleep." He referred to magnetism as <u>concentration</u> performed by a <u>concentrationist</u> (or magnetizer) on a <u>concentrater</u> (or subject). He referred to highly susceptible subjects as époptes, a term he derived from Greek which roughly translated means "he who sees all to be discovered." It simply means someone who can experience all the phenomena of hypnosis, though it is connected also with a set of mystical beliefs that need not concern us here.

2) A second point is that Faria was the first investigator not only to report some of the individual differences in hypnotic ability, but also to give them prominence in his theorizing. Mesmer had observed individual differences in response around the baquet and had been puzzled by them. The Benjamin Franklin Commissioners had also noticed these differences, but had used them only to point out that responsivity to the baquet was much more variable than commonly supposed. Faria was the first to make them the cornerstone of his theoretical position. Equally as important, he proceeded to document some of these individual differences. He observed (on the basis of experience with over 5,000 people) that "experiments and observations demonstrate that lucid sleep, which adapts itself to climates, temperature, and to the quality of foods, is in France in the ratio of one in five or six of the population (Faria, 1906,

p. 142)." This figure of between 16 and 20 percent of highly susceptible people is not unlike what is still being found in present-day experimental settings.

3) Faria's third major contribution was in his induction procedures. Whereas with animal magnetism a variety of elaborate rituals developed in relation to the baquet and magnetized trees, Faria induced lucid sleep by having his subjects sit down, close their eyes, and focus their attention on sleep. After a period, he would instruct them with one word: "Sleep." If that failed, he would have the subject fixate on his open hand which he would move slowly towards the person's face. If that failed, he would touch the person lightly on the head, face and body. To terminate lucid sleep, he would instruct the person: "Wake up." These austere induction procedures yielded similar phenomena to those obtained using the elaborate techniques of the animal magnetists.

Faria developed a very interesting theory, which was mistaken on certain points but which is still relevant to many current-day attempts to understand the nature of hypnosis. Although his era was dominated by magnetic beliefs, the germs of several psychologically oriented views that were later to become prominent were nevertheless in the air at this time. There was the belief that hypnosis was all a matter of the will (i.e., positive motivation) of the hypnotized person, a view which de Puységur espoused. By contrast, Faria pointed out that people entered lucid sleep with favorable motivation, with no motivation, and even negative motivation. And he also pointed out that people, whom he had never met previously, would sometimes enter lucid sleep immediately as they crossed the threshold of his salon, before he could even speak to them. At the same time, he used this observation to dismiss the view of the magnetists that hypnosis was primarily a matter of powers of the magnetist over the magnetized person.

There was also the view of the Benjamin Franklin Commission that hypnosis was a matter of the hypnotized person's imagination - a view that, ironically enough, after almost 200 years of neglect, has regained considerable currency among many present-day investigators. Faria's main reason for rejecting imagination was based on the close parallels he drew between lucid and nocturnal sleep. He felt it was sufficient to reject imagination by recourse to the phenomenon of post-hypnotic amnesia. He observed that a person remembers all that is imagined, whereas after lucid sleep a person will forget some or all of the events that have transpired. While this view constitutes too sweeping a dismissal of imagination, it shows that he thought seriously about its possible contribution to hypnotic events.

Although Bernheim and Gilles de la Tourette regarded him as the originator of suggestibility theory, Faria placed minor emphasis upon suggestion as decisive for understanding lucid sleep. This is because he drew some very important distinctions between experimental and clinical hypnosis. On the one hand, he believed that the performance of époptes (the top 15 to 20 percent of subjects) depended upon natural abilities they possessed, particularly their powers of concentration. As he put it, "We cannot induce concentration in individuals whenever we desire; rather we find individuals who are inherently susceptible (Faria, 1906, p. 34)."

On the other hand, Faria performed a considerable amount of clinical hypnosis and seems to have regarded suggestion as more important in the therapeutic setting. For instance, he had an almost amazing awareness of placebo effects. He noted that an ineffective medicine, taken with confidence, is often more beneficial than an effective medicine, and that such confidence could be induced by suggestion. He seems to have understood a dilemma regularly encountered even today among clinical and experimental practitioners of hypnosis. That is, when the experimentalist talks of hypnosis, he is usually referring to the behavior of the top 10 to 15 percent of subjects high in hypnotic ability. By contrast, the clinician is usually speaking of an unselected group of subjects who are responsive to therapeutic suggestions given in conjunction with a hypnotic induction.

It indicates something of Faria's breadth that he could say that suggestion was relatively unimportant in determining the behavior of époptes, and yet maintain that suggestion was highly important in therapeutic settings.

Finally, Faria's own theory was a mixture of physiological and psychological observations. The physiology was wrong, mainly because it was based on the medical knowledge of his period. The psychological ingredients contain a number of hypotheses that are still highly tenable. On the physiological side, there was a medical belief, current at the time, that blood could be thick or thin, though arterial blood flow was always thick. Thus, Faria believed that hypnotic ability depended upon thinness of the blood. To demonstrate this point, he made the first known attempts to modify hypnotic susceptibility by extracting blood from initially recalcitrant subjects, and attempting to hypnotize them 24 hours later. At the same time, he believed that various psychological characteristics were important - in particular, the characteristic of impressionability. This may be why later investigators saw him as the originator of suggestibility theory.

But to borrow from Hilgard (1965), Faria saw more than one pathway into hypnosis. To him, the best époptes were anemics (because of their thin blood), hysterics and women (because of their greater impressionability), and people who fall asleep easily or perspire profusely (again on the grounds of impressionability). In addition to possessing these requisite predispositions, époptes had also to possess the skill of being able to concentrate their senses on the idea of lucid sleep. Faria does not always make this clear, but he appeared to be saying that impressionability or thin blood were not in themselves sufficient conditions to create an épopte; the skill of concentration was also required. In addition, he recognized the role of interpersonal factors. All of the foregoing abilities were of no avail unless the épopte perceived the hypnotist as competent; this, in turn, engendered trust, or "intimate conviction," as Faria put it. In other words, he was saying that it was necessary for the hypnotist to inspire confidence in order to provoke what he called "the development of natural phenomena."

From the foregoing analysis, it is clear that many currently plausible theories of hypnosis owe their debt to Faria. Unfortunately, his contributions have continued to be seriously underestimated at best, and ignored at worst. He is important for drawing attention to hypnotizability as a phenomenon requiring explanation, for emphasizing the inner workings of the hypnotized person in an era of almost universal belief in external influence by magnetic means, and for his observations of experimental and therapeutic suggestions.

REFERENCES

Barracund, D. Histoire de l'hypnose en France. Paris: Presses Universitaires de France, 1967.

Bertrand, A. Traité du somnambulisme et des différentes modifications qu'il présente. Paris: Dentu impr., 1823.

Bertrand, A. Du magnétisme animal en France et des jugements qu'en ont portés les sociétés savantes. Paris, 1826.

Binet, A., & Féré, C. Animal magnetism. (English Translation). New York: Appleton, 1888. (Originally published in French in 1886).

Braid, J. Neurypnology; or the rationale of nervous sleep considered in relation with animal magnetism. London: Churchill, 1843.

Bramwell, J.M. Hypnotism. Its history, practice, and theory. London: Alexander Moring, 1906.

Ellenberger, H. The discovery of the unconscious: The history and evolution of dynamic psychiatry. New York: Basic Books, 1970.

Faria, J.C. di Abbé. De la cause du sommeil lucide: ou étude sur la nature de l'homme, 2nd edition. (D.G. Dalgado, editor) Paris: Henri Jouve, 1906. (Originally published in 1819).

Hilgard, E.R. Hypnotic susceptibility. New York: Harcourt, Brace and World, 1965.

Hull, C.L. Hypnosis and suggestibility: An experimental approach. New York: Appleton-Century-Crofts, 1933.

Janet, P. Psychological healing: A historical and clinical study. (English translation by E. Paul and C. Paul). New York: Macmillan, 1925. 2 vols. (Originally published in French, 1919).

Podmore, F. From Mesmer to Christian Science. A short history of mental healing. New Hyde Park, New York: University Books, 1964. (Originally published in 1909).

Sheehan, P.W., & Perry, C.W. Methodologies of hypnosis: A critical appraisal of contemporary paradigms of hypnosis. Hillsdale, New Jersey: Erlbaum, 1976.

WHAT DID HE (BERNHEIM) SAY?

André M. Weitzenhoffer

Veterans Administration Hospital

Oklahoma City, Oklahoma, U.S.A.

Abstract: Bernheim was not the first to call attention to the fact that suggestions can be effective in the absence of hypnosis or to claim that hypnosis itself is a product of suggestion. However, he does appear to have been the first to state explicitly that _all_ hypnotic phenomena can be produced by suggestion in the absence of hypnosis. This important discovery is thus at least a hundred years old.

Bernheim is perhaps best known for his dictum that, "There is no hypnosis, there is only suggestion." This has often been misunderstood to mean that he denied the existence of a hypnotic state. That was not his intention. Bernheim expressly made the point that hypnosis was a specific condition of enhanced suggestibility brought about through the characteristic ideodynamic action of appropriate suggestions. He viewed the induction of hypnosis as setting into motion psychophysiological changes that lead to a decrease in ego participation and to increasingly complex automatisms. Thus, in addition to evidence that Bernheim viewed hypnosis as an altered state of awareness, one finds evidence of his anticipation of Janet's dissociation theory of hypnosis. Bernheim, however, also held a "modern" view of suggestion as a manifestation of normal, healthy processes and, hence, as belonging to the domain of normal psychology. In doing so he anticipated features of some modern ego psychological theories of hypno-suggestive phenomena.

> The non-voluntary character of responses to suggestions emphasized by Bernheim's theory has essentially been ignored in modern research. The resulting failure to distinguish between individuals who respond voluntarily and non-voluntarily may have been an important source of confusion in recent research. This failure may also mean that hypnotism as defined by modern research methods is not the same entity originally studied and described by Bernheim and his contemporaries.

In a recent article, Krauss, Katzell and Krauss (1974) assert, "...Barber (e.g., 1969) appears to have demonstrated that all phenomena once felt to characterize the hypnotic state can be produced without hypnosis (p. 144)." Although these authors do not specifically assert that Barber was the first to do this, or even to make this point, there is the implication of it. Quite apart from this, the above quote reflects an increasing trend, starting some fifteen years ago, to giving Barber credit for first calling attention to, if not for discovering or demonstrating, the above important fact.

To whom the credit should go will probably never be fully established. One can certainly point out, however, that at least three years before Barber's first publication, Weitzenhoffer (1953) had stated, after an extensive review of the available data, "Actually, most, if not all, of the phenomena one can obtain with suggestions given to a hypnotized subject can also be obtained without going through the preliminary process of hypnotizing him (p. 6)." And, much earlier, Wells (1924) had written an article aimed expressly at detailing procedures he used to produce hypnotic-like behavior in the absence of any formal induction of hypnosis. Still earlier, such well-known authorities as Moll and Forel, writing at the start of the century, had explicitly recognized the potentialities existing in "waking-suggestions" for eliciting hypnotic phenomena.

In fact, there are indications as early as 1784 that the scientific community was aware of the role suggestion played in the production of mesmeric phenomena, even though the term "suggestion" does not appear to have been in use then. Braid, who coined the term "hypnotism" in 1841, was very much aware of this role of suggestion and performed experiments to demonstrate it, even though he, too, did not specifically make use of this term in his early writings. One of the first to do so in connection with hypnotic phenomena was William B. Carpenter. In a rather remarkable paper in 1852, in which he explicitly spoke of suggestion, Carpenter also developed the thesis that hypnotic phenomena and, in particular, the sleep characteristics of hypnosis, were products of suggestions whose effects, he proposed further, came about through the physiological mechanism of "ideo-motor action." Although he does not explicitly say so, there are clear indications in his paper that he did not view hypnosis as essential for the production of suggested phenomena. On the other hand, he also held that certain mental conditions involving the abeyance of the will, such as he believed occurred with hypnosis, favored the effects of suggestion. In later writings, Carpenter went on to amplify these ideas.

Although Bernheim (1886) indicated that he first stated at a scientific meeting in 1833 that suggestion alone can produce all hypnotic phenomena, he certainly was not the first to introduce this possibility. In fact, Bernheim (1886) credits Braid with having partially anticipated him around 1846 in a paper titled "Phenomena of the Waking Condition." Bernheim does, however, appear to have been the first to take that position explicitly and unambiguously, a position he was to hold and develop throughout the years, and to expound upon voluminously. Carpenter clearly anticipated Bernheim in this regard, but it seems to have been mainly through Bernheim's efforts that the doctrine of suggestion has come down to us. Furthermore, while Carpenter may have done some experimentation of his own, it appears to have been minimal at best, and it remained for Bernheim to develop the suggestion theory of hypnotic phenomena on a solid ground of clinical and experimental findings of his own as well as of others.

The clearest and most detailed exposition of Bernheim's ideas in this connection is to be found in his 1886 work where he writes, "I insist upon the fact that all or some of these suggestions may be realized with and without sleep (p. 15)." A little further on he continues, "...Hypnotism is not then the necessary prelude to suggestion; it facilitates suggestion when it can be induced;" and, significantly, he adds, "but other suggestions may sometimes succeed when the suggestion of sleep is inefficious (p. 15)." As the years went by, his further experience only confirmed this view for him, and twenty years later (1903) we find him writing, "I have definitely established that induced sleep is not necessary in order to obtain so-called hypnotic phenomena...they may be elicited in some non-hypnotized subjects (p. 78)." In making this unambiguous statement born out of his investigations of hypnotic phenomena, Bernheim definitely antedates Barber by about half a century.

As a matter of fact, Bernheim made at least one other statement which, taken out of context, could be viewed as indicating that he had also anticipated both Barber and Sarbin (e.g., 1972) in respect to another matter: that there is no hypnosis. For in 1903 we find him writing, "In my opinion, the best thing one could do would be to completely delete the word hypnotism and replace it by suggestion state (p. 78)." In further affirmation and explanation, he added, "There is no hypnotism: by this I mean to say there is no special, anormal, antiphysiological state, meriting this name; there are only more or less suggestible subjects, to whom one may suggest ideas, emotions, actions, hallucinations (p. 80)."

But wait. What exactly did Bernheim say here? That we ought to replace the term "hypnotism" by "suggestion state" - not just by "suggestion," but by "suggestion state." Granted, he may have intended nothing more by appending the term "state" to "suggestion." But, then, maybe he did intend to make an essential distinction.

As a matter of fact, there is ample evidence in the two works quoted that this is the case. For Bernheim, as with Barber, a central issue was that of causality. Contrary to what Barber (1969) has recently asserted, Bernheim clearly considered suggestion to be the prime cause of all the observed phenomena; however, again in contrast to Barber, he also believed in the possibility of inducing a state of hypersuggestibility in some individuals by means of suggestion. The latter state he identified with what had been and was then being called hypnotism.

Thus, he states in 1886, "I define hypnotism as the induction of a peculiar psychical condition which increases the susceptibility to suggestion. Often, it is true, the sleep that may be induced facilitates suggestion, but it is not the necessary preliminary. It is suggestion that rules hypnotism (p. 15)." Here, then, Bernheim clearly tells us three things: There is a special condition of hypersuggestibility that can be induced. It may have sleep-like characteristics. It is not the prime cause, suggestion is. Significantly, he adds, "the hypnotic condition is not an abnormal one, it does not create new functions nor extraordinary phenomena; it develops those which are produced in the waking condition; because of a psychic modality, it exaggerates the normal susceptibility to suggestion, which we all possess to some extent; our psychical condition is modified...(p. 149)."

Can any clearer statement be made regarding the existence of an induced state characterized by hypersuggestibility? Or of the continuity between normal everyday behavior and hypnotic or suggested behavior?

The association of sleep with induced states of hypersuggestibility is mentioned frequently by Bernheim. He did not view sleep as a requisite for hypersuggestibility, but felt that, when sleep could be induced, it was often associated with the highest degrees of suggestibility. It was for this combination of great suggestibility and sleep that he reserved the label "somnambulism." Bernheim did not have access to electroencephalographic data. Partial-to-complete spontaneous amnesia upon waking was his one criterion for induced sleep as well as for natural sleep. Because of this, Bernheim viewed the two conditions as indistinguishable. His conception of hypnosis as an altered state of awareness is well summarized in the following quote (1886): "...I repeat that sleep, whether it be artificial or spontaneous, does not mean the abolition of the intellectual faculties; it is a cerebral condition other than the waking...a condition in which the phenomena of automatic life predominate...Without developing this view...let us be content to know that the mind may still think and work during sleep...we are conscious of it, as the somnambulist is conscious of what he is doing, only it is another state of consciousness. The mind keeps up its intellectual work during sleep. In some cases this work during sleep is accomplished in a visible manner... (p. 153)."

The role and primacy of suggestion in the production of hypnotic sleep and the mechanism of its production are expressed further in the following quote (1886): "The sleep is itself but a suggested effect in no ways different than are catalepsy, anesthesia, and hallucinations...All dynamic activities of the body can be enhanced, inhibited or distorted by suggestion; motility, sensation, imagination, etc. Each subject has his specific suggestibilities; this one is suggestible only with regard to movement, this other one only so with regard to pain...this third subject is suggestible, in addition, with respect to certain sensory images: one may induce in him gustatory and auditory hallucinations. Each person, has, I repeat, his own modes of suggestibility...A certain number of persons succeed in actualizing the suggestion of sleep (p. 78)." And, further on, "Sleep exaggerates physiological automatism, it does not create it (p. 191)."

Regarding suggestion itself, Bernheim (1903) writes the following: "I define suggestion in the widest sense; it is the act through which an idea is introduced into the brain and accepted by it (p. 24)." Suggested phenomena, he explains further, result from a combination of beliefs, that is, of non-critical acceptance of ideas, and from automatisms founded upon ideo-dynamic reflex action. "It is a psychological law," writes Bernheim (1903), "which derives from observation: Each cell activated by an idea activates the nerve fibers which actualize this idea (p. 31)." Normally, he explained, the critical faculties interfere with this reflex and prevent it from manifesting itself, or greatly modify its manifestations. But when the critical faculties or ego processes are held in abeyance, or in the absence of contrary information, the immediate response of an individual to incoming information is one of believing it. That is, there is then "direct acceptance" by the brain of this information and of the ideas which it conveys and generates by association. This acceptance, which is a centripetal action, is suggestion proper. It is followed immediately by the reflexive, centrifugal actualization of the associated ideas. "Every suggestion," wrote Bernheim (1903), "tends toward becoming action, to realize itself. The idea becomes sensation, that is, a tactile, gustatory, olfactory, auditory, visual image. It becomes movement. It becomes emotion (p. 4)."

Furthermore, according to Bernheim, the primary ideas that are suggested produce further ideas by association, and these secondary ideas can also lead to direct action. Additionally, he emphacized, responses to suggestion show great diversity and are a function of the innate qualities of each individual's brain, of his acquired aptitudes, and of prior suggestions. The response to suggestion can, therefore, be complex behavior that is not always fully predictable.

In view of Carpenter's earlier writings, it needs to be recognized once again that Bernheim's theory of suggestion was not original. However, he did develop the theory more fully and gave it a more solid empirical foundation. He wrote extensively about it, and his writings not only influenced his contemporaries greatly but have had considerable impact on the development of modern hypnotism.

The best and most explicit account of his theory of suggestion is found in his 1886 volume. There he develops most fully his conception of ideo-motor and ideo-sensory-based automatisms, a concept that was to become a main topic in his much later book, published in 1917.

By the term automatism, he means any simple or complex activity not mediated by the volitional apparatus (i.e., by the conscious mind). "Automatic acts," he writes (1917), "are those which are realized through a somatic mechanism, without the psychic cerebral action, will and conscious intelligence, intervening in its realization (p. 1)." The relevance of automatisms to suggestions is direct. It is in the nature of suggestion to elicit automatisms.

Automatisms range from such relatively simple effects as the contracture of a specific muscle to the most complex behaviors that have been attributed to natural and artificial somnambulism. Simple or complex, they are all based upon ideo-dynamic action. Furthermore, (and this is a point about which Bernheim was emphatic) automatisms, simple and complex, are all a part of normal, everyday functioning. All that suggestion does is to make use of already existing normal mechanisms and processes which, normally, are subject to the overriding, modulating influence of the executive functions, that is, of the conscious, volitional apparatus.

An obvious corollary of Bernheim's theory of suggestion is that any process or agent that can eliminate interference by the executive functions should facilitate suggestion. This is how Bernheim views the suggestibility-enhancing properties of natural sleep and induced sleep. And, in line with his position that very real physiological changes do take place when sleep is induced, he warned against inducing too complete a sleep, lest the subject become unresponsive to stimuli from the same kind of depression of brain activity as seen in profound sleep.

The fundamental automatism and non-voluntariness that Bernheim associates with suggested behavior clearly anticipates later dissociation theories of hypnotic behavior. Indeed, consider one of the definitions of suggestion that Pierre Janet, the so-called father of the dissociation theory of hypnosis, gives in his classic 1925 work: "Suggestion is a peculiar reaction to certain perceptions; the reaction consists in the activation, more or less complete, of the tendency aroused by the suggestion, in the absence of a completion of the activation by the collaboration of the remainder of the personality (p. 230)."* The rest of the text makes it quite clear that he is referring to the lack of participation of the ego in the production of the suggested behavior. Indeed, in an earlier work, Janet (1889) states concisely: "The name suggestion has been given to this influence of one man upon another which exerts itself without mediation of voluntary consent (p. 139)." Could one hope for any clearer statement than this?

Basically, both Janet and Bernheim see circumvention of ego control (hence, of mediation by the critical faculties and by volition) as the specific mark of suggested behavior. This, of course, is what we find implicitly, if not explicitly, in all discussions of hypnotic behavior since then until fairly recently. For both investigators, induced somnambulism, the ultimate form of hypnotic behavior, is nothing more than a complex, elaborate, automatism, possibly a superordinate automatism built upon more elementary automatisms through suggestion. In the final analysis, one can find very little fundamental difference between the theories of Janet and of Bernheim.

Bernheim's view of hypnotism and, especially, suggestion has important implications for modern hypnotism, and especially for the research in it which has gone on during the last fifteen to twenty years and even longer. As the present writer (1972, 1973) has previously observed, there has been a tendency on the part of modern clinical and experimental hypnotists to ignore the criteria of enhanced suggestibility and of non-voluntariness in judging, respectively, whether or not a state of hypnosis was present and whether or not responses to communications intended to function as suggestions were adequate. The common practice has been to use an induction of hypnosis and then, and only then, to measure the subject's suggestibility. If the subject's suggestibility has gone through an enhancement as a result of the induction procedure, this important information has been lost and subjects with, as well as without, enhancement have been treated identically with respect to the presence or absence of hypnosis and its depth. Similarly, subjects responding voluntarily as well as non-voluntarily to communications intended to serve as suggestions have, more often than not, been treated the same, with no account taken of this difference. The development of modern scales of suggestibility and hypnotizability

---

* Underlining by the present author.

has been particularly instrumental in spreading this potentially deleterious practice over the last 47 years. The inability on the part of several generations of investigators to find meaningful correlations between personality variables and suggestibility or hypnotizability may very well have its basis in the above mentioned confoundings. Similarly, many of the discrepancies and disagreements which continue to crop up regarding the facts of hypnotism may have at least partial roots in these confoundings.

As the present writer has been able to demonstrate recently (Weitzenhoffer 1972, 1974), it is possible, with a small procedural modification, to provide empirical support for Bernheim's view of suggestion, using the same test situations that form the basis of such scales as the Stanford Scale of Hypnotic Susceptibility, Forms A and B (Weitzenhoffer and Hilgard, 1959) and other similar scales. That is, one can demonstrate with modern tools and methods, that presumably hypnotized and non-hypnotized subjects fall into two groups: those experiencing voluntary responses and those experiencing non-voluntary responses. Furthermore, the data have shown that the induction of hypnosis enhances suggestibility through its specific contribution to the non-voluntary group. Thus, it does not seem possible to continue to ignore Bernheim's conception of suggestions and suggested responses.

Bernheim's writings are historically important, not only because of the influence they had on his contemporaries and subsequent generations of investigators, but also because they reflect a concensus existing in his time regarding the non-voluntary or automatic aspect of suggested behavior. This is one particular feature attested to by a majority of his contemporaries as well as earlier investigators. One implication of the present paper is that the modern approach to hypnotism, particularly as it is reflected in the Stanford scales and other similar instruments, amounts to a redefinition of hypnotism and suggestion at variance with that held by Bernheim. A further implication is that hypnotism today may not be the same thing as hypnotism was in Bernheim's time. If this is indeed the case, it seems to this writer that we may need to reexamine our priorities carefully. It is certainly legitimate to continue to study the kinds of behaviors that are currently being studied under the heading of hypnotism. It may not be, however, to the best advantage of scientific progress in hypnotism to continue to assume that all such behaviors are identical with those serving as the basis for the hypnotism of the nineteenth century.

REFERENCES

Barber, T.X. Hypnosis: A scientific approach. New York: Van Nostrand Reinhold Co., 1969.

Bernheim, H. Suggestive therapeutics. (English translation by Christian A. Herter). New York: London Book Co., 1947. (The original work was De la suggestion et de ses applications therapeutiques. Paris: Octave Doin, 1886).

Bernheim, H. Hypnotisme, suggestion, psychotherapie. Paris: Octave Doin, Editeur, 1903.

Bernheim, H. Automatisme et suggestion. Paris: Librairie Felix Alcan, 1917.

Carpenter, W.B. On the influence of suggestion modifying and directing muscular movement, independently of volition. Proceedings, Royal Institution of Great Britain, 1852, 1, 147-153.

Janet, P. L'Automatisme psychologique. Paris: Felix Alcan, Editeur, 1889.

Janet, P. Psychological healing. Vol. I. (Translation by Eden and Cedar Paul). London: George Allen and Unwin Ltd., 1925. (Originally published as "Les medications psychologiques." Paris: Alcan, 1919).

Krauss, H.H., Katzell, R., & Krauss, B.J. Effect of hypnotic time distortion upon free-recall learning. Journal of Abnormal Psychology, 1974, 83, 140-144.

Sarbin, T.R., & Coe, W.C. Hypnosis: A social psychological analysis of influence communication. New York: Holt, Rinehart, and Winston, 1972.

Weitzenhoffer, A.M. Hypnotism: An objective study in suggestibility. New York: John Wiley and Sons, Inc., 1953.

Weitzenhoffer, A.M., & Hilgard, E.R. The Stanford Scale of Hypnotic Susceptibility, Form A. Palo Alto, California: Consulting Psychologists Press, 1959.

Weitzenhoffer, A.M. A re-examination of the concept of suggestion. I. The classical suggestion-effect. Unpublished manuscript, 1972.

Weitzenhoffer, A.M. Lectures on hypnotism and hypnotherapy. Six taped lectures. Fort Lee, New Jersey: Behavioral Sciences Tape Library, 1973.

Weitzenhoffer, A.M. When is an "Instruction" an "Instruction?" International Journal of Clinical and Experimental Hypnosis, 1974, 22, 258-269.

Wells, W.R. Experiments in waking hypnosis for instructional purposes. Journal of Abnormal and Social Psychology, 1924, 18, 389-404.

II: Experimental

A PRELIMINARY REPORT ON SOCIAL LEARNING BEHAVIOR IN THE HYPNOTIC SITUATION: MODELING OR MIMICRY*

Ronald W. Botto** and Seymour Fisher

Boston University Medical School, U.S.A.

Abstract: In a review of research employing a model to enhance hypnotizability, it was noted that in most cases the model portrayed all, or nearly all, of the behaviors to be later elicited. In such cases, there is no way to determine whether the resultant behavior is true modeling - with its implication of generalization - or merely mimicry (in the sense of specific imitation). In the present study, subjects observed either a Good or a Poor Model who passed or failed, respectively, 4 of 12 suggestions from the HGSHS:A. When total scores were analyzed, enhancement (Good Model) and decrement (Poor Model) of hypnotizability were observed. However, when the analysis compared those items demonstrated by the model with those not demonstrated, only subjects exposed to the Poor Model exhibited any suggestion of generalization. Furthermore, when these results were compared to previously obtained norms, not even the subjects exposed to the Poor Model showed changes greater than those normally occurring in a test-retest situation. Because the comparison norms could serve only a quasi-control, conclusions must be tentative. However, there is sufficient evidence to call for a much closer examination of what hypnotic researchers have been labeling as "modeling."

---

* This research was supported by U.S. Public Health Service grant DA-00099 (S. Fisher, principal investigator).

** Currently at Behavioral Science Section, Department of Community Dentistry and Human Behavior, School of Dental Medicine, Southern Illinois University at Edwardsville, Edwardsville, Illinois 62026.

Many methods have been suggested as viable means of altering hypnotic susceptibility. Among these are motivation, sensory deprivation, therapeutic counseling, and, more recently, modeling. Of these methods, modeling appears to be one of the more efficient, and is, furthermore, adaptable to most clinical and experimental settings. In addition to its relatively shorter administration time, it has the advantage of being adaptable to videotape so that the clinician or researcher can operate in relative ease and independence. Furthermore, it has been shown that one can obtain significant differences in levels of hypnotizability without demand characteristics playing a potentially major role (Botto, Fisher, & Soucy, 1977).

In view of the many possibilities that modeling possesses as a useful empirical and clinical tool, it is important that one understands as much about the phenomenon as possible. A number of studies have been carried out to test various questions related to modeling in the hypnotic setting, such as the effect of vicarious reinforcement and prestige of the model (DeVoge & Sachs, 1973), effectiveness of a good versus poor model (Klinger, 1970), various components of modeling (Diamond, 1972), order of item presentation (Brown & Krasner, 1969), and subject-model identification (DeStephano, 1971).

What most of these studies seem to be addressing is the basic question of whether or not modeling in the hypnotic setting adheres to the general principles of learning which have been demonstrated repeatedly in the social learning literature. One of the basic concerns of social learning researchers is the differentiation between modeling behavior and imitation. As pointed out by Bandura (1972) in a recent review of the modeling paradigm in social learning theory,

> the term [modeling] was adopted because modeling influences have much broader psychological effects than the simple response mimicry implied by the term imitation. Depending on how they are used, modeling influences can thus produce not only specific mimicry but also generative and innovative behavior.

The foundation for this statement has come from a number of studies in the social learning field which have shown that, indeed, the behavior about which these researchers speak is modeling and not merely imitation (Parke, 1972). The most critical criterion, as indicated, is in the application of the effect of generalization, for this is the vehicle by which "generative and innovative behavior" can express itself, thereby providing the critical difference between mimicry and modeling.

Of those researchers investigating modeling in hypnosis, only two have employed a paradigm which did not exhibit the exact behaviors they wished to elicit. In an attempt to break modeling down into verbal and non-verbal facets, Diamond (1972) divided low susceptible subjects into groups that tested the various combinations of these two components using a good model. His subjects were fairly refractory to hypnosis, scoring 0 - 4 on an abridged Harvard Group Scale of Hypnotic Susceptibility, Form A (Shor & Orne, 1962), and 0 - 8 on a follow-up Stanford Scale of Hypnotic Susceptibility, Form B (Weitzenhoffer & Hilgard, 1959). Furthermore, all subjects, in addition to being recruited for an experiment to "increase hypnotic susceptibility," received a five-minute motivational session dealing with the positive aspects of hypnosis. His model performed seven tasks, all of which were similar in context, if not content, to 7 of the actual 12 items on which the subjects were retested. Thus, generalization, if it occurred, could be shown for only five additional items. While Diamond obtained enhanced hypnotic scores for his verbal conditions, the non-verbal behavioral model showed no enhancement, but, rather, a slight decrement in score. Furthermore, since generalization was not a concern in the study, the presentation of the results failed to make clear whether or not it had occurred.

DeStephano (1971) had his models exhibit behavior on eleven tasks which represented items factorally similar to those in the Harvard Group Scale of Hypnotic Susceptibility, Form A, used for the subjects' posttest. Also, the subjects observed the induction as well as the testing procedure, and had the opportunity for verbal interaction with, and explanation by, the experimenter, as well as the opportunity to question the models following the demonstration. This procedure seems very closely aligned to the verbal-and-behavioral condition of Diamond. DeStephano found an increase in hypnotizability only for subjects with moderate pretest hypnotizability scores. As with Diamond, he did not analyze his data in terms of imitation vs. modeling.

As can be seen from these studies, it is still not clear whether modeling truly occurs in hypnosis, or whether the behaviors observed are simply produced by mimicry. The purpose of the present study was to examine more closely the effect of generalization in the hypnotic modeling paradigm. Pursuant to this, subjects viewed the modeling of only 4 of the 12 items in the Harvard Group Scale of Hypnotic Susceptibility, Form A, and were not shown the induction.

METHOD

On the basis of pretest scores on a low demand version of the Harvard Group Scale of Hypnotic Susceptibility, Form A (Botto, Fisher, & Soucy, 1977), subjects were divided into two groups: those scoring 0 - 6 were placed in the Good Model group, while those scoring 7 - 12 were placed in the Poor Model group.

Upon arrival, subjects were asked to sit quietly in one of two laboratories. All subjects were separated by a partition, and all procedures, aside from some introductory remarks and specific test directions, were conducted by means of a tape recording and videotape. After some preliminary introductory remarks, the lights were dimmed, the taped introduction was played, and the videotaped model was shown. As was stated to the subjects, the modeled videotape was a simulation of hypnosis by a member of the laboratory staff.* Only four items of the modified Harvard Group Scale of Hypnotic Susceptibility, Form A, were modeled: #1 - head falling, #3 - arm lowering, #7 - hands moving together, and #9 - fly hallucination. The induction was also omitted. In the Good Model condition, the model responded successfully to all suggestions; in the Poor Model condition, the model, while responding to some degree, failed to pass any of the criteria (see Botto & Fisher, 1973). The tape-recorded low demand Harvard Group Scale of Hypnotic Susceptibility, Form A, was then administered a second time.

RESULTS

Hypnosis scores for the two conditions (Good Model, Poor Model), both before and after the presentation of the model, are shown in Table 1. As can be seen in this table, both the increase in total score for the Good Model and decrease in total score for the Poor Model are statistically significant** (GM: $t = 3.27$, $df = 8$, $p < .01$; PM: $t = 2.45$, $df = 11$, $p < .025$).

In Table 2, the scores are broken down further into the two groups of component items of the Harvard Group Scale of Hypnotic Susceptibility, Form A: the four modeled items (#1, 3, 7, 9) and the eight non-modeled items (#2, 4, 5, 6, 8, 10, 11, 12). In the Good Model condition, there was a significant increase in scores for the modeled items ($t = 3.41$, $df = 8$, $p < .01$) after the model was viewed; however, the increase in scores for the non-modeled items was not significant ($t = 1.08$, $df = 8$, $p > .05$). Furthermore, there was no significant difference in the change scores between the two conditions ($t = 1.74$, $df = 8$, $p > .05$). In the Poor Model condition, scores of both the modeled items and the non-modeled items decreased significantly (M: $t = 2.35$, $df = 11$, $p < .025$; NM: $t = 1.84$, $df = 11$, $p < .05$). There was no significant difference in the amount of change between the modeled and the non-modeled items ($t = 0.66$, $df = 11$, $p > .05$).

---

* The authors would like to thank Mr. Gerald Soucy for his portrayal.

** All tests are one-tailed unless otherwise indicated.

TABLE 1

Total HGS:A Scores Before and After Presentation of the Model

	Pre		Post		Diff.	
	$\bar{X}$	S.D.	$\bar{X}$	S.D.	$\bar{X}$	S.D.
Good Model (N = 9) (low susceptibility)	4.22	1.56	5.56	1.33	1.34***	1.22
Poor Model (N = 12) (high susceptibility)	9.58	1.38	8.00	2.26	-1.58**	2.23

** $p < .025$
*** $p < .01$

TABLE 2

Modeled and Non-Modeled HGS:A Item Scores Before and After Presentation of the Model

		Pre		Post		Diff.	
		$\bar{X}$	S.D.	$\bar{X}$	S.D.	$\bar{X}$	S.D.
Good Model (N = 9) (Low susceptibility)	Modeled Items	1.89	1.05	2.78	0.44	0.89***	0.78
	Non-Modeled Items	2.33	1.66	2.78	1.30	0.45	1.24
Poor Model (N = 12) (High susceptibility)	Modeled Items	3.42	0.67	2.75	0.87	-0.67**	0.98
	Non-Modeled Items	6.17	1.03	5.25	1.60	-0.92*	1.73

* $p < .05$
** $p < .025$
*** $p < .01$

It appears, therefore, that there is at least partial support for the contention that modeling occurs in the hypnotic situation. Before conclusive statements can be made, however, not only must support be found in Good as well as Poor Modeling paradigms, but there must also be appropriate comparisons with a No Model control group to rule out any effect attributable to a regression towards the mean. This is especially important in the present study, since groups were selected on the basis of a score above or below a pre-test mean. In an attempt to rule out such regression factors, data collected previously have been examined to give some tentative indications about the effectiveness of the model. One must be cautious, however, in using these data for comparison, since the subjects were all males over 21, and they were tested on the standardized versions of the Harvard Group Scale of Hypnotic Susceptibility, Forms A and B.

The data for this quasi-control group are presented in Table 3. When the change in total scores between the two administrations of the Harvard Group Scale (without a model) was compared with that of the Good Model condition (Table 1), the difference between the two conditions was not statistically significant ($t = 1.04$, $df = 29$, $p > .05$).

With the high susceptible subjects of this No Model condition, a comparison of change in total scores with that for the Poor Model group (Table 1) indicated a significantly greater decrease in scores for the Poor Model group ($t = 2.34$, $df = 30$, $p < .025$). However, when scores were examined further on the basis of specific items, the relative difference betwen the two groups in decrease of scores was significant only for the modeled items ($t = 3.83$, $df = 30$, $p < .01$). This would suggest that the behavior being exhibited is imitative rather than modeled.

DISCUSSION

While the use of a somewhat inappropriate control group limits the conclusions that can be drawn from the present experiment, we should like to note that similar findings were obtained in another study that was carried out employing the Poor Model condition only (Table 4). In comparison with the No Model control group (Table 3), the total decrease in the Poor Model condition (Table 4) was significantly greater than that shown by the No Model control group ($t = 2.41$, $df = 47$, $p < .025$). However, the reduction in scores was significant only for the modeled items ($t = 3.04$, $df = 47$, $p < .01$).

Thus, when within group analyses are performed, there are significant changes that appear to be attributable to generalization. However, when the experimental groups are compared to a No Model

TABLE 3

Total and Item Scores on Successive Administrations of the HGS:A and HGS:B for a No Model Control Group

		HGS:A		HGS:B		Diff.	
		$\bar{X}$	S.D.	$\bar{X}$	S.D.	$\bar{X}$	S.D.
	Total	5.09	1.04	5.64	2.27	0.55	2.11
Low Susceptibility (N = 22)	Items #1, 3, 7, 9	2.54	0.66	3.04	0.64	0.50	0.86
	Items #2, 4, 5, 6, 8, 10, 11, 12	2.54	1.03	2.59	1.88	0.05	1.65
	Total	9.10	1.30	9.10	2.21	0.00	1.59
High Susceptibility (N = 20)	Items #1, 3, 7, 9	3.35	0.73	3.75	0.54	0.40	0.60
	Items #2, 4, 5, 6, 8, 10, 11, 12	5.75	1.14	5.35	1.85	-0.40	1.63

TABLE 4

Total and Item HGS:A Scores Before and After Presentation of a Poor Model Only

	Pre		Post		Diff.	
	$\bar{X}$	S.D.	$\bar{X}$	S.D.	$\bar{X}$	S.D.
Total (N = 29)	8.62	1.37	7.31	2.17	-1.31***	2.04
Modeled Items	3.10	0.67	2.76	0.91	-0.34*	2.97
Non-Modeled Items	5.52	1.40	4.55	1.68	-0.97***	1.82

* $p < .05$
*** $p < .01$

control group, despite its shortcomings, there is little evidence for anything other than mimicry. It must be stressed that the limited appropriateness of the No Model control group used in the present experiment calls for much additional research before firm conclusions about the ability of the hypnotized individual to exhibit "generative and innovative" behavior can be drawn. The experiment does, however, point to the need for concern in the use of the term "modeling" as applied currently in the hypnotic literature.

REFERENCES

Bandura, A. Modeling theory: Some traditions, trends, and disputes. In R.D. Parke (editor), Recent trends in social learning theory. New York: Academic Press, 1972. Pp. 35-61.

Botto, R.W., & Fisher, S. Modeling effects on hypnotizability in a low demand situation. Paper presented at the Annual Meeting of the Society for Clinical and Experimental Hypnosis, Newport Beach, November, 1973.

Botto, R.W., Fisher, S., & Soucy, G.P. The effect of a good and a poor model on hypnotic susceptibility in a low demand situation. International Journal of Clinical and Experimental Hypnosis, 1977, 25, 175-183.

Brown, H.A., & Krasner, L. The role of subject expectancies in hypnosis. International Journal of Clinical and Experimental Hypnosis, 1969, 17, 180-188.

DeVoge, J.T., & Sachs, L.B. The modification of hypnotic susceptibility through imitative behavior. International Journal of Clinical and Experimental Hypnosis, 1973, 21, 70-77.

DeStephano, M.G. The modeling of hypnotic behavior. Paper presented at the Annual Meeting of the Society for Clinical and Experimental Hypnosis, Chicago, 1971.

Diamond, M.J. The use of observationally presented information to modify hypnotic susceptibility. Journal of Abnormal Psychology, 1972, 79, 174-180.

Klinger, B.I. Effect of peer model responsiveness and length of induction procedure on hypnotic responsiveness. Journal of Abnormal Psychology, 1970, 75, 15-18.

Parke, R.D. (editor). Recent trends in social learning. New York: Academic Press, 1972.

Shor, R.E., & Orne, E.C. Harvard Group Scale of Hypnotic Susceptibility, Form A. Palo Alto, California: Consulting Psychologists Press, 1962.

Weitzenhoffer, A.M., & Hilgard, E.R. The Stanford Scale of Hypnotic Susceptibility, Form B. Palo Alto, California: Consulting Psychologists Press, 1959.

ANIMAL HYPNOSIS AND PAIN

Giancarlo Carli

Istituto di Fisiologia Umana dell'Universita' di Siena, Italy

Abstract: Animal hypnosis is usually defined as a state of prolonged, reversible immobility which is brought about by different types of sensory stimulation and is characterized by passivity and lack of responsiveness. An easy method for producing this phenomenon consists of holding the animal in a fixed position (supine, prone, on one side, etc.) and keeping it there until it stops moving. Once immobility occurs, it persists in the absence of further restraint. Termination of this condition may occur either spontaneously or following certain sudden stimuli.

In our laboratory, animal hypnosis in the rabbit has been studied in the following ways: a) comparison, in the same subjects, of neurophysiological characteristics (EEG, EMG, spinal reflexes, blood pressure, and heart rate) during animal hypnosis, sleep, and wakefulness; b) determination of the rabbit's capacity, during hypnosis, to perform and to extinguish an avoidance response learned in the non-hypnotic state; and, c) assessment of the effects of long-lasting nociceptive stimuli applied in a control condition and during hypnosis. In other experiments, the effect of morphine and naloxone on hypnotic duration was examined.

Based on the results obtained by using these various approaches, it is suggested that a pain-suppressing mechanism is active during animal hypnosis, and that this mechanism exhibits effects similar to the analgesic mechanism of morphine.

Animal hypnosis is a very different phenomenon from human hypnosis, and any comparison between the two conditions leads only to confusing speculation. The term animal hypnosis is commonly used to indicate a response of immobility which is easily elicited by placing an animal on its back and maintaining it in that position until struggling ceases (Carli, 1977; Gallup, 1974; Klemm, 1971). Once immobility occurs, it persists in the absence of restraint for periods varying from a few seconds to several minutes. Termination of this condition may occur either spontaneously or following different types of sensory stimuli. Animal hypnosis is present in several animal species; in mammals, it is easily obtained in guinea pigs and rabbits. In this condition, the general responiveness of the animal to external stimuli is apparently reduced (Gilman & Marcuse, 1949). Sporadic reports (Rapson & Jones, 1964) indicating that surgery can be performed during animal hypnosis without the interruption of the immobility have provided some support for the old hypothesis (Gilman & Marcuse, 1949) that an analgesic mechanism may be responsible for the suppression of the pain response.

The principal characteristics of animal hypnosis in the rabbit (see Table 1) are a tendency to develop high voltage slow waves in the EEG, coupled with myosis (Carli, 1969; Klemm, 1966) and a tonic depression of spinal reflexes (Carli, 1969). Moreover, rabbits trained to avoid an electric shock by moving the hind limb in response to a 4-second sound, can learn to interrupt the hypnotic episode at the time the conditioned stimulus is presented (Carli, 1975). Although blood pressure and heart rate do not change during animal hypnosis (Carli, 1974), regional cerebral blood flow - which is related to the ongoing neural activity - significantly increases in the thalamus, hypothalamus, and corpus striatum, but decreases in the medulla and in the pons (Battistini, Carli, Farabollini, Fontani, Lenzi, & Passero, 1977). This is in contrast to the generalized vasodilation recorded in the brain during slow wave and REM sleep (Reivich, 1975).

The neuroendocrine system appears to be strongly affected by hypnotic induction. For example, the biological action of testosterone in several brain regions - mainly in the anterior hypothalamus (Naftolin & Ryan, 1975) - is known to be associated with its conversion to estradiol (aromatization) (Perez-Palacios, Larsson, & Beyer, 1975). The conversion of testosterone to estradiol is sharply reduced 15 minutes after the termination of an episode of animal hypnosis (Lupo di Prisco, Farabollini, & Carli, 1976).

As for the duration of animal hypnosis, it has been shown that when this condition is produced at regular intervals, a reduction in duration (habituation) is recorded (Nash & Gallup, 1976; Smith & Klemm, 1977). On the other hand, fear-producing stimuli (e.g., an electric shock, loud noise, suspension over a visual cliff, con-

TABLE 1

Characteristics of Animal Hypnosis

Physiological Manifestations	Modifications
EEG	Tendency to high voltage slow waves
Spinal reflexes	Depressed
Blood pressure, heart rate	No change
Regional cerebral blood flow	Increased in thalamus, hypothalamus, and striatum
	Decreased in medulla oblongata and pons
Central testosterone conversion to estradiol (aromatization)	Depressed
Duration of hypnosis	Increased by fear stimuli
	Increased by nociceptive stimulation
	Decreased by habituation procedures

frontation with a simulated predator) result in a significant increase in hypnotic duration (Gallup, 1977) if presented just before hypnotic induction.

We have found that the subcutaneous injection of formalin into the dorsal region of the rabbit foot elicits several aversive reactions (running and shifting movements, licking of the affected foot, etc.) which are associated in the EEG with the low voltage fast waves typical of intense emotional states. In the nonhypnotic condition, these manifestations of discomfort persist with decreasing intensity for about one hour. Animal hypnosis can be induced in this condition of apparent continuous pain (Carli, Lefebvre, Silvano, & Vierucci, 1976). Moreover, if hypnosis is induced when the pain reactions are less intense, i.e., five minutes after formalin injection, the animal exhibits a predominance of high voltage slow activity EEG rhythms. At the end of the hypnotic episode, both the discomfort reactions and the activation rhythms are again observed.

These results of prolonged nociceptive stimulation deserve a more detailed discussion. It is well known that termination of animal hypnosis can be produced by a sudden phasic excitation of sensory afferents (tactile, acoustic, etc.) or by trains of electrical pulses activating flexor reflex afferents. Moreover, hypnosis is terminated in almost all cases when high intensity electrical shocks are delivered directly to the animal's foot through the floor. This implies that both painful and nonpainful stimuli may interrupt the hypnotic episode by overriding the depression of spinal reflexes that occurs during hypnosis. A critical factor might be stimulus duration, since it is known that long-lasting tonic stimuli are likely to produce peripheral and central adaptation and sleep (Pompeiano & Sweet, 1962). However, formalin injection has never elicited high voltage slow waves in the non-hypnotic state. Furthermore, the EEG patterns during hypnosis are not abnormal, but, on the contrary, are identical to the spontaneous activity occuring during sleep, or during hypnosis induced in the absence of nociceptive stimulation.

Analgesia in animals may be defined operationally as the selective abolition of discomfort behavior following painful stimulation. At the present time, however, we prefer to consider analgesia in animal hypnosis a stimulating working hypothesis to be substantiated by more adequate experimental evidence.

As summarized in Table 2, there are striking similarities between the effects of morphine and those of animal hypnosis. Injection of morphine (at doses of from 1 to 5 mg/kg) elicits depression of spinal reflexes, high voltage slow waves in the EEG, and myosis. Moreover, morphine can block the pain manifestations elicited by formalin by producing catalepsis and high voltage slow waves in the EEG. Finally, sudden external stimuli produce an arousal reaction in the EEG as well as pupil dilation.

Several important new discoveries in the pharmacology, physiology, and biochemistry of opiate action deserve careful consideration. There is evidence that opiate receptors exist in the neural tissue, although morphine is not a normal body constituent. Analgesia can be produced by implantation of opiates into selected brain regions or by electrical stimulation of the same regions where stereospecific binding with opiates occurs. More recently, endogenous substances have been extracted and purified from the brains of several mammals. Intracerebroventricular or intracerebral injections into the periaqueductal gray matter of endogenous peptides, which act as agonists at morphine receptor sites, produce analgesia and prolonged immobility reactions, and may be counteracted by the narcotic antagonist naloxone. Naloxone, a synthetic narcotic antagonist, occupies opiate receptor sites and completely reverses the analgesic effects of morphine. Moreover, it is able to antagonize

TABLE 2

Effects of Animal Hypnosis and of Morphine

Condition	Effects
Animal hypnosis or morphine	Depression of spinal reflexes
	High voltage slow waves in the EEG
	Pupil constriction
	Immobility
	Suppression of pain manifestations
	No change in other sensory modalities
	Antagonized by naloxone
Morphine	Potentiates hypnotic duration

the analgesia elicited by the injection of endogenous peptides like enkefalin and endorphins, as well as the analgesic response to focal electrical stimulation of the periaqueductal gray matter. Both morphine and electrical stimulation of the periaqueductal gray matter block the response of interneurons in lamina five of the spinal cord to nociceptive stimulation. This effect is also antagonized by naloxone.

In a recent series of experiments, we have tested the hypothesis that a morphine-like mechanism is active during animal hypnosis. Animal hypnosis was produced by placing each animal (rabbit) on its back, restraining it in a wooden U-shaped trough, and maintaining it there until it relaxed (Klemm, 1966). The disappearance and reappearance of righting reflexes indicated the beginning and the end of hypnosis respectively. A period of manual restraint shorter than 30 seconds was employed to produce immobility and relaxation. Failure to obtain hypnosis was followed by the immediate repetition of the procedure up to a maximum of three attempts. A reduction in duration was obtained by repetitive inductions (5 trials a day, 2-minute intertrial interval) for two to three weeks until the habituation criterion (10 consecutive trials, i.e., 2 experimental days, below

45 seconds) was reached. The subjects were tested on the day following the attainment of the habituation criterion. For all groups studied, N = 5.

In habituated rabbits, there was an increase in hypnotic duration when animal hypnosis was induced under a condition of continuous pain, i.e., 5 minutes after formalin injection. Formalin was injected between trials 2 and 3 of the testing day. A comparison of the mean duration of trials 3, 4, and 5 (104 ± 9.9 seconds) following formalin injection with the corresponding trials of the previous (control) day (6.7 ± 4.2 seconds) showed a significant ($p < .001$) difference. The potentiation of hypnotic duration lasted as long as the EEG and behavioral manifestations of pain were present. In another group of subjects, naloxone (5 mg/kg, i.m.), injected 2 minutes after formalin, abolished the potentiation of hypnotic duration produced by formalin injection.

To study this decrease in hypnotic duration further, naive susceptible rabbits were used, i.e., rabbits who displayed long-lasting episodes (5 trials, 2-minute intertrial interval, all trials longer than 45 seconds). Figure 1 shows the reduction in hypnotic duration following naloxone injection (B: 15 mg/kg, i.m.; C: 20 mg/kg). A comparison of the mean duration of trials 3,4, and 5 of the previous (control) day with the corresponding trials after naloxone revealed a significant decrease ($p < .02$ in B; $p < .01$ in C) for both groups. No change in hypnotic duration was recorded following injections of saline (Figure 1:A), or of naloxone at smaller doses (5 mg/kg).

The pharmacological effects of naloxone deserve some attention. It has been shown in different laboratories (Jacob, Tremblay, & Colombel, 1974; Walker, Berntson, Sandman, Coy, Schally, & Kastin, 1977) that naloxone at doses of 1 - 2 mg/kg increases pain sensitivity in rats. On the other hand, Goldstein, Pryor, Otis, and Larsen (1976), have determined that 50 mg/kg is the maximum dose of naloxone that can be used without producing a change in the threshold for escape from foot shock. In our experiments, no apparent change in behavior and EEG activity followed the injection of 15 and 20 mg/kg of naloxone.

As for morphine, it has frequently been observed (Davis, 1963; Hicks, Maser, Gallup, & Edson, 1975) to potentiate hypnotic duration in rabbits and chickens. A final point in favor of the morphine hypothesis comes from findings with animals whose serotonin has been depleted by p-chlorphenylalanine (p-CPA). In several species, but not in rabbits, p-CPA strongly reduces morphine analgesia. In our rabbits, who were apparently experiencing prolonged pain, p-CPA blocked neither the analgesic effect of morphine nor the high voltage slow waves in the EEG during animal hypnosis.

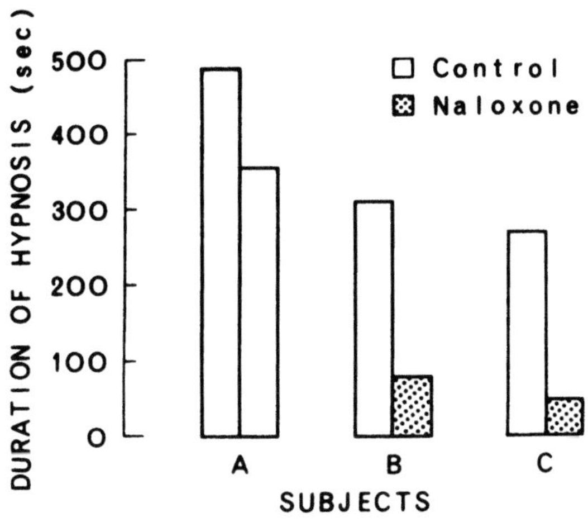

Fig. 1. Effect of naloxone and saline injection on the duration of animal hypnosis. A: saline injection; B: 15 mg/kg naloxone injection; C: 20 mg/kg naloxone injection.

In conclusion, it is suggested that a pain-suppressing mechanism is active during animal hypnosis, and that this mechanism exhibits effects similar to the analgesic mechanism of morphine.

REFERENCES

Battistini, N., Carli, G., Farabollini, F., Fontani, G., Lenzi, G. L., & Passero, S. Changes in regional blood flow during animal hypnosis in the rabbit. Archivio di Fisiologia, 1977, in press.

Carli, G. Dissociation of electrocortical activity and somatic reflexes during rabbit hypnosis. Archives Italiennes de Biologie, 1967, 107, 219-234.

Carli, G. Blood pressure and heart rate in the rabbit during animal hypnosis. Electroencephalography and Clinical Neurophysiology, 1974, 37, 231-237.

Carli, G. Neurophysiological and behavioral correlates of animal hypnosis. In P. Levin and P. Koella (editors), Sleep 1974. Basel: Karger, 1975. Pp. 250-251.

Carli, G. Animal hypnosis in the rabbit. Psychological Record, 1977, Suppl. 27, 123-143.

Carli, G., Lefebvre, L., Silvano, G., & Vierucci, S. Suppression of accompanying reactions to prolonged noxious stimulation during animal hypnosis in the rabbit. Experimental Neurology, 1976, 53, 1-11.

Davis, W.M. Neurophysiological basis and pharmacological modification of inhibitory emotional behavior in the rabbit. Archives Internationales de Pharmacodynamie et de Thérapie, 1963, 142, 349-360.

Gallup, G.G., Jr. Animal hypnosis: Factual status of a fictional concept. Psychological Bulletin, 1974, 81, 836-853.

Gallup, G.G., Jr. Tonic immobility: The role of fear and predation. Psychological Record, 1977, Suppl. 27, 41-61.

Gilman, T.T., & Marcuse, F.L. Animal hypnosis. Psychological Bulletin, 1949, 46, 151-165.

Goldstein, A., Pryor, G.T., Otis, L.S., & Larsen, F. On the role of endogenous opioid peptides: Failure of naloxone to influence shock escape threshold in the rat. Life Sciences, 1976, 18, 599-604.

Hicks, L.E., Maser, J.D., Gallup, G.G., Jr., & Edson, P.H. Possible serotonergic mediation of tonic immobility: Effects of morphine and serotonin blockade. Psychopharmacologia, 1975, 42, 51-56.

Jacob, J.J., Tremblay, E.C., & Colombel, M.C. Facilitation de réactions nociceptives par la naloxone chez la souris et chez le rat. Psychopharmacologia, 1974, 37, 217-223.

Klemm, W.R. Electroencephalographic-behavioral dissociations during animal hypnosis. Electroencephalography and Clinical Neurophysiology, 1966, 21, 365-372.

Klemm, W.R. Neurophysiologic studies of the immobility reflex ("animal hypnosis"). In S. Ehrenpreis and O.C. Solnitzky (editors), Neurosciences Research. New York: Academic Press, 1971. Pp. 165-212.

Lupo di Prisco, C., Farabollini, C., & Carli, G. Correlati umorali dell'ipnosi animale nel coniglio. II: Effetto sul metabolismo del testosterone nell'ipotalamo anteriore. Bollettino della Societa' Italiana di Biologia sperimentale, 1976, 52, 144.

Naftolin, F., & Ryan, K.J. The metabolism of androgens in central neuroendocrine tissues. The Journal of Steroid Biochemistry, 1975, 6, 993-997.

Nash, R.F., & Gallup, G.G., Jr. Habituation and tonic immobility in domestic chickens. Journal of Comparative and Physiological Psychology, 1976, 90, 870-876.

Perez-Palacios, G., Larsson, K., & Beyer, C. Biological significance of the metabolism of androgens in the central nervous system. The Journal of Steroid Biochemistry, 1975, 6, 999-1006.

Pompeiano, O., & Sweet, J.E. EEG and behavioral manifestations of sleep induced by cutaneous nerve stimulation in normal cats. Archives Italiennes de Biologie, 1962, 100, 311-342.

Rapson, W.S., & Jones, T.C. Restraint of rabbits by hypnosis, Laboratory Animal Care, 1964, 14, 131-133.

Reivich, M. Discussion - J. Seylaz. In D.H. Ingvar and N.A. Lassen (editors), Brain work: The coupling of function, metabolism, and blood flow in the brain. Copenhagen: Monksgaard, 1975. Pp. 247-249.

Smith, G.W., & Klemm, W.R. Fear hypothesis revisited: Other variables affecting duration of the immobility reflex (animal hypnosis). Behavioral Biology, 1977, 19, 76-86.

Walker, J.M., Berntson, G.G., Sandman, C.A., Coy, D.H., Schally, A.V., & Kastin, A.J. An analog of enkephalin having prolonged opiate-like effects in vivo. Science, 1977, 196, 85-87.

IMAGERY, ABSORPTION, AND THE TENDENCY TOWARD "MIND EXPLORATION" AS CORRELATES OF HYPNOTIC SUSCEPTIBILITY IN MALES AND FEMALES

Ruben C. Gur

University of Pennsylvania, U.S.A.

Abstract: Hypnotizability, when measured by standardized hypnotic susceptibility scales, is an extremely stable personality characteristic (e.g., Morgan, Johnson, & Hilgard, 1974) which is as hard to modify as scores on an intelligence test (cf. Shor & Cobb, 1968; Gur, 1974). It is therefore rather surprising to find that very few personality correlates of this trait have been identified, in spite of considerable efforts (Hilgard, 1967).

Recently, R.C. Gur and R.E. Gur (1974) suggested that one of the reasons for this failure is the powerful moderating effects of variables such as sex and handedness on correlates of hypnotic susceptibility. Thus, Bowers (1971) found sex to moderate the relationship between creativity and hypnotic susceptibility, and Gur and Gur (1974) found both handedness and sex to moderate the relationship between hypnotizability and functional brain asymmetry. Specifically, they reported hemisphericity, i.e., the characteristic tendency of an individual to rely on one or another cerebral hemisphere, to be a good predictor of hypnotic susceptibility in right-handed males, but not in left-handers or in females.

The purpose of the present paper is to report a series of studies in which the role of sex as a moderating variable in correlates of hypnotizability is further elucidated. In the process of clarifying the role of sex as a moderator, a number of hypotheses are suggested to explain its effect. The results in general support the hypothesis that males and females have different "paths" into hypnosis, and constitute a further step toward exploring what these avenues might be.

Hypnotic susceptibility, when measured on a standardized scale, appears to be a highly stable characteristic of an individual (Hilgard, 1965; London, 1967). Test-retest reliabilities of the standard scales are in the .80's and even an interval of 10 years produced a retest correlation of .60 (Morgan, Johnson, & Hilgard, 1974). There is even some evidence suggesting hereditary components in susceptibility (Morgan, 1973). Such a high stability, comparable to that obtained with I.Q. tests, would seem to justify the application of the label "trait" to hypnotic susceptibility. This would imply that whether a subject is high or low in susceptibility depends on a number of relatively enduring antecedent factors that have had a shaping influence on this trait throughout the subject's development. Such constitutional and/or environmental factors should, theoretically, be identifiable and also result in producing other personality traits which would be correlated with hypnotic susceptibility.

Attempts to correlate hypnotic susceptibility with broad paper and pencil inventories, however, have failed to fulfill these expectations, leading Hilgard (1967) to conclude his comprehensive review of these endeavors by commenting that "The results to date seem rather skimpy in view of the efforts expended (p. 439)." In retrospect, this failure of the broad personality inventories to produce measures that would correlate substantially with hypnotic susceptibility is not surprising. Such tests, when given without prior theoretical expectations, are not likely to produce very informative and reliable results when each of their numerous indices is correlated separately with susceptibility, since even when a few significant correlations do emerge, there is a considerable chance of their being spurious. Furthermore, as Tellegen and Atkinson (1974) have pointed out, when factor analytic methods are used it is commonly found that purportedly multidimensional inventories such as the MMPI, CPI, and 16PF are heavily saturated with two major dimensions (Block, 1965; Eysenck & Eysenck, 1969; Sells, Demares, & Wills, 1971), labeled by Eysenck as Stability versus Neuroticism and Introversion versus Extraversion. None of these dimensions should necessarily be related to hypnotizability.

More recent attempts to relate hypnotic susceptibility to rather specific measures which were theoretically hypothesized to correlate with hypnotizability have met considerable success. J. Hilgard's (1970) characterization of the hypnotizable subject as a "mental space adventurer" who is capable of deep imaginative involvement has led to a number of studies designed to assess the validity of these primarily clinical impressions. Van Nuys (1972) found, in a sample of 47 male undergraduates, that those who reported using "mind expanding drugs" such as marijuana and LSD scored significantly higher on the Harvard Group Scale of Hypnotic Susceptibility (Shor & Orne, 1962). This finding was independently duplicated by Franzini & McDonald (1973), who also reported significant relations in their sample between marijuana use and sex, academic major, practice of yoga or transcendental meditation, previous hypnotization, and nonmedical use of other psychedelic and narcotic drugs. The corresponding relations between hypnotizability and these variables are not reported, unfortunately. Such relations should be expected, however, in view of the positive correlations found in their sample between hypnotizability and marijuana usage. Van Nuys (1973) also found a substantial correlation between hypnotizability and a behavioral measure of the ability to become absorbed in objects in a non-analytic, meditation-like manner.

J. Hilgard's concept of "imaginative involvement" has also influenced Tellegen and Atkinson (1974), who used a rather substantial sample of 481 female undergraduates (divided into two subsamples of 142 and 171) in an attempt to construct and validate a scale to measure this trait and to correlate it with hypnotizability. They administered two "broad band" paper and pencil questionnaires in addition to a scale, designed specifically for their study, which assessed the subjects' tendency to become immersed in movies, acting, nature, past events and voices, fantasies, day dreaming, and the individual's tendency and ability to have dissociative experiences, to trust, to be impulsive, and to relax. As expected from earlier research, none of the standard questionnaires correlated significantly with hypnotizability. Their specific "Absorption" scale, on the other hand, correlated reliably with hypnotic susceptibility both in the initial (.27, $p < .01$) and in the replication subsamples.

A series of investigations has also related hypnotic susceptibility to vividness of imagery (Palmer & Field, 1968; Perry, 1973; Sutcliffe, Perry, & Sheehan, 1970). These studies reveal a small but rather reliable positive correlation between hypnotizability and vividness of imagery as measured by the Betts (1909) questionnaire.

Hilgard's description of the hypnotizable subject has led Bakan (1969) to investigate the relation between hypnotic susceptibility and functional brain asymmetry, as measured by conjugate lateral eye movements during face-to-face questioning. In this situation, subjects tend to move their eyes in a characteristic direction when they reflect upon their answers. This direction is correlated with a number of personality variables which are indicative of preferential activation of the cerebral hemisphere contralateral to the direction of movement (Bakan, 1971; Day, 1964, 1967a, 1967b; Gur, 1975; Gur & Gur, 1975; Gur, Gur, & Harris, 1975). Bakan (1969) found that hypnotizability was correlated moderately with the tendency to shift the eyes to the left, a finding which was replicated by Morgan, McDonald, & MacDonald (1971).

Our own research into correlates of hypnotic susceptibility has utilized these findings as a basis for further explorations of the psychological meaning of individual differences in hypnotic susceptibility. Most of the research to be reported in this paper was done in collaboration with Raquel Gur and some in collaboration with Harold Sackeim and Brachia Marshalek.

Our first purpose was to investigate the role of handedness and of sex as possible moderators of the correlation between hypnotic susceptibility and hemispheric activation. The small size of the correlations reported in the past could have been due to the inclusion in the samples of left-handers and of females, two groups which appear to differ in hemispheric organization from right-handed males. Studies with normals and with brain-damaged patients have revealed that left-handers do not always show the commonly observed lateralization of verbal functions to the left hemisphere and of spatial functions to the right hemisphere. Some 40% of them show the reversed pattern and some show evidence of ambilateralization. In females, whether right- or left-handed, the picture is even more complicated. To begin with, a number of studies have shown that females are less well lateralized for hemispheric function than males. Whether this is due to a greater tendency toward ambilaterality or due to a different pattern of cognitive organization is not at all clear; there is evidence to support both propositions. A number of theoretical accounts have been proposed to explain these sex differences, an outline of which would be beyond the scope of this paper (see Harris, 1975, for a thorough review). Suffice it to say that all of these theories would lead to the expectation that correlates of hemispheric activation should be lower for females than for males. This expectation was further strengthened by Bowers' (1971) study in which sex was found to moderate the relation between creativity and hypnotizability.

In our first study in this vein, we tested 30 right-handed males, 30 right-handed females and 30 left-handers, 11 of whom were females. We administered the Harvard Group Scale of Hypnotic Susceptibility as well as the Stanford Hypnotic Susceptibility Scale, Form C (SHSS:C) in individual sessions. The eye movements were monitored during face-to-face presentation of 20 questions, 10 verbal and 10 spatial. The hypnotic susceptibility scores were averaged for each subject across the two scales. The results showed an overall small but significant negative correlation between hypnotic susceptibility and number of eye movements to the right, indicating a relation, for the total sample, between hypnotizability and right-hemisphere activation. When the sample was divided into the handedness and sex groups, however, the pattern displayed in Figure 1

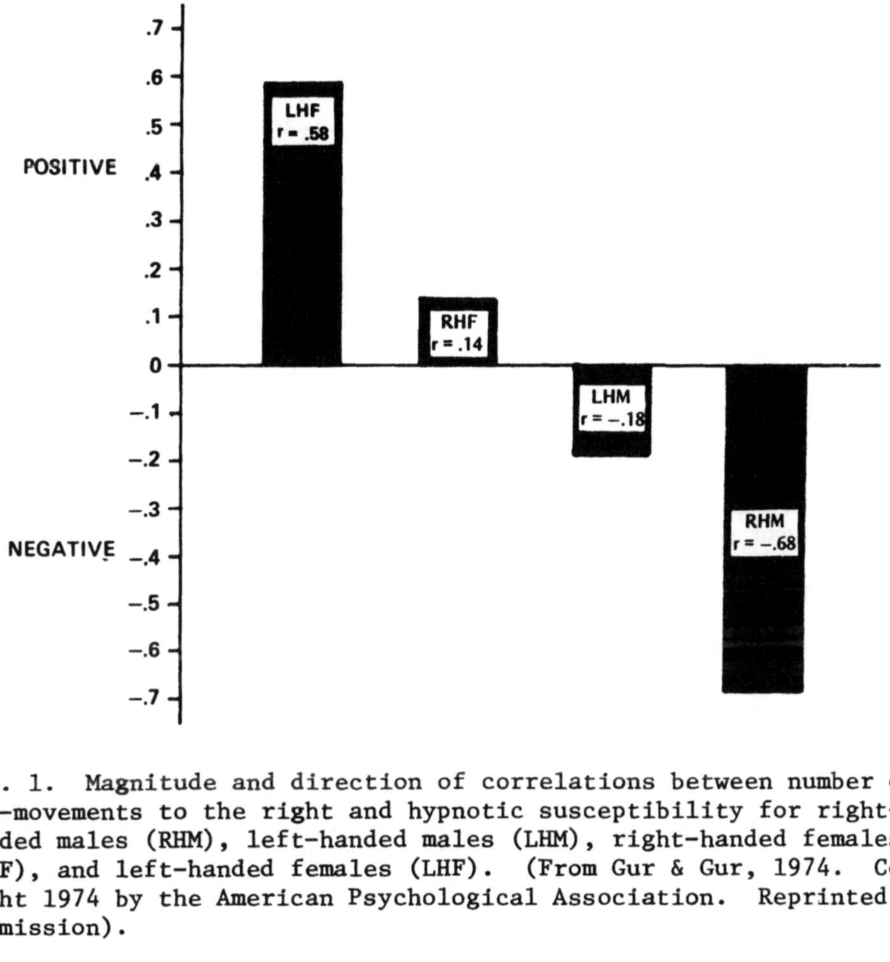

Fig. 1. Magnitude and direction of correlations between number of eye-movements to the right and hypnotic susceptibility for right-handed males (RHM), left-handed males (LHM), right-handed females (RHF), and left-handed females (LHF). (From Gur & Gur, 1974. Copyright 1974 by the American Psychological Association. Reprinted by permission).

emerged. As can be seen from this figure, the correlation is strong for right-handed males and in the opposite direction for left-handed females. It is virtually nonexistent for right-handed females and for left-handed males.

Thus it appeared that the study, although confirming the association between hypnotizability and hemispheric activation in right-handed males and in left-handed females, has failed to identify laterality correlates in females. A subsequent study (Gur & McKinley, 1975) has attempted to achieve just that. We tested 40 subjects on the SHSS:C and administered to them three measures which were theoretically and empirically expected to relate to hypnotizability. The first measure was Tellegen's Absorption Scale (Tellegen & Atkinson, 1974). The second measure was Marks' (1973) scale for measuring vividness of visual imagery. Third was a measure developed by Levy and Teger (unpublished) which assesses the tendency to use a variety of "mind exploration" devices such as marijuana, LSD, meditation, etc. This questionnaire was previously found to be related to the tendency toward right-hemisphere activation. Sex differences have emerged again. Whereas the "Mind Exploration" questionnaire predicted hypnotic susceptibility in males, it did not predict it in females. Conversely, in females, the "Absorption" scale and the "Vividness of Visual Imagery Questionnaire" were good predictors of hypnotizability. These scales did not predict hypnotizability in males. The multiple correlation between the three scales and hypnotic susceptibility was .53, not a better predictor than the "Mind Exploration" scale alone ($F = 3.25$, df = 2, 17; not significant). In females, by contrast, a regression analysis showed that combining "Absorption" and vividness of imagery resulted in a multiple correlation of .76, which is a significant improvement in the predictive power over each measure alone ($F = 11.76$, df = 2, 17; $p < .0001$). Adding "Mind Exploration" scores to the regression equation did not increase the multiple correlation.

Sex differences continue to appear in virtually every study we do in which correlates of laterality are explored. In the present paper, we will limit ourselves to only a brief glimpse at some of these studies. In one study, we looked at differences in psychopathology between people who sit on the right side of a classroom and those who sit on the left. The reason we expected to find such differences lies in previous findings (Gur & Gur, 1975), which related right hemisphere activation to psychosomatic complaints in right-handed males (left-movers had significantly more of those) and another study (Gur, Gur, & Marshalek, 1975) in which classroom seating was related to eye movement directionality in both males and females (see Figure 2) (left-movers tend to sit on the right side of the classroom and right movers tend to sit on the left).

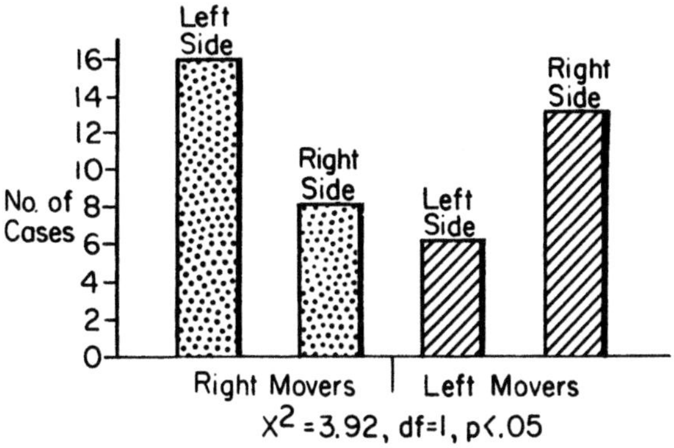

Fig. 2. Seating preference of left-movers and right-movers (From Gur, Gur, & Marshalek, 1975. Copyright 1975 by the American Psychological Association. Reprinted by permission).

We administered a symptom questionnaire to a group of undergraduates and recorded their seating location. The questionnaire is a translation of the DSM-II (American Psychiatric Association, 1968) into simple English. The subject is asked to rate himself on each question regarding the extent to which he suffers from the symptom described in it. The results are presented in Figure 3.

As can be seen from the figure, "healthy" men sit with "sick" women and "healthy" women sit next to the "sick" males. (This statement should be qualified, of course, as we are dealing with a group of well-functioning students).

In a study recently completed by Raquel Gur, an attempt was made to compare schizophrenics to normals on hemispheric activation in response to verbal and spatial questions (Gur, 1977). Half of the questions in each group were emotional and half were nonemotional. This variable was introduced in view of a recent finding by Schwartz, Davidson, and Maer (1975) which indicated, in normal subjects, that eye movements to the right are elicited by face-to-face questioning in response to nonemotional questions, whereas eye movements to the left occur in response to emotional questions. An overall effect of spatial vs. verbal questions was obtained, with more movements to the right being elicited by the verbal questions; also an overall effect of emotionality was obtained in that eye movements to the left were elicited in response to the emotional questions. When the sample was divided by diagnosis and sex, however, the results showed that normal males responded mostly on the basis of the verbal-spatial dimension - thus replicating Kinsbourne's (1972) and Gur, Gur, & Harris' (1975) earlier findings with right-handed males -

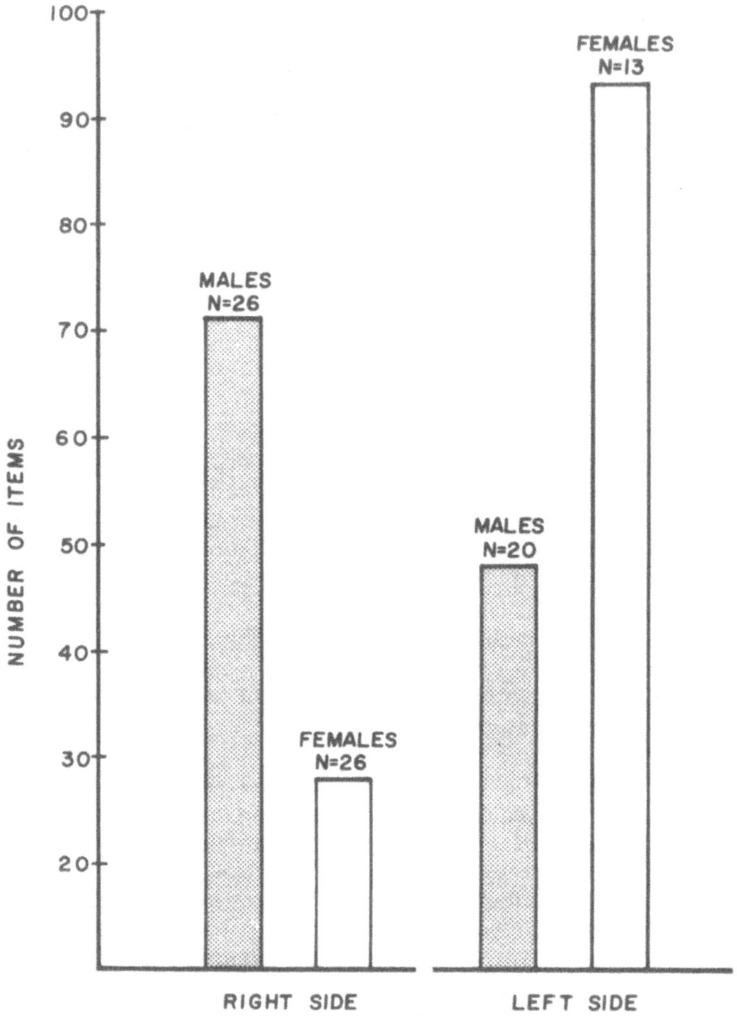

Fig. 3. Number of Manifest Symptom Questionnaire items on which left-siders and right-siders differ in mean response, grouped by sex (From Gur, Sackeim, & Gur, 1976).

whereas normal females responded primarily on the basis of the emotional-nonemotional dimension. The schizophrenic males and females showed opposite tendencies. Males responded according to the emotional dimension and females according to the cognitive dimension. Again, and in an entirely different setting, "sick" males behave like "healthy" females and vice versa.

What are we to make of such sex differences?

In order to answer this question we need to know a lot more about the nature of sex differences in laterality. In three studies which were recently completed in our laboratory, we found the two sexes to differ not only in the way in which motoric and cognitive aspects of laterality are organized, but also in the course of development of lateral differentiation (Gur & Gur, 1977). The extent to which these differences are due to hereditary, hormonal, or environmental factors is not clear. The best guess would be that all of these factors interact to produce the effects (see Levy & Gur, 1977, for a more detailed discussion). Much more research is needed before a more refined statement can be made in this regard. One conclusion, however, appears quite clearly: sex differences exist in correlates of hypnotizability, and these should be carefully scrutinized if we are ever to understand their implications for theories of hypnosis.

REFERENCES

American Psychiatric Association. Diagnostic and statistical manual of mental disorders (DSM-II) (2nd ed.). Washington, D.C.: American Psychiatric Association, 1968.

Bakan, P. Hypnotizability, laterality of eye movement and functional brain asymmetry. Perceptual and Motor Skills, 1969, 28, 927-932.

Bakan, P. The eyes have it. Psychology Today, 1971, 4, 64-69.

Betts, G.H. The distribution and function of mental imagery. Columbia University Contributions to Education, 1909, 26, 1-99.

Block, J. The challenge of response sets. New York: Appleton-Century-Crofts, 1965.

Bowers, K.S. Sex and susceptibility as moderator variables in the relationship of creativity and hypnotic susceptibility. Journal of Abnormal Psychology, 1971, 78, 93-100.

Day, M.E. An eye-movement phenomenon relating to attention, thought and anxiety. Perceptual and Motor Skills, 1964, 19, 443-446.

Day, M.E. An eye-movement indicator of type and level of anxiety: some clinical observations. Journal of Clinical Psychology, 1967a, 23, 443-441.

Day, M.E. An eye-movement indicator of individual differences in the physiological organization of attentional process and anxiety. The Journal of Psychology, 1967b, 66, 51-62.

Eysenck, H.J., & Eysenck, S.B.G. Personality structures and measurement. San Diego, California: Knapp, 1969.

Franzini, L.R., & McDonald, R.D. Marijuana usage and hypnotic susceptibility. Journal of Consulting and Clinical Psychology, 1973, 40, 176-180.

Gur, R.C. An attention-controlled operant procedure for enhancing hypnotic susceptibility. Journal of Abnormal Psychology, 1974, 83, 644-650.

Gur, R.C., & Gur, R.E. Handedness, sex and eyedness as moderating variables in the relation between hypnotic susceptibility and functional brain asymmetry. Journal of Abnormal Psychology, 1974, 83, 635-643.

Gur, R.C., & McKinley, P. Imagery, absorption and the tendency toward "mind exploration" as correlates of hypnotic susceptibility in males and females. Paper presented at the 27th Annual Convention of the Society for Clinical and Experimental Hypnosis, Chicago, 1975.

Gur, R.C., Sackeim, H.A., & Gur, R.E. Classroom seating and psychopathology: Some initial data. Journal of Abnormal Psychology, 1976, 85, 122-124.

Gur, R.E. Conjugate lateral eye movements as an index of hemispheric activation. Journal of Personality and Social Psychology, 1975, 31, 751-757.

Gur, R.E. Left hemisphere overactivation in schizophrenia: Evidence from measures of lateral eye movements directionality. Paper submitted for publication, 1977.

Gur, R.E., & Gur, R.C. Defense mechanisms, psychosomatic asymptomatology, and conjugate lateral eye movements. Journal of Consulting and Clinical Psychology, 1975, 43, 416-420.

Gur, R.E., & Gur, R.C. Sex differences in the relations among handedness, sighting dominance and eye acuity. Neuropsychologia, 1977, 15, 481-498.

Gur, R.E., Gur, R.C., & Harris, L.J. Cerebral activation, as measured by subjects' lateral eye movements, is influenced by experimenter location. Neuropsychologia, 1975, 13, 35-44.

Gur, R.E., Gur, R.C., & Marshalek, B. Classroom seating and functional brain asymmetry. Journal of Educational Psychology, 1975, 67, 151-153.

Harris, L.J. Sex differences in spatial ability, possible environmental, genetic and neurological factors. In M. Kinsbourne (editor), Hemispheric asymmetry of function. Cambridge, England: Cambridge University Press, 1975.

Hilgard, E.R. Hypnotic susceptibility. New York: Harcourt, Brace, and World, 1965.

Hilgard, E.R. Individual differences in hypnotizability. In J.E. Gordon (editor), Handbook of clinical and experimental hypnosis. New York: MacMillan, 1967.

Hilgard, J.R. Personality and hypnosis: A study of imaginative involvement. Chicago: University of Chicago Press, 1970.

Kinsbourne, M. Eye and head turning indicates cerebral lateralization. Science, 1972, 179, 539-541.

Levy, J., & Gur, R.C. Individual differences in psychoneurological organization. In J. Herron (editor), The sinistral mind. New York: Academic Press, 1977 (in press).

London, P. The induction of hypnosis. In J.E. Gordon (editor), Handbook of clinical and experimental hypnosis, New York: MacMillan, 1967.

Marks, D.F. Visual imagery differences in the recall of pictures. British Journal of Psychology, 1973, 64, 17-24.

Morgan, A.H. The heritability of hypnotic susceptibility in twins. Journal of Abnormal Psychology, 1973, 82, 55-61.

Morgan, A.H., Johnson, D.L., & Hilgard, E.R. The stability of hypnotic susceptibility: A longitudinal study. International Journal of Clinical and Experimental Hypnosis, 1974, 22, 249-257.

Morgan, A.H., McDonald, P.J., & MacDonald, H. Differences in bilateral alpha activity as a fucntion of experimental task with a note on lateral eye movements and hypnotizability. Neuropsychologia, 1971, 9, 459-469.

Palmer, R.D., & Field, P.B. Visual imagery and susceptibility to hypnosis. Journal of Consulting and Clinical Psychology, 1968, 32, 456-461.

Perry, C. Imagery, fantasy and hypnotic susceptibility; A multidimensional approach. Journal of Personality and Social Psychology, 1973, 26, 208-216.

Schwartz, G.E., Davidson, R.J., & Maer, F. Right hemisphere lateralization for emotion in the human brain: Interactions with cognition. Science, 1975, 190, 286-288.

Sells, S.B., Demares, R.G., & Wills, D.P., Jr. Dimensions of personality: II. Separate factor structures in Guilford and Cattell Trait Markers. Multivariate Behavioral Research, 1971, 6, 135-385.

Shor, R.E., & Cobb, J. An exploratory study of hypnotic training using the concept of plateau responsiveness as a reference. The American Journal of Clinical Hypnosis, 1968, 10, 178-193.

Shor, R.E., & Orne, E.C. Harvard Group Scale of Hypnotic Susceptibility. Palo Alto, California: Consulting Psychologists Press, 1962.

Sutcliffe, J.P., Perry, C.W., & Sheehan, P.W. Relation of some aspects of imagery and fantasy to hypnotic susceptibility. Journal of Abnormal Psychology, 1970, 76, 279-287.

Tellegen, A., & Atkinson, G. Openness to absorbing and self-altering experiences ("absorption"), a trait related to hypnotic susceptibility. Journal of Abnormal Psychology, 1974, 83, 286-297.

Van Nuys, D. Drug use and hypnotic susceptibility. International Journal of Clinical and Experimental Hypnosis, 1972, 20, 31-37.

Van Nuys, D. Meditation, attention and hypnotic susceptibility: A correlational study. International Journal of Clinical and Experimental Hypnosis, 1973, 21, 59-69.

A NONSUGGESTED EFFECT OF TRANCE INDUCTION*

A. Gordon Hammer

Macquarie University, Australia and
Institute of Pennsylvania Hospital, U.S.A.

Wendy-Louise Walker and A. D. Diment

Sydney University, Australia

Abstract: The historical association of hypnosis with suggestion has distracted theorists from the task of giving a comprehensive account of the effects of the trance state. Characteristics of this state may be revealed by the qualities of responses made to stimuli which are free of suggestions about expected responses. It was hypothesized that trance involves a regressive change in ego functions, and it was inferred that subjective responses to a poem spoken aloud to hypnotized subjects would involve increased primary process thinking in the absence of explicit suggestions to that effect. This prediction was confirmed in a study in which introspective reports were systematically recorded and content-analyzed. Comparison with one control group indicated that the high level of primary process functioning was the outcome of hypnosis and not just of hypnotizability, while comparison with a second control group suggested that this finding could not be attributed to subtle demand characteristics.

---

* Presentation of this report was made possible by assistance from Macquarie University, Australia, and in part by Grant # 19156 from the National Institute of Mental Health, Public Health Service, to the Unit for Experimental Psychiatry, The Institute of Pennsylvania Hospital, Philadelphia, Pa., U.S.A.

It is a matter of history that hypnotists routinely first put their clients through an induction procedure, and then proceed to use experimental or therapeutic maneuvers. Nevertheless, the nature and effects, and, indeed, the relevance of the induction procedure are far from understood. The implicit rationale for it is that it changes the client's state of mind in a helpful, preparatory way, as does an analgesic before a dental extraction or the starter's warning before a race.

Currently there is skepticism about this notion of a hypnotic state. As early as 1933, Hull had reservations: "The only thing which...gives any justification for the practice of calling it a 'state' is its generalized hypersuggestibility...The essence of hypnosis lies in the fact of change in suggestibility." This pronouncement, however, may have exerted a misleading influence on the study of hypnosis, and there are certainly some difficulties about it. First, if by using the word "essence," Hull means that he is offering a definition, there is the difficulty of defining a state in terms of changes. A "state" surely is some condition present here and now, irrespective of what preceded it. It would be meaningful to define trance as a state of high suggestibility (however caused); but, in fact, it is not widely claimed that all highly suggestible people are, ipso facto, all the time in a state of hypnosis. On the other hand, an empirical assertion that hypnosis, defined in some independent way, increases or tends to increase responsiveness to suggestion is quite legitimate in form, and well supported by evidence. Secondly, there seems to be little warrant for the assertion that the induction of the state which increases responsiveness to suggestions does not have any other characteristics or effects. Rather, if there be a distinguishable trance state, then research psychologists have as yet concentrated almost exclusively on the enhanced suggestibility aspect and, with a few notable exceptions, given only slight attention to whether it has features or outcomes independent of suggestion. Two assumptions of the present paper are that the hypothetical construct of a trance state is a viable one, and that evidence about its existence and nature should be looked for not only in the sphere of suggestibility, but also elsewhere.

There is nothing inherently obscure or deceptive about the notion of a "state." Substances, for example, are known to exist in various states, such as solid, liquid, and gaseous, clearly distinguished before the nature of these differences was fully understood. Some examples of mental states are depression, alertness, boredom, and absentmindedness. Psychologists must distinguish states from other dependent variables. A state is different from a response (e.g., a startle reflex), from an act (e.g., running a race), and from a trait or disposition (e.g., a liking for music); and, less clearly, from a stream of activity (e.g., daydreaming), and from a preparatory set (e.g., waiting for the luncheon bell).

A state differs from a response inasmuch as it continues for some time after the initiating circumstance. An act also continues, but it is a changing process with an end goal to which it is meaningfully directed, whereas a state is relatively unchanging and not goal-directed; it simply affects or colors most other ongoing responses and acts. Traits influence and color ongoing behavior, but only when they are touched upon relevantly. Traits tend to last for years, and are dispositions rather than current actualities, while states last only for minutes or hours, and are currently active and then gone. Streams of activity differ somewhat from states by virtue of their constantly changing content. Preparatory sets differ by virtue of their goal-directedness. States vary from one another in quality, degree, and duration. They may be initiated rapidly or slowly.

Psychological research concerned with the characterization and measurement of particular states is still rather primitive. Some states may be distinguished by direct observation (objective or subjective) of their continuing qualities, but sometimes states are indicated by their differential effects on "probe" stimuli, as when sleep is evidenced, albeit uncertainly, by diminished reaction to a whispered comment.

A few investigators have paid some attention to nonsuggested features of hypnotic behavior. Milton Erickson (1941), concerned both with distinguishing genuine hypnotic responses from compliance and with identifying essential features of trance, nominated waxy flexibility, rapport, and posthypnotic amnesia as a triad of spontaneous phenomena; however, despite his astuteness in observation, he was mistaken in failing to recognize that these phenomena are often implicitly suggested. Evans (1968) drew attention to a number of "counter-expectational" properties of responses in trance, properties which appear not to have been suggested even though the responses themselves were. For example, some typical but nonsuggested strategies were employed by genuinely hypnotized subjects to solve arithmetic problems in the face of a suggested amnesia for the number 6. Kihlstrom and Edmonston (1971) used Hull's term "neutral hypnosis" to underline the notion of nonsuggested effects in a study in which they found that going into trance appeared spontaneously to bring about changes in the experienced meanings of certain concepts, as indicated by shifts on Osgood's Semantic Differential. They stress the occurrence rather than the nature of the changes, but also point to some evidence that an altered awareness of self, involving diminished defensiveness, may be one component. Sherman (1971), using suitably trained subjects, allowed them to go into extremely deep trance, told them to "let whatever happens happen," and then at intervals simply asked for reports on current experience. A pervasive and common experience was "feeling oneness with everything."

There have also been a few attempts to give a theoretical account of the essence of the trance state. Shor (1959) described two main components of the depth of hypnosis: the extent of the subject's role-taking involvement, and the diminution of generalized reality testing. Later (1962), he added a third component, the degree of archaic involvement, which he describes in terms of transference relationships, but which is also consistent with concepts of regression and increased liability to primary process thinking, as those concepts are broadly understood in psychoanalytic theory. Kubie and Margolin (1944), and Gill and Brenman (1961), psychoanalytically oriented and working with clinical rather than laboratory data, independently worked out similar positions to the effect that the hypnotic state involves regressive changes in ego functions including some movement toward the primary process.

Against this background, it was hypothesized that hypnotic induction changes the state of mind of susceptible subjects and that this change involves a regressive diminution of the ego's realistic appraisal of experience. Further, it was inferred that such regression will tend to involve not only increased suggestibility, but also other consequences, one of which is increased proneness to make spontaneous use of primary process (or dream-like) thinking.

METHOD

The experimental subjects were undergraduates, five men and five women, who had scored 10, 11, or 12 on a pre-test with the Harvard Group Scale of Hypnotic Susceptibility, Form A (Shor & Orne, 1962). In individual familiarizing and practice sessions, an eye-closure induction was used, and then the subjects were asked to imagine a garden scene. Then the experimenter* said: "I am going to play a piece of music. It is entitled 'Spring' from 'Four Seasons' by Vivaldi. When it is finished I will start to talk to you again." After the piece was played, the subjects were aroused with instructions to remember the session fully, and an appointment was made for another session. In the second session, which was the main one, induction by a combination of relaxation and eye closure was used, and deepening was attempted by simple counting. The experimenter then said: "I am going to play a piece of poetry. It is entitled 'Prayer before Birth,' by Louis MacNiece. When it is finished I will start to talk to you again." A tape-recorded rendition of the poem was played, and then the subjects were aroused. Here is a short extract from the poem (Auden, 1964):

---

* The experimental procedures were carried out with all subjects by A. D. Diment.

I am not yet born, console me.
I fear that the human race may, with tall
walls wall me,
with strong drugs dope me, with wise lies lure
me, on
black racks rack me, in blood-baths roll me.

To discover the nature of the subjects' responses to the poem, a retrospective account was obtained of what was in consciousness while the poem was being played. The method of Interpersonal Process Recall (Kagan, 1972) was used, with audio instead of video feedback. Just after subjects were roused, the experimenter said: "Now I can reveal the true purpose of this experiment. I want to find out in as much detail as possible any thoughts or feeling or any reactions at all you may have had while the poem was being played. To help you recall these thoughts and feelings, I shall shortly replay the poem and if at any time during the replay you can recall what you were thinking or anything at all while it was playing the first time just let me know and I will stop the tape and you can tell me about them." The recall was taped on another recorder. The experimenter asked for elaborations in the manner standardized by Kagan. To ensure that the recall was carried out in the same state by all subjects - since the control subjects were not hypnotized - the experimental subjects were dehypnotized before the retrospective inquiry, after receiving suggestions counteracting any spontaneous amnesia.

The control group was drawn from the same population as the experimental group. The two groups were matched on age, prior studies of and interest in poetry, and on previously assessed hypnotic susceptibility. The control subjects were given the same familiarizing and practice session as were the experimental subjects, including the trance induction, and a second session was arranged. In the second session, they were comfortably seated, asked to relax, and, without a formal trance induction, told that the poem would be played. When the poem was completed, they were told they would remember their experiences, and a retrospective inquiry was carried out as with the experimental subjects.

When hypnotizable subjects who understand that hypnosis is being studied are not explicitly hypnotized, it is possible that they infer that they are controls, and obligingly, albeit unconsciously, strive to behave in what they take to be an unhypnotized way. The "demands" in the present enigmatic situation are not obvious, but, nevertheless, it was thought necessary to include a second control group of subjects who had no idea that the experiment was concerned with hypnosis. A large group who had volunteered ostensibly for a relaxation experiment were given a few moments of relaxation, and then told immediately in the standard way that a poem would be played. On its completion, they were told they would remember their experiences, and a retrospective inquiry was carried out in the prescribed way. Subsequently, all of these subjects were tested with the Harvard Group Scale, and, as the second control group, ten of them were selected at random from those who scored 10, 11, or 12.

A typist transcribed the 30 recorded recall reports, and ensured that the protocols were free of any information that would indicate which group they came from. It is assumed that these protocols indicate important components of subjects' experiences during the playing of the poem, and they constitute the raw data. This material was independently treated in two ways, globally and analytically.

RESULTS

In the global method, a judge who was experienced in hypnosis research, who had participated in planning this study and understood fully its purpose, and who was familiar with imaginal productions of hypnotized subjects,* read through entire transcripts and made impressionistic judgments about whether the descriptions of the experiences had or had not been given by a hypnotized subject. All ten transcipts from experimental subjects were included, in addition to five selected at random from each of the two control groups. The judge was aware that an equal number of experimental and control protocols were included in the set of 20, and made no attempt to discriminate between those of the two control groups. She correctly identified eight of the ten experimental records and eight of the controls. The chances of achieving this or a better "hit" rate as a sampling accident, calculated by Fisher's exact probability method for fixed margins, are between one and two in a hundred ($.01 < p < .02$). It seems very likely, then, that there are at least some features which distinguish the protocols of one group from those of the other.

In the analytic method, a systematic content analysis of the protocols was made, using an adaptation of Perry's (1964) method for analyzing dream content.** Technical details will be included in a full report in preparation, but the following information is sufficient to indicate what the findings are. The criteria of primary process that were used were elaboration of responses, high incidence of perceptual (as opposed to conceptual) components, high incidence of imagery not obviously and directly related to stimulus material, high incidence of phrases implying the current involvement of self in the experience, and high incidence of unrealistic concepts, involving distortions, contaminations or other bizarre responses.

---

* These judgments were made by W.-L. Walker.

** The authors express their appreciation of the contribution of Ms. Jeanna Sutton in carrying out these ratings.

Each protocol was divided into meaning units or elements. Each of the 1,863 elements was then rated on each of four different, and experimentally independent, classes of response by a psychologist experienced in this kind of content analysis who was unaware of the source of the protocols. The four response classes were:

I: a. concrete, b. abstract, c. mixed, d. not-applicable.
II: a. involves relevant imagery, b. involves imagery not obviously relevant, c. does not involve imagery.
III: a. implies involvement of subject in the action, b. does not.
IV: a. involves unrealistic or distorted ideation, b. does not.

The following are examples of the response classes:

Ia. concrete (perceptual): "...and suddenly it changed to a stone."
Ib. abstract (conceptual): "...almost a horror of bureaucracy of man and the callousness of men."
IIa. relevant imagery: "...an image of a baby."
IIb. not obviously relevant image: "...an image of a whole mass of people just walking..."
IIIa. involvement of subject: "...like I was searching for something."
IVa. distorted ideation: "...I felt closing in" (distortion of body image).

The proportion of the total number of elements that fell into six principal categories of the response classes was calculated for each subject, and constituted each person's score on that category. Table 1 gives the mean scores for the total number of elements and for the six principal categories. The scores for the last six variables are percentages of the total number of elements.

The differences between the experimental group and each of the control groups on variables 1, 3, 5, 6, and 7 (the ones directly relevant to the major hypotheses) are all significant at the .005 level. The deductions from the hypothesis clearly are not disconfirmed. For variables 2 and 4 (percentage of abstract elements and percentage of obviously relevant images), where no firm predictions were made - the variables were in a sense controls for "concrete elements" and "not obviously relevant images" - percentage scores in the hypnosis group were smaller than in the controls. Since, however, no element can be both concrete and abstract, nor both relevant and irrelevant, there is some artifactual tendency toward negative correlation between the alternatives, and these two findings are not independent of the other five.

The correlations over the 30 cases among the five specified relevant variables are all positive, ranging from .30 to .79, and

TABLE 1

Means of Groups on Principal Content Variables

Variables	Groups		
	Hypnotized	Control I	Control II
1. Number of elements	106	40	40
2. Percentage of abstract elements	5%	15%	18%
3. Percentage of concrete elements	42%	7%	16%
4. Percentage of relevant images	15%	28%	33%
5. Percentage of irrelevant images	21%	3%	5%
6. Percentage of ego-involved experiences	31%	4%	8%
7. Percentage of unrealistic ideas	19%	1%	3%

have a mean of .63, which clearly is consistent with the assumption that these variables are all in part influenced by some general factor, presumably the hypothesized primary process thinking.

DISCUSSION

From the above data, it is clear that a combination of the various signs of primary process enables a fairly satisfactory separation of experimental from control subjects. As yet, no multiple regression analysis of the data has been carried out, but by rough "eyeball" procedures, eight of the hypnotized subjects are easily identified, as are 18 of the controls. The latter result is particularly impressive since these control subjects were all highly hypnotizable. However, there is still some overlap of the groups, and the presence of primary process can no more bear the full burden of defining trance than can suggestibility. It is concluded that a trance induction procedure, carried out with susceptible subjects, causes a greatly increased occurrence of primary process thinking in response to some sorts of verbal stimuli (in this case, to poetry), and does so without there being any suggestions to that effect. This result is consistent with the view that an induction, when effective, brings about a state of mind different from the normal waking state, and that this state probably has a number of effects, one of which is an increase in primary process thinking.

REFERENCES

Auden, W.H. (editor) Selected poems of Louis MacNiece. London: Faber and Faber, 1964.

Erickson, M.H., & Erickson, E.M. The nature and character of posthypnotic behavior. Journal of General Psychology, 1941, 24, 95-133.

Evans, F.J. Recent trends in experimental hypnosis. Behavioral Science, 1968, 13, 477-487.

Gill, M.M., & Brenman, M. Hypnosis and related states. New York: International University Press, 1961.

Hull, C.L. Hypnosis and suggestibility. New York: Appleton-Century, 1933.

Kagan, N. Influencing human interaction. East Lansing, Michigan: Author, 1972.

Kihlstrom, J.F., & Edmonston, W.E. Jr. Alterations in consciousness in neutral hypnosis: Distortions in semantic space. American Journal of Clinical Hypnosis, 1971, 13 (4), 243-248.

Kubie, L.S., & Margolin, S. The process of hypnotism and the nature of the hypnotic state. _American Journal of Psychiatry_, 1944, _100_, 611-622.

Perry, C.W. A manual of procedures for analysing manifest dream content into narrative elements and for classifying such elements with respect to distortion from reality. Unpublished manual, University of Sydney, 1964.

Sherman, S.E. _Very deep hypnosis: An experimental and electroencephalographic investigation_. Ann Arbor, Michigan: University Microfilms, 1971.

Shor, R.E. Hypnosis and the concept of the generalized reality-orientation. _American Journal of Psychotherapy_, 1959, _13_, 582-602.

Shor, R.E. Three dimensions of hypnotic depth. _International Journal of Clinical and Experimental Hypnosis_, 1962, _10_, 23-38.

Shor, R.E., & Orne, E.C. _Harvard Group Scale of Hypnotic Susceptibility, Form A_. Palo Alto, California: Consulting Psychologists Press, 1962.

HYPNOTIC ANALGESIA VS. ACUPUNCTURE ANALGESIA IN HIGH AND LOW HYPNOTICALLY SUSCEPTIBLE SUBJECTS*

V. Jane Knox, Kit Shum, and Deborah M. McLaughlin

Queen's University, Canada

Abstract: The present study was designed to compare the effect of hypnotic analgesia with that of acupuncture analgesia. The cold pressor pain of 12 high and 12 low hypnotically susceptible subjects was assessed under three conditions: 1) no treatment baseline; 2) hypnotic analgesia; and, 3) acupuncture analgesia. Pain intensity, as measured by Hilgard's verbal report scale (Hilgard, Cooper, Lenox, Morgan, & Voevodsky, 1967) did not differ between the groups on the no treatment baseline trial. For all subjects, hypnotic analgesia was the more effective treatment. As expected, hypnotic analgesia was significantly more effective for highs than it was for lows. Acupuncture analgesia was also more effective for highs than it was for lows, but the difference between the groups only approached statistical significance. The data suggested that for high susceptibles acupuncture analgesia may be more effective when it is preceded by an experience with hypnotic analgesia.

Acupuncture analgesia does not work for everybody. When it is applied clinically in China, candidates are carefully screened, and only about 10% of all surgical patients are selected to receive acupuncture analgesia (Bonica, 1974). Subjects in whom pain is experi-

---

* This study was supported by Ontario Ministry of Health Grant #AC6 to V.J. Knox.

mentally induced do not all respond alike to acupuncture analgesia either. A number of researchers have reported that the effect of acupuncture analgesia ranges from one of marked alteration in the pain of some subjects to no changes in the pain of others (e.g., Andersson & Holmgren, 1975).

Hypnotizability is one dimension of individual difference which has been proposed to account for the observed differences in response to acupuncture analgesia. In 1974, Katz, Kao, Speigel, and Katz reported some support for this view in a sample of acute and chronic pain patients; those who were good hypnotic subjects showed a better response to acupuncture than those who were poor hypnotic subjects. Further support for the relevance of hypnotic susceptibility to response to acupuncture was provided by Knox and Shum (in press). In the latter study, experimentally induced pain in high susceptibles was significantly more affected by acupuncture than was the pain of low susceptibles.

The study to be reported here is a further investigation of the relationship between acupuncture and hypnosis. It was designed to assess the similarity between the effect of acupuncture analgesia and that of hypnotic analgesia on the experimentally induced pain of high and low hypnotically susceptible subjects.

METHOD

Subjects were 24 undergraduates at Queen's University who had been screened for hypnotic susceptibility on both the Harvard Group Scale (HGSHS) (Orne & Shor, 1962) and the individually administered Stanford Scale of Hypnotic Susceptibility, Form C (SSHS:C) (Weitzenhoffer & Hilgard, 1962). Twelve of these subjects were chosen because they scored in the high susceptible range on both scales; the remaining 12 scored in the low susceptible range on the two scales.

Cold pressor pain was produced by immersing the hand and forearm in a tank of circulating ice water. The apparatus has been described in detail elsewhere (Knox & Shum, in press). The subject put his arm on an arm rest hinged to one end of the tank, and the experimenter used a pulley arrangement to lower the arm rest into the water at the beginning of a trial. The ice water trials were always 60 seconds long. At the 60 second mark, the experimenter raised the arm rest from the water and immediately wrapped the subject's arm in a warm towel. During each 60 second trial, the subject was asked to rate the intensity of his pain every 5 seconds, so that 12 pain reports were obtained on each trial. The scale the subject used to rate his pain is one used extensively by E.R. Hilgard (e.g., Hilgard, 1969; Hilgard, Cooper, Lenox, Morgan, & Voevodsky, 1967; Hilgard, Ruch, Lange, Lenox, Morgan, & Sachs, 1974).

It is an open-ended numerical scale for which the subject is given two reference points: "0" is defined as no pain and "10" is defined as intense pain. All subjects in the present experiment were given a practice trial with the ice water and the pain rating scale before the experiment proper was begun.

The design of the experiment called for each subject to receive three ice water trials: 1) an acupuncture analgesia trial; 2) a hypnotic analgesia trial; and 3) a no treatment baseline trial. These trials spanned two days and were arranged in a counterbalanced order. No subjects received acupuncture and hypnosis trials on the same day.

Acupuncture analgesia was induced by the second author, a Nanking trained physician and acupuncturist. The treatment involved two needles - one inserted between the thumb and forefinger of the experimental arm (Hoku), and the other into the experimental forearm (Hsishang). These locations are assumed to produce analgesia in the hand and forearm. After insertion, the needles were attached to a model 71.1 battery operated Acupuncture Anesthesia Apparatus manufactured in the People's Republic of China and were electrically stimulated with the maximum current defined by the subject as non-painful. Stimulation time was approximately 20 minutes. At the end of the 20-minute induction period, the needles were removed and the subject began the 60-second ice water trial. The time from needle removal to completion of the ice water trial never exceeded 90 seconds.

The hypnotic analgesia trial was preceded by a standard hypnotic induction, followed by suggestions of hand and arm analgesia. Together, these instructions took approximately 20 minutes.

Finally, the baseline dip was simply a 60-second ice water trial preceded by no experimental manipulation.

RESULTS

The results of the numerical ratings of pain intensity will be presented first. The data analysis reported here examined the pain intensity ratings at 30 seconds in ice water.

At the 30-second mark of the no treatment baseline trial, high susceptibles reported a mean pain intensity of 8.5, while the mean for low susceptibles was 10.25. The difference between these two means does not approach statistical significance ($t = 0.85$, $df = 22$, $p > .10$). Consequently, we then examined the percent decrease from this baseline in each of the two treatment trials. The percent decrease from baseline in reported pain at 30 seconds under acupuncture and under hypnosis is shown in Figure 1. It may be seen

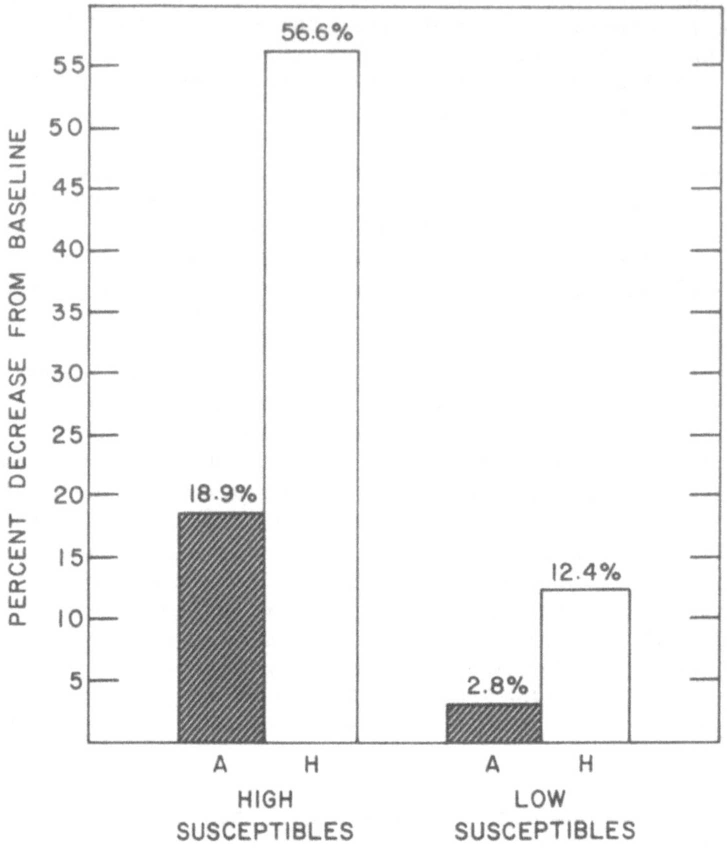

Fig. 1. Mean reduction in pain reports at 30 seconds in ice water as a function of treatment and susceptibility level (A = acupuncture; H = hypnosis).

that overall, hypnotic analgesia was the more effective treatment. That is, both high and low susceptibles showed a greater decrease in reported pain under hypnotic analgesia than under acupuncture analgesia ($F = 27.98$, $df = 1, 18$; $p < .0001$). As one would expect, hypnotic analgesia was more effective for highs than for lows; the difference between high and low susceptible subjects in pain reduction under hypnotic analgesia was highly significant ($t = 4.73$, $df = 22$, $p < .0005$).

On the basis of our earlier study in which acupuncture analgesia was significantly more effective for high susceptibles than it was for low susceptibles, we expected highs in the present experiment to show a greater pain reduction than lows under acupuncture.

The reported pain of highs was more affected by acupuncture than was the reported pain of lows, but not significantly so. The comparison of the two susceptibility groups' pain reduction under acupuncture analgesia only approached significance ($t = 1.38$, $df = 22$, $p < .10$).

Recall that the three ice water trials - no treatment baseline, hypnotic analgesia, and acupuncture analgesia - were presented to subjects in a counterbalanced order. Three orders of trials were used in the study, with four high susceptibles and four lows per order. The three orders are depicted on the abscissa of Figure 2. In order A, subjects received the baseline and acupuncture trials on day 1, and the hypnosis trial on day 2; in order B, hypnosis was on day 1, with baseline followed by acupuncture on day 2; order C was acupuncture, day 1, and hypnosis then baseline on day 2. While acupuncture analgesia was always less effective than hypnotic analgesia, the difference between the effectiveness of acupuncture and hypnosis was not the same for all orders (treatment x order, $F = 3.44$, $df = 2, 18$; $p < .053$). This finding is evident in Figure 2, which shows the percent pain reduction over baseline in each order of treatments for high and low susceptibles combined. When acupuncture is experienced <u>before</u> hypnosis (as in orders A and C), pain reduction under acupuncture is on the order of 6%, and hypnotic analgesia provides a significantly greater reduction in felt pain (order A, $t = 3.53$, $df = 7$, $p < .01$; order C, $t = 2.69$, $df = 7$, $p < .05$). In contrast, when acupuncture is experienced <u>after</u> hypnosis, it reduces pain 19.7% over baseline, and while hypnosis again provides greater reduction, the difference between the two treatments is no longer significant (order B, $t = 1.08$, $df = 7$, $p > .10$). One is tempted to conclude that there is a beneficial effect on acupuncture of having experienced hypnotic analgesia beforehand. However, it should be noted that although the effect of acupuncture is maximized by a preceding experience with hypnosis, the resultant 19.7% reduction in felt pain is not significantly different from the 6.4% reduction associated with experiencing acupuncture before hypnosis ($t = 1.06$, $df = 22$, $p > .10$).

While the number of high and low susceptible subjects in each order is too small to warrant statistical analysis of the data, there appear to be differences between the two groups in their response to acupuncture when acupuncture follows hypnotic analgesia (order B). High susceptibles in order B reduced their pain an average of 41.6% after acupuncture. In contrast, lows in order B actually reported an <u>increase</u> of 2.3% in their pain after acupuncture.

DISCUSSION

The study reported here provides only limited support for the proposition that hypnotic susceptibility and successful acupuncture

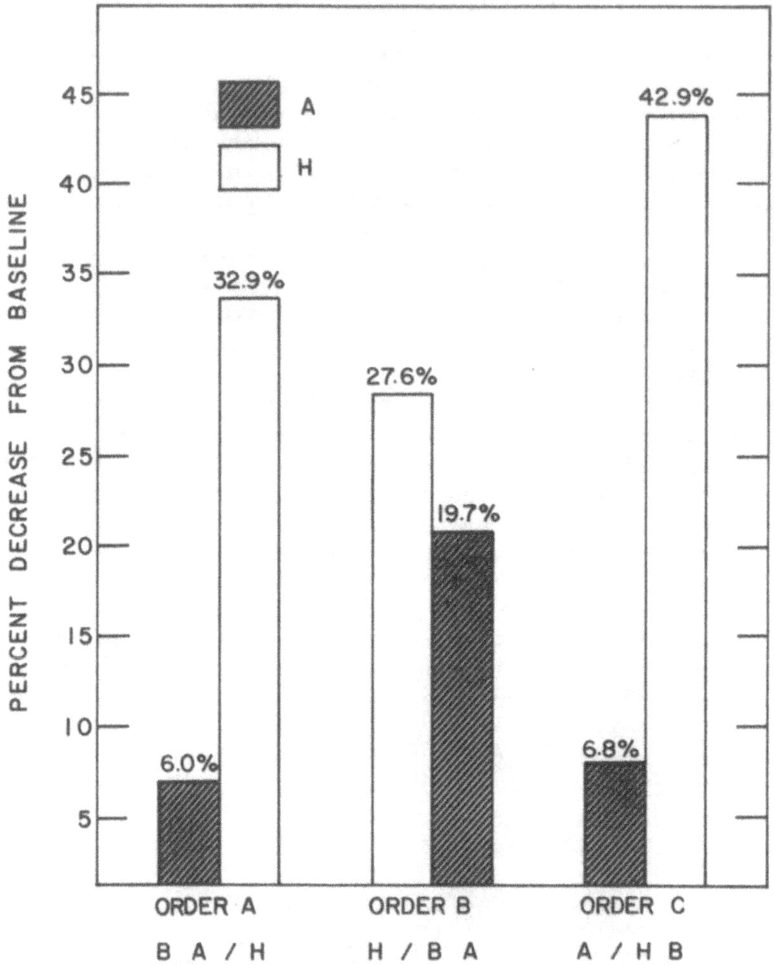

Fig. 2. Mean reduction in pain reports at 30 seconds in ice water as a function of treatment and order of trials (A = acupuncture; H = hypnosis; B = baseline).

analgesia are related. Previous experiments, both in our laboratory and elsewhere, have shown high susceptible subjects to be significantly more responsive to acupuncture than low susceptibles (e.g., Katz et al., 1974; Knox & Shum, in press). In the present study, highs were also more affected by acupuncture than were lows, but not significantly so. It is our conclusion that the relationship between hypnotic susceptibility and response to acupuncture is, at best, weak.

Overall, the effect of acupuncture was to reduce, but not to eliminate, felt pain. In this respect, our findings are consistent with the results reported by other investigators; when a positive effect of acupuncture has been demonstrated with laboratory pain, this effect invariably has been a limited one (e.g., Anderson, Jamieson, & Man, 1974; Chapman, Wilson, & Gehrig, 1976; Smith, Chiang, Kitz, & Antoon, 1974). Further, the data presented here do not mask individual cases of pain elimination. All subjects in the present study and in our previous study reported some pain on the acupuncture trial.

On the other hand, not only was hypnotic analgesia more effective than acupuncture in reducing pain over all subjects, but, also, 4 of our 12 high susceptibles reported virtual elimination of pain under hypnosis. It would appear that at least with cold pressor pain, hypnosis is the more effective analgesic not only for highs but for lows as well.

However, our data do suggest that it may be possible to augment the effect of acupuncture analgesia. Our most responsive subjects were high susceptibles who had previously experienced hypnotic analgesia. One might speculate that, having experienced hypnotic analgesia, these subjects could contribute to an acupuncture effect by adding aspects of hypnotic analgesia to the situation. However, not only were our subjects instructed to avoid using hypnotic techniques during the acupuncture trial, but they were questioned extensively on this point after the experiment was over. All of our subjects reported that they were able to avoid using hypnotic techniques during acupuncture. It is our opinion that if the finding of a relation between previous treatment and the efficacy of acupuncture analgesia is replicated, systematic investigation of this relation would be warranted.

REFERENCES

Anderson, D.G., Jamieson, J.L., & Man, S.C. Analgesic effects of acupuncture on the pain of ice water: A double-blind study. Canadian Journal of Psychology, 1974, 28, 239-244.

Andersson, S.A., & Holmgren, E. On acupuncture analgesia and the mechanism of pain. American Journal of Chinese Medicine, 1975, 3 (4), 311-334.

Bonica, J.J. Acupuncture anesthesia in the People's Republic of China. Journal of the American Medical Association, 1974, 229 (10), 1317-1325.

Chapman, C.R., Wilson, M.E., & Gehrig, J.D. Comparative effects of acupuncture and transcutaneous stimulation on the perception of painful dental stimuli. Pain, 1976, 2, 265-283.

Hilgard, E.R. Pain as a puzzle for psychology and physiology. American Psychologist, 1969, 24, 103-113.

Hilgard, E.R., Cooper, L.M., Lenox, J., Morgan, A.H., & Voevodsky, J. The use of pain-state reports in the study of hypnotic analgesia to the pain of ice water. Journal of Nervous and Mental Disease, 1967, 144 (6), 506-513.

Hilgard, E.R., Ruch, J.C., Lange, A.F., Lenox, J.R., Morgan, A.H., & Sachs, L.B. The psychophysics of cold pressor pain and its modification through hypnotic suggestion. American Journal of Psychology, 1974, 87, 17-31.

Katz, R.L., Kao, C.Y., Speigel, H., & Katz, G.L. Pain, acupuncture, hypnosis. In J.J. Bonica (editor), Advances in neurology, Vol. 4. New York: Raven Press, 1974.

Knox, V.J., & Shum, K. Reduction of cold pressor pain with acupuncture analgesia in high and low hypnotic subjects. Journal of Abnormal Psychology, 1977, 86, 639-643.

Orne, E., & Shor, R.E. Harvard Group Scale of Hypnotic Susceptibility. Palo Alto, California: Consulting Psychologists Press, 1962.

Smith, G.M., Chiang, H.T., Kitz, R.J., & Antoon, A. Acupuncture and experimentally induced ischemic pain. In J.J. Bonica (editor), Advances in neurology, Vol.4. New York: Raven Press, 1974.

Weitzenhoffer, A.M., & Hilgard, E.R. Stanford Hypnotic Susceptibility Scale: Form C. Palo Alto, California: Consulting Psychologists Press, 1962.

INDIVIDUAL AND GROUP ASSESSMENT OF HYPNOTIC RESPONSIVITY IN COERCED VOLUNTEER CHRONIC SCHIZOPHRENICS

Germain Lavoie*
Hôpital Louis-H. Lafontaine and Université de Montréal

John Lieberman and Michel Sabourin
Université de Montréal

Andrée Brisson
Hôpital des Laurentides, L'Annonciation, Canada

Abstract: This paper reviews the results obtained with chronic schizophrenic patients on the SHSS:A (N = 106) and on the HGSHS:A (N = 142), and the correspondence between these two scores for 73 patients. Results indicate that in these randomly chosen samples, in which the only reason for exclusion was a patient's explicit refusal to participate, no more than 1% to 2% of the patients could experience deep hypnosis. Nevertheless, 20% of this group did succeed in attaining a score of 7 or more on the SHSS:A; also, these patients had a significantly better index of adaptive regression on the Rorschach test, although the probability of their discharge was not any higher. The discussion stresses the influence of the sampling and testing procedures used on the results obtained, and suggests that further research is needed to determine the diagnostic and prognostic usefulness of hypnotic susceptibility in chronic schizophrenia.

---

* The authors wish to thank G. Ally, L. Girard-Robin, J. Godon and J. Langlois, who shared in obtaining some of the data presented or discussed in this paper.

At the beginning of this century, many clinicians beleived that psychotics and especially schizophrenics were not hypnotizable, and hypnosis was even used as an instrument for the differential diagnosis of neurotics and psychotics (Travis, 1924; Copeland & Kitching, 1937).

The majority of clinical and experimental studies which followed (Abrams, 1964; Biddle, 1967; Bowers, 1961; Bowers, Brecher-Marer, & Polatin, 1961; Brenman & Knight, 1943; Erickson, 1941; Erickson, 1964; Friedman & Keup, 1963; Gale & Herman, 1956; Gill & Brenman, 1959; Gordon, 1973; Greene, 1969; Heath, Hoaken & Sainz, 1960; Illovsky, 1962; King, 1957; Kramer & Brennan, 1964; Lavoie, Sabourin, & Langlois, 1973; Lavoie, Sabourin, Ally, & Langlois, 1976; Lieberman, Lavoie, & Brisson, 1978; Polak, Mountain, & Emde, 1964; Stauffacher, 1958; Vingoe & Kramer, 1966; Wilson, Cormen, & Cole, 1949; Wolberg, 1945) demonstrated that a certain proportion of psychotics including schizophrenics could be hypnotized. In agreement with the pioneer work of Schilder & Kauders (1926), many of these studies pointed out the particular difficulties inherent in the hypnosis of schizophrenics. The reponse to hypnosis appears to be stronger at the time of onset of schizophrenia rather than in chronic cases (Friedman & Keup, 1963). When reality testing is better (Gale & Herman, 1956), and there exists a capacity for time limited regression in the service of the ego (Lavoie et al., 1976), the response to hypnosis in schizophrenics is also better. Recently (Spiegel, 1976), there has been a renewed interest in hypnotic responsivity as a diagnostic instrument.

We will first report data collected over the last several years concerning the assessment of hypnotic susceptibility in 194 chronic schizophrenics. We will then describe some parameters of the hypnotic responsivity of chronic schizophrenics.

METHOD

Subjects

Sample A is a random sample of 56 chronic psychotic patients (including 48 schizophrenics) tested in 1968 with the Stanford Hypnotic Susceptibility Scale, Form A (Weitzenhoffer & Hilgard, 1959) (Lavoie et al., 1973).

Sample B is a random sample of 142 chronic schizophrenic patients tested in 1975 with the Harvard Group Scale of Hypnotic Susceptibility, Form A (Shor & Orne, 1962).

Sample C is composed of 73 subjects in sample B who had a score of 5 or more or 2 or less on the HGSHS:A, and who were also tested with the SHSS:A.

Sample D is composed of 54 subjects in sample C who were tested in the usual "passive" condition of the SHSS:A, the 19 others being tested in an "active" condition (Lieberman et al., 1978).* Four additional patients were tested with the SHSS:A, but not with the HGSHS:A. This is a total of 58 subjects in sample D tested with the SHSS:A in the usual passive condition.

All patients were male and French speaking. The mean length of hospitalization was 15 years (range 4 - 34 years) for sample A, and 10 years (range 2 - 37 years) for sample B. Most patients were receiving routine drug treatment which consisted mainly of phenothiazine derivatives.

Examiners

At least two examiners were used on each occasion (i.e., one observer (O) and one experimenter (E)). For the 1968 sample, there were three: one _E_ and two _O_'s.

Procedure

The patients came to the department knowing only that they were to participate in a research project. They were told that hypnosis was involved. Proper care was taken in establishing rapport, and very few patients refused to participate in the experiment.

Hypnotic Scales

HGSHS:A. For the group testing situation (sample B), a French adaptation (M. Sabourin, translator) of the HGSHS:A was used to provide a standard hypnotic induction and evaluation procedure. A pilot study of the psychometric characteristics of this adapted scale had been carried out on a sample of 82 university students (43 females and 39 males), whose mean age was 21 years (S.D. = 2.55) (Sabourin, Lavoie, Melanson, Seklow, & Brisebois, 1972). The mean

---

* Hilgard (1965) remarks that "the hypnotic subject is not making his own plans, but is doing what the hypnotist directs; hence episodes are not tied together as they are in intentional study or memorizing, but more as they are in passive incidental learning." Lieberman et al., (1976) compared this condition to a condition of "active" learning or intentional memorizing. Immediately before the suggestion of amnesia, the patients were required to memorize the previous items of the scale to make sure that they actually recorded the material _before_ the suggestion of amnesia.

score for the French adaptation was 7.08, as compared with the mean of 7.39 published by Shor & Orne (1963) for the Harvard sample. Furthermore, the distribution of the scores in the French sample seemed closer to the normal distribution than the distribution of the Harvard sample. Both patients and subjects were tested in groups of 10.

Because the patients reported in this paper have difficulties answering written questionnaires, proper evaluation of recall amnesia would have required individual inquiries after group testing. Therefore, for practical reasons the amnesia item was omitted. Consequently, the HGSHS:A consisted of 11 items instead of 12.

SHSS:A. A French translation (M. Sabourin, translator) of the SHSS:A was used. For sample A, the hypnotic induction and the measurement of hypnotic responsivity were carried out according to the standardized procedure of the SHSS:A. The patients in Sample C were tested with 14 items (i.e., the usual 12 items plus "taste hallucination" and "dream," borrowed from the Stanford Hypnotic Susceptibility Scale, Form C and administered immediately before the posthypnotic suggestion) (Lieberman et al., 1978). Since only 11 of the 12 items of the HGSHS:A were used, only 11 equivalent items of the SHSS:A (i.e., item 1 through 11 for both scales, with the amnesia item excluded) will be considered when the two scales are compared. An additional reason for excluding the amnesia item from the SHSS:A when this group of 73 subjects is studied as such, is the fact that 19 of these subjects were submitted to an active learning procedure immediately before the amnesia suggestion. Although it did not affect the other items of the scale, this procedure (Lieberman et al., 1978) invalidated the standard amnesia item.

Tests of Intelligence and Personality

A battery of psychological tests was administered to the patients in sample A. These included the Rorschach test (administered and scored according to the Holt, Eagle, Havel, Goldberger, Phillip, Rabkin, Safrin et al., (1963) system), the MMPI (Hathaway & McKinley, 1943), the Eysenck Personality Inventory (Eysenck & Eysenck, 1964), and the IPAT Anxiety Scale (Cattel, 1957), for a total of 69 personality variables. They were also tested for I.Q. with the Revised Beta Examination (Kellog & Morton, 1946), and for M.Q. with the Wechsler Memory Scale (Wechsler, 1945). Sub-types of schizophrenia, age, and time spent in the hospital were also considered.

RESULTS

Table 1 indicates the percentage of schizophrenics who were high, medium or low on the SHSS:A and on the HGSHS:A. Column 1 shows that with 12 items, the SHSS:A produced 4% high susceptible subjects, 44% medium susceptible subjects, and 52% low susceptible subjects. Column 3 shows that with 11 items, the HGSHS:A produced 6% high susceptible subjects, 18% medium susceptible subjects, and 76% low susceptible subjects. If one takes the individual procedure as a safer estimate of hypnotic susceptibility, 4% of the chronic schizophrenic patients obtained a score of 8 or more. If the criterion had been 9 or more, as in the Nace, Orne, and Hammer (1972) study for example, the figure would fall to 3%. Probably only 1% would prove to be really highly susceptible subjects, according to Hilgard's (1976) criterion. It seems, therefore, that although it is rare very high hypnotic susceptibility does occur among chronic schizophrenic patients. We have evidence, however, that some patients can be very deeply and quickly hypnotized in clinical settings even if they score rather poorly on standard scales in experimental settings.

Figure 1 presents (solid line) the distribution of scores on the SHSS:A in sample A (N = 56). The dotted line indicates the distribution of scores in sample D (N = 58). The central depressed portion of the dotted line results from the fact that subjects who had scores of 3 or 4 on the HGSHS:A were not tested with the SHSS:A in 1975. This figure demonstrates that, with chronic schizophrenics, the SHSS:A produced an approximation of the normal curve that suffers from positive asymmetry.

TABLE 1

Percentage of Chronic Schizophrenics Obtaining High, Medium and Low Scores on SHSS:A and HGSHS:A

Depth of Hypnosis	SHSS:A (N = 48) (12 items)	SHSS:A (N = 48) (11 items)	HGSHS:A (N = 142) (11 items)
High (8 - 12)	4%	4%	6%
Medium (5 - 7)	44%	36%	18%
Low (0 - 4)	52%	61%	76%

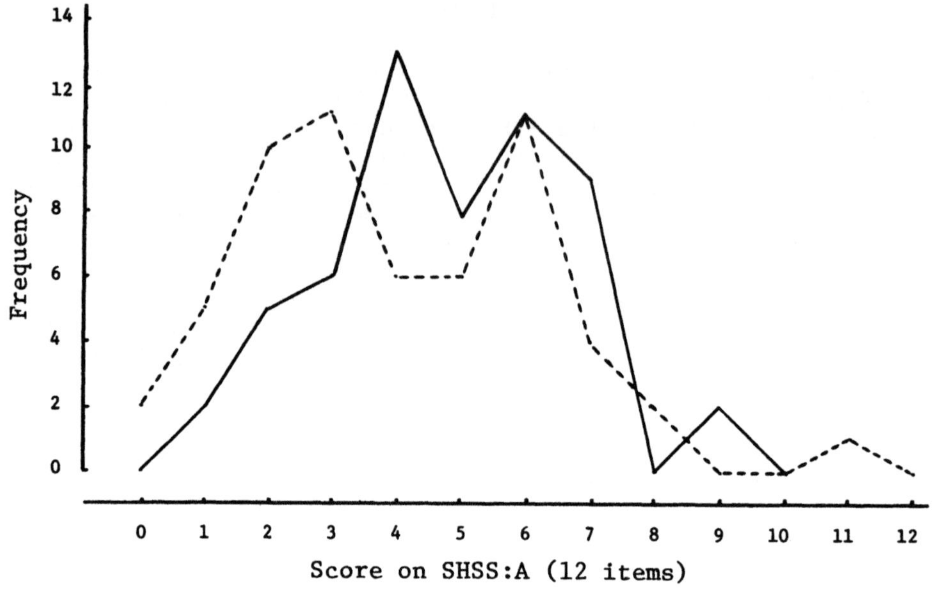

Fig. 1. Distribution of scores on the SHSS:A for a random sample of chronic psychotics (solid line; N = 56, including 48 schizophrenics), and for a second sample of chronic schizophrenics who obtained either 0 - 2, or 5 - 9, on the HGSHS:A (dotted line; N = 58).

Figure 2 presents (solid line) the actual distribution of scores on the HGSHS:A, based on 11 items, for a random sample of 142 chronic schizophrenics (sample B). The dotted line presents the theoretical distribution for the HGSHS:A based on 12 items instead of 11, that is, including the amnesia item. This distribution assumes that the response to the amnesia item would have been comparable to that obtained with the SHSS:A in both sample A and sample D, that is, an 80% passing rate unrelated to hypnotic susceptibility.*

---

* This means that 80% (i.e., 26) of the 33 subjects who obtained a score of zero would have obtained a score of 1; we therefore added 26 to the number of subjects (23) who had obtained a score of 1 on the HGSHS:A <u>without</u> the amnesia item. However, if we assume that 80% of <u>these</u> 23 subjects (i.e., 18) would also have passed the amnesia

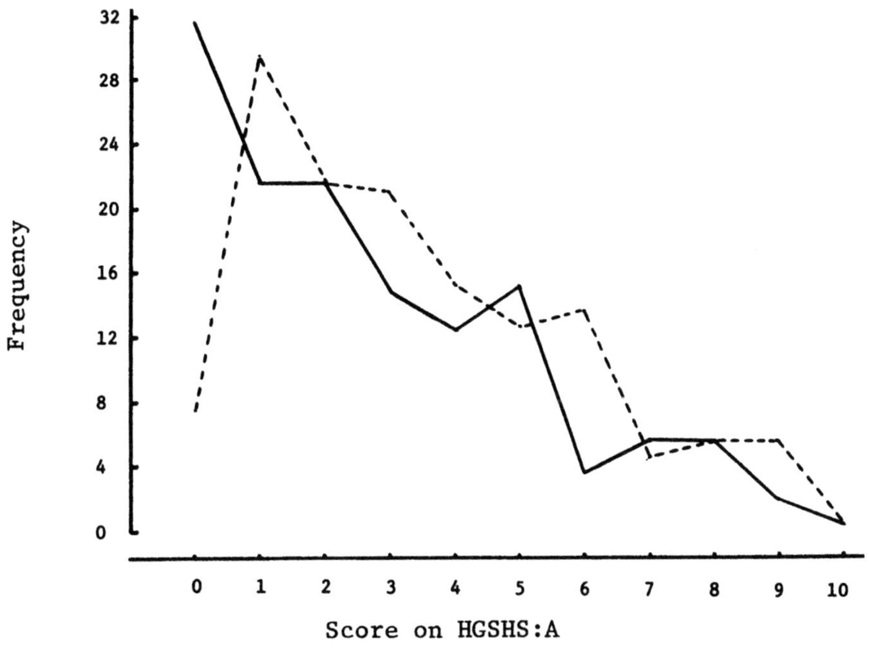

Fig. 2. Distribution of scores on the HGSHS:A for a random sample of chronic schizophrenics (N = 142), excluding the amnesia item (observed distribution, solid line) and including the amnesia item (theoretical distribution, dotted line).

Since most patients "pass" the amnesia item, i.e., fail to recall more than three items on the amnesia test, the inclusion of this item in the scale (dotted line of Figure 2) drastically reduces the frequency of patients obtaining a hypnotic score of zero.

The distribution of the HGSHS:A includes an excessive proportion of low scores. Furthermore, there is a continuous decrease in the frequency of scores as one proceeds from 1 to 10. This seems to result mainly from disturbing factors inherent in the group testing situation with unselected chronic schizophrenics, a fact

---

item, we must subtract this number (18) from the total number of subjects who scored 1, and add it to the number who scored 2 (without the amnesia item). Similar correction for each susceptibility level would produce the curve represented by the dotted line in Figure 2.

that has also been observed in a number of other psychometric situations. Possible limitations of the HGSHS:A (Hartman, 1965; Levitt, Aronoff, & Morgan, 1974; Orne, 1971) might therefore be amplified with schizophrenic samples, in light of their special psychological deficit (Shakow, 1969).*

Comparison of HGSHS:A and SHSS:A

Figure 3 presents the scores of 73 chronic schizophrenics tested with both the SHSS:A and with the HGSHS:A. The horizontal axis presents the scores on the HGSHS:A, and the vertical axis, the scores on the SHSS:A. The oblique line shows that when compared with the SHSS:A, the HGSHS:A overestimates high scores, and underestimates low scores. In effect, most of the patients having 0, 1, or 2 on the HGSHS:A obtained <u>higher</u> scores on the SHSS:A (88%). On the other hand, most of the patients having 5 or more on the HGSHS:A obtained <u>lower</u> scores on the SHSS:A (92%).

In spite of these observations, the HGSHS:A still remains very useful for the screening of susceptible chronic schizophrenics. In effect, the horizontal and vertical middle lines in Figure 3 show that most patients who scored 5 or less on the HGSHS:A also scored 5 or less on the SHSS:A (96%). On the other hand, 72% of the patients who scored 6 or more on the HGSHS:A also scored 6 or more on the SHSS:A. Consequently, the HGSHS:A permits the establishment of a dichotomy between more susceptible and less susceptible chronic schizophrenic patients.

When looking at this figure, one should remember that it is based on 11 of the 12 items of the scales. Had the amnesia item been included in the comparison, the criterion for differentiating more susceptible and less susceptible subjects would be a score of 7 or more on both scales, instead of 6 or more.

---

* The two groups of patients whose SHSS:A scores are presented in Figure 1 differ significantly from Hilgard's (1965) normative group. That is, the proportion of patients obtaining high scores is lower than what is found in the normative group. Similarly, the HGSHS:A scores presented in Figure 2 differ significantly from the normative data published by Shor and Orne (1963) and those presented by Sabourin et al., (1972) for a French population of university students. Again, the proportion of patients obtaining high scores is lower than that found in normative groups.

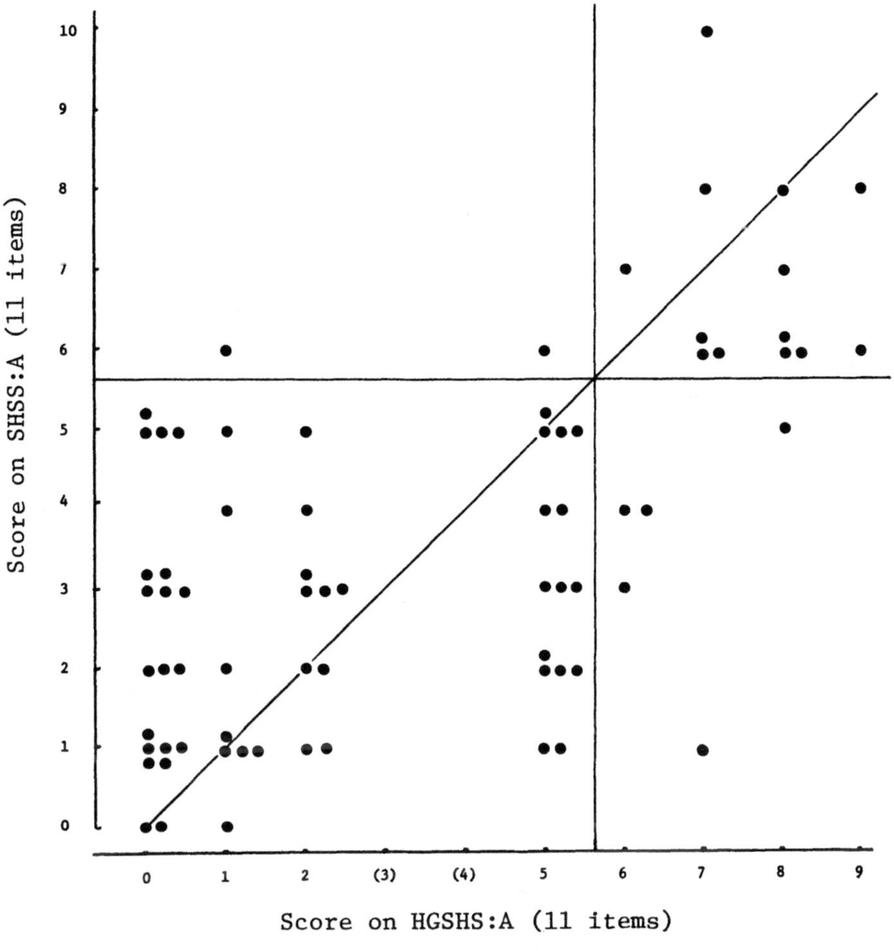

Fig. 3. Distribution of scores of 73 chronic schizophrenics on the HGSHS:A and the SHSS:A. Each dot represents an individual. Patients who scored 3 or 4 on the HGSHS:A were not tested with the SHSS:A.

Hypnosis, Thinking Disorders, and Adaptive Regression

Correlations of SHSS:A with age, time of hospitalization, subtypes of schizophrenia, I.Q., M.Q., and personality variables derived from the personality inventories were small and nonsignificant. However, an expected relation with the capacity for time limited adaptive regression was found. These results, based on Gill and Brenman's (1959) theory of hypnosis, have been analyzed in detail in a previous study (Lavoie et al., 1976). In summary, it was demonstrated that a score of 7 or more on the SHSS:A, attained by approximately 20% of the patients, significantly predicted a fairly good capacity for adaptive regression as measured with Holt's system of scoring the Rorschach test. It was found that 10 of the 11 subjects (90.9%) with high SHSS:A scores (7 - 9) were high on Holt's index of adpative regression (AR index), while only 5 of the 19 subjects (26.3%) with medium SHSS:A scores (5 - 6) and 4 of the 26 subjects (15.4%) with low SHSS:A scores (1 - 4) were high on this index (Lavoie et al., 1976). Furthermore, gross formal deviations of thinking were negatively related to both hypnotic susceptibility and the AR index. However, neither hypnotic susceptibility nor the AR index correlated significantly with duration of hospitalization.

DISCUSSION

Our results indicate that high hypnotic susceptibility is rare among chronic schizophrenic patients. Comparisons with available SHSS:A and HGSHS:A norms for normal subjects, however, are of questionable value, since in all cases the normal groups have been younger and of a higher socio-economic level than our groups of chronic patients.

In the present study, patients were told that hypnosis was involved before the procedure to hypnotize them was initiated. As many as possible were invited to join the experiment and only the few patients who clearly refused to participate were excluded from the sample. This procedure of choosing the sample suggests that it can most accurately be described as composed of "coerced volunteers" (Boucher & Hilgard, 1962), even if all subjects had agreed to participate (see also Rosenthal & Rosnow, 1975).* This is a basic

---

* Such a group may be referred to as composed of "coerced" volunteers, according to the criteria set out by Boucher and Hilgard (1962). These individuals differ from "true" volunteers who seek out the hypnotic experience on their own, i.e., after a public announcement. There is a certain amount of coercion when a profes-

issue for the interpretation of our results, since discrepancies in the findings of some previous studies (v.g., Barber, Karacan, & Calverley, 1964; Greene, 1969; Kramer & Brennan, 1964; Vingoe & Kramer, 1966) suggest that the sampling process may strongly influence the results.

Girard-Robin (1977), studied patients from the same population as the one described in this study, but retained only those who were truly eager to participate (hence, true volunteers). By her procedure, 59% (47/80) were retained for hypnosis, while in the studies reported in the present paper, 93% of the sample initially invited to participate were actually tested with the hypnotic scales. The more permissive selection procedure of Lucie Girard-Robin led not only to a higher percentage of patients who obtained 8 or more on the SHSS:A (i.e., 17%), as compared with only 4% in the present study, but also to a higher percentage (51%) of low scores (0 - 3), as compared with 25% for the more coerced sample used in the present study ($p < .01$, two-tailed Kolmogorov-Smirnov test). Obviously, the meaning and effect of volunteer bias with hospitalized chronic schizophrenics deserves further investigation.

In summary, given the conditions of the present study, we found that no more than 1% to 2% of hospitalized chronic schizophrenic patients are very highly susceptible to hypnosis. There were, however, some personality differences between those who obtained 7 or more on the SHSS:A and those who obtained 6 or less. The proportion of patients who scored 7 or more was approximately 20%. These patients were likely to have a fairly good adaptive regression index on the Rorschach and less thinking disorder, a pattern that suggests a positive prognosis. However, the fact that neither hypnotic susceptibility nor the adaptive regression index correlated significantly with duration of hospitalization suggests that the underlying adaptive potential may be obscured, perhaps by other personal or situational factors. A follow-up study of the patients already examined for hypnotic susceptibility should clarify this issue.

---

sional person asks a schizophrenic patient who has lived in a hospital for many years if he would agree to participate in a research project, just as there is some coercion when a teacher asks a student to participate in a hypnosis experiment as part of his curriculum.

REFERENCES

Abrams, S. The use of hypnotic techniques with psychotics: A critical review. American Journal of Psychotherapy, 1964, 18, 79-94.

Barber, T.X., Karacan, I., & Calverley, D.S. "Hypnotizability" and suggestibility in chronic schizophrenics. Archives of General Psychiatry, 1964, 11, 439-451.

Biddle, W.E. Hypnosis in the psychoses. Springfield, Illinois: Charles C. Thomas, 1967.

Boucher, R.G., & Hilgard, E.R. Volunteer bias in hypnotic experimentation. American Journal of Clinical Hypnosis, 1962, 5, 49-51.

Bowers, M.K. Theoretical considerations in the use of hypnosis in the treatment of schizophrenia. International Journal of Clinical and Experimental Hypnosis, 1961, 9, 39-46.

Bowers, M.K., Brecher-Marer, S., & Polatin, A.H. Hypnosis in the study and treatment of schizophrenia: a case report. International Journal of Clinical and Experimental Hypnosis, 1961, 9, 119-138.

Brenman, M., & Knight, R.P. Hypnotherapy for mental illness in the aged: Case report of hysterical psychosis in a 71 year old woman. Bulletin of the Menninger Clinic, 1943, 7, 188-198.

Cattell, R.B. IPAT Anxiety Scale. Champaign, Illinois: Institute for Personality and Ability Testing, 1957. Echelle d'anxiété IPAT (Trad. and adapt. by D. Cormier). Montréal: Institut de Recherches Psychologiques, 1962.

Copeland, C.L., & Kitching, H.E. Hypnosis in mental hospital practice. Journal of Mental Science, 1937, 83, 328-352.

Erickson, M.H. Hypnosis: A general review. Disease of the Nervous System, 1941, 2, 13-34.

Erickson, M.H. An hypnotic technique for resistant patients: The patient, the technique and its rationale and field experiments. American Journal of Clinical Hypnosis, 1964, 7, 8-32.

Eysenck, H.J., & Eysenck, S.B.G. Manual of the Eysenck Personality Inventory. London: University of London Press, 1964. (Inventaire de personnalité d'Eysenck. Paris: Editions du Centre de Psychologie Appliquee, 1970.

Friedman, J.J., & Keup, W.K. Hypnotizability of newly admitted psychotic patients. Psychosomatics, 1963, 4, 95-98.

Gale, C., & Herman, M. Hypnosis and the psychotic patient. Psychiatric Quarterly, 1956, 30, 417-424.

Gill, M.M., & Brenman, M. Hypnosis and related states: Psychoanalytic studies in regression. New York: International Universities Press, 1959.

Girard-Robin, L. L'amnésie post-hypnotique et ses rapports avec les fonctions cognitives chez les schizophrènes chroniques. (Posthypnotic amnesia and cognitive functioning in chronic schizophrenic patients). Unpublished Master's dissertation. Université de Montréal, 1977.

Greene, J.T. Hypnotizability of hospitalized psychotics. International Journal of Clinical and Experimental Hypnosis, 1969, 17, 103-108.

Hartman, B.J. Self-scoring and observer-scoring estimates of hypnotic susceptibility in a group situation. Perceptual and Motor Skills, 1965, 20, 452.

Hathaway, S.R., & McKinley, J.C. Manual for the Minnesota Multiphasic Personality Inventory. New York: Psychological Corporation, 1943. (Inventaire multiphasique de la personnalité (Minnesota). Trad. and adapt. by Jean-Marc Chevrier. Montréal: Institut de Recherches Psychologiques, 1963).

Heath, E.S., Hoken, P.C.S., & Sainz, A.A. Hypnotizability in state-hospitalized schizophrenics. Psychiatric Quarterly, 1960, 34, 65-68.

Hilgard, E.R. States of consciousness in hypnosis: Divisions or levels? Presidential address, 7th International Congress of Hypnosis and Psychosomatic Medicine, Philadelphia, Pennsylvania, July, 1976 (this volume, p. 15).

Holt, R.R., Eagle, C., Havel, J., Goldberger, L., Phillip, A., Rabkin, J., Safrin, R. et al. Manual for scoring of primary process manifestation in Rorschach responses (9th edition). New York: Research Center for Mental Health, New York University, 1963.

Illovsky, J. Experiences with group hypnosis in schizophrenics. Journal of Mental Science, 1962, 108, 685-693.

Kellog, C.E., & Morton, N.W. Examen bêta (nouvellé edition revisée) (revised beta examination). (Translation of 1946 edition, J.L. Launay, translator), Montreal: Institut de Recherches Psychologiques, 1966.

King, P.D. Hypnosis and schizophrenia. Journal of Nervous and Mental Disease, 1957, 125, 481-486.

Kramer, E., & Brennan, E.P. Hypnotic susceptibility of schizophrenic patients. Journal of Abnormal and Social Psychology, 1964, 69, 657-659.

Lavoie, G., Sabourin, M., & Langlois, J. Hypnotic susceptibility, amnesia and I.Q. in chronic schizophrenia. International Journal of Clinical and Experimental Hypnosis, 1973, 21, 157-168.

Lavoie, G., Sabourin, M., Ally, G., & Langlois, J. Hypnotizability as a function of adaptive regression among chronic psychotic patients. International Journal of Clinical and Experimental Hypnosis, 1976, 24, 238-257.

Levitt, E.E., Aronoff, G., & Morgan, D.C. A note on possible limitations of the use of the Harvard Group Scale of Hypnotic Susceptibility, Form A. International Journal of Clinical and Experimental Hypnosis, 1974, 22, 234-238.

Lieberman, J., Lavoie, G., & Brisson, A. Suggested amnesia and order of recall as a function of hypnotic susceptibility and learning conditions in chronic schizophrenic patients. International Journal of Clinical and Experimental Hypnosis (to appear, 1978).

Nace, E.P., Orne, M.T., & Hammer, G.A. Posthypnotic amnesia as an active psychic process: The reversibility of amnesia. Archives of General Psychiatry, 1974, 31, 257-260.

Orne, M.T. The simulation of hypnosis: Why, how and what it means. International Journal of Clinical and Experimental Hypnosis, 1971, 19, 183-210.

Polak, P.R., Mountain, H.E., & Emde, R.N. Hypnotizability and prediction of hypnotizability in hospitalized psychotic patients. International Journal of Clinical and Experimental Hypnosis, 1964, 12, 252-257.

Rosenthal, R., & Rosnow, R.L. The volunteer subject. New York: John Wiley, 1975.

Sabourin, M., Lavoie, G., Melanson, D., Selkow, V., & Brisebois, J.P. L'évaluation de la susceptibilité hypnotique d'étudiants universitaires québecois par une échelle de groupe (HGSHS:A): rapport préliminaire. Paper read at the Congrés de l'ACFAS, Ottawa, October, 1972.

Schilder, P., & Kauders, O. Lehrbuch der hypnose. Vienna: Julius Springer 1926. Hypnosis (Translated by S. Rotherberg). New York: Nervous and Mental Disease Publ. Co., 1927. A textbook of hypnosis. (Translated by G. Corvin). In P. Schilder: The nature of hypnosis. New York: Internatonal Universities Press, 1956, 45-184.

Shakow, D. On doing research in schizophrenia. Archives of General Psychiatry, 1969, 20, 618-642.

Shor, R.E., & Orne, E.C. Harvard Group Scale of Hypnotic Susceptibility, Form A. Palo Alto, California: Consulting Psychologists Press, 1962. (Echelle collective de susceptibilité hypnotique de Harvard, Forme A (M. Sabourin, trans). Unpublished manuscript, Montreal, 1971).

Shor, R.E., & Orne, E.C. Norms on the Harvard Group Scale of Hypnotic Susceptibility, Form A. International Journal of Clinical and Experimental Hypnosis, 1963, 11, 39-47.

Spiegel, H. The Hypnotic Induction Profile as a diagnostic instrument. Paper read in J.F. Kihlstrom (Chairman), On the assessment of hypnotic responsivity. Symposium presented at the 7th International Congress of Hypnosis and Psychosomatic Medicine. Philadelphia, Pennsylvania, July, 1976.

Stauffacher, J.C. Recovery from paranoid delusions following hypnotic uncovering of repressed episodes. Journal of Clinical Psychology, 1958, 14, 328-331.

Travis, L.E. A test for distinguishing between schizophrenoses and psychoneuroses. Journal of Abnormal and Social Psychology, 1924, 19, 283-287.

Vingoe, F.J., & Kramer, E. Hypnotic susceptibility of hospitalized psychotic patients: A pilot study. International Journal of Clinical and Experimental Hypnosis, 1966, 14, 47-54.

Wechsler, D. A standardized memory scale for clinical use. Journal of Psychology, 1945, 19, 87-95. Echelle clinique de mémoire. Paris: Editions du Centre de Psychologie Appliquée, 1968.

Weitzenhoffer, A.M., & Hilgard, E.R. Stanford Hypnotic Susceptibility Scale, Form A. Palo Alto, California: Consulting Psychologists Press, 1959 (Echelle de susceptibilité hypnotique de Stanford, Forme A (M. Sabourin, trans). Unpublished manuscript, Montréal, 1969).

Wilson, C.P., Cormen, H.H., & Cole, A.H. A preliminary study of the hypnotizability of psychotic patients. Psychiatric Quarterly, 1949, 23, 657-666.

Wolberg, L.R. Hypnoanalysis. New York: Grune and Stratton, 1945.

TOWARDS UNDERSTANDING THE NATURE OF HYPNOSIS

V. E. Rozhnov

Central Institute of Postgraduate Medical Training,
Moscow, U.S.S.R.

Abstract: Changes in infraslow oscillations of brain potentials were studied during different stages of hypnosis and during hypnotic suggestions for olfactory hallucinations. It is concluded that hypnosis is a special psychophysiological state which differs from both sleep and wakefulness.

The nature of hypnosis and related phenomena has long been controversial and been the subject of investigation and debate by many researchers and therapists. The theory that likens hypnosis to sleep has had the greatest number of proponents, including such noted researchers as Braid, Liébeault, Bernheim, Forel, and Bekhterev. The identity of hypnosis and sleep was maintained most categorically by Pavlov, who considered hypnosis to be partial sleep during which there exists, against a background of general cortical and subcortical inhibition, a waking, look-out station that creates rapport between the hypnotized subject and the hypnotist.

Though marking a very important stage in the study of hypnosis and related states, an understanding of hypnosis as merely partial sleep cannot explain a whole range of phenomena of both a clinical and experimental nature. With this in mind, Professor N.A. Aladjalova, Dr. S.L. Kamenetsky and the present writer, working at the Psychotherapy Clinic of the Central Institute of Postgraduate Medical Training in Moscow, have obtained experimental data that warrant a new view of the nature of hypnosis.

Our investigations were based on a study of electrophysiological processes in the brain of hypnotized persons at different stages and depths of hypnosis. Since the classical EEG does not demonstrate definite changes during hypnosis, we studied infraslow oscillations of the potentials (ISOP) of the brain, which cover the intermediary frequency range between 24-hour and EEG rhythms. Specific details regarding the method employed may be found in Aladjalova, 1962.

According to their period, the ISOP are distinguished as multi-second (T = 1 to 10 sec), decasecond (T = 10 to 60 sec), multiminute (T = 1 to 10 min), decaminute (T = 10 to 60 min), and one-hour long waves. The principal regularities of ISOP dynamics were established by means of electrodes implanted in an animal's brain (Aladjalova, 1962).

A peculiarity of the ISOP is their interhemispheric asymmetry. ISOP of different frequencies and amplitudes may appear in different areas of the head's convex surface at the same time. This dynamic changes at the moment of psychic activity. The character of the distribution is not stable; it is variable even when the same psychological load is applied repeatedly. This suggests that the dynamics of ISOP reflect the organizational form of psychic functions, which is not in direct relation to the load, but is formed out of many specifics of cerebral activity at any given moment.

Infraslow rhythmic oscillations of the potentials of the brain reflect the global processes which unite cerebral activity into a dynamic organization larger than the one reflected in the EEG. This level of integration of nervous processes comes closer to the highest specialized cerebral act.

In order to evaluate the specifics of the functional state of the human brain during hypnosis, we studied the ISOP during the development of the hypnotic state and during hallucinations suggested in that state. The results of this study allowed us to distinguish fundamental characteristics in the changing ISOP of the brain at different hypnotic stages (Aladjalova, Rozhnov, & Kamenetsky, 1973) and to depict them schematically.

Predominating in the waking state in all the areas of the brain are multisecond oscillations with a period of T = 7 - 10 sec and an amplitude of A = 0.1 mv. The oscillation periods differ somewhat in different areas of the brain. At the beginning of the session, with relaxation, sleepiness, and sensory limitation (somnolence) setting in, the hemispheres of the brain are encompassed by homogenous slow oscillations of T = 30 - 40 sec, resembling oscillations during drowsiness. In addition, multiminute oscillations appear with T = 2 - 4 min and A = 0.5 - 0.8 mv, which are characteristic of transitions at the waking state level.

The transition from somnolence to a deep hypnotic state is not, it turns out, gradual. The ISOP pattern shows that this transition occurs as a leap, with a sudden drastic shift in the potential level of one of the ISOP leads in the shape of a retracting curve, with a short series of multisecond oscillations of increased frequency (T = 5 sec) appearing at its depression. These phenomena last about two minutes (see Figure 1). If the subject is brought out of the hypnotic state at this moment, he will assess his condition as loss of self-control. The process resembles the operation of a trigger mechanism which suddenly brings about a new, stable hypnotic state with symptoms of catalepsy, while the decasecond rhythm (T = 12 - 20 sec) specific to this state sets in in some regions of the brain. The somnambulistic stage of hypnosis is characterized by the domination of a similar decasecond rhythm, which in some leads, however, alternates with a low-amplitude multisecond rhythm of a somewhat higher frequency (T = 6 sec). The latter usually accompanies intensive mental activity.

The decasecond oscillatory process becomes particularly regular in areas of the hemispheres where its amplitude increases to 0.3 mv. This rhythm occurs in the frontal areas twice as frequently as in any other. Moreover, an attempt to bring the hypnotized subject out of hypnosis may not succeed if at this moment there are regular high-amplitude decasecond oscillations in both frontal areas. A repetition of the order to awaken gradually upsets this rhythm and the hypnotized subject awakens.

The emphasis on the functional state of the frontal areas of the brain during hypnosis parallels the significance ascribed to these areas in the mediation of conscious goal-directed behavior by such investigators as A.R. Luria. Altering their activity may be regarded in terms of selectively limiting the exchange of information with the external environment. The data presented here provide an objective confirmation of facts long known to hypnotists which suggest that as the hypnotic state develops, and particularly when it reaches the deep stage of somnambulism, this external sensory influx becomes selectively restricted. One may think of the external sensory influx as being divided into two streams. While susceptibility to some of its components rises steeply, there appears to be a corresponding reduction of reactivity to others. This change in response selectivity results in a shift of consciousness with accompanying changes in the decasecond rhythm of the brain's bioelectric activity.

That the decasecond rhythms are actually related to hypnotic suggestions is confirmed by their enhancement during the process of hallucinating. Hallucinatory experiences are accompanied by a steep flare-up of the ISOP: high-amplitude (1 mv and higher) decasecond rhythms appear in several regions of the brain, and disappear with the cessation of the hallucinatory experience (see Figure 2). ISOP of such intensity do not occur in the quiet waking

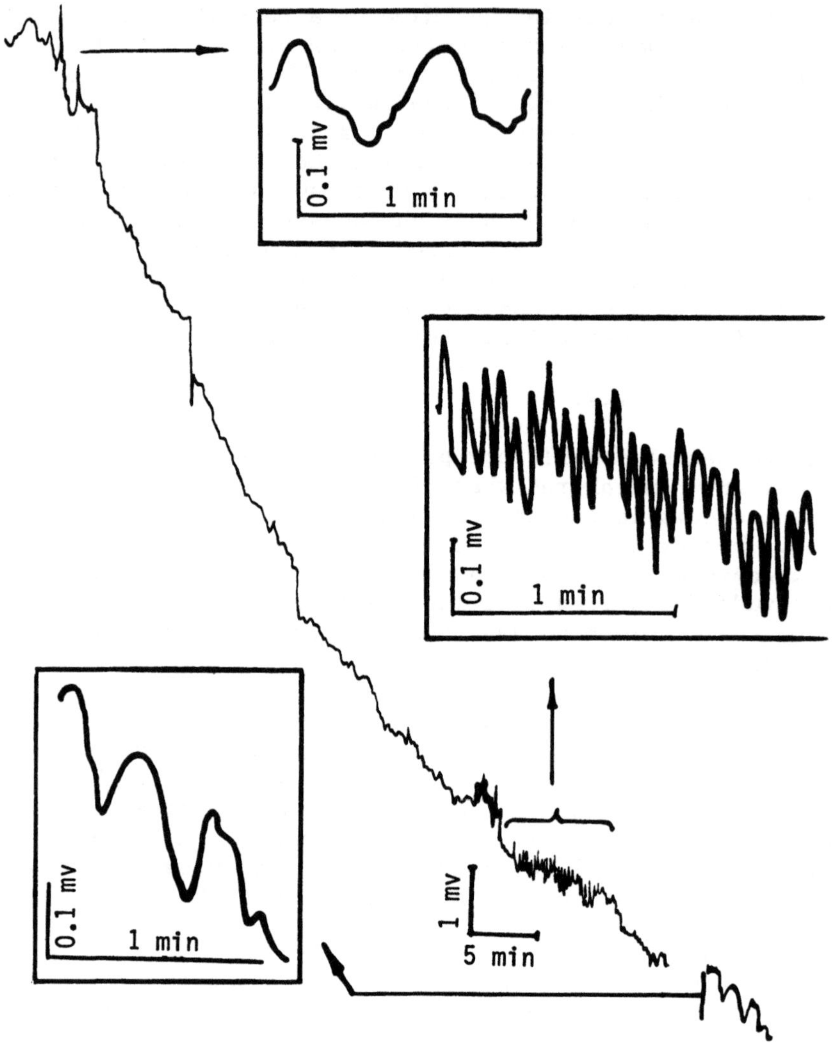

Fig. 1. The transformation of ISOP on the convex surface of a man's head at the moment of his passing from somnolence into a deep hypnotic state (temporoparietal zone of right hemisphere).

The top frame shows the decasecond rhythm of the state of somnolence (2 oscillations per minute). The center frame shows a series of regular multisecond oscillations (14 oscillations per minute) at the moment of the switch-on of a postulated trigger mechanism. The bottom frame shows the decasecond rhythm (4 oscillations per minute) in a state of deep hypnosis. Scale indicated in the frames: 1 minute, 0.1 mv.

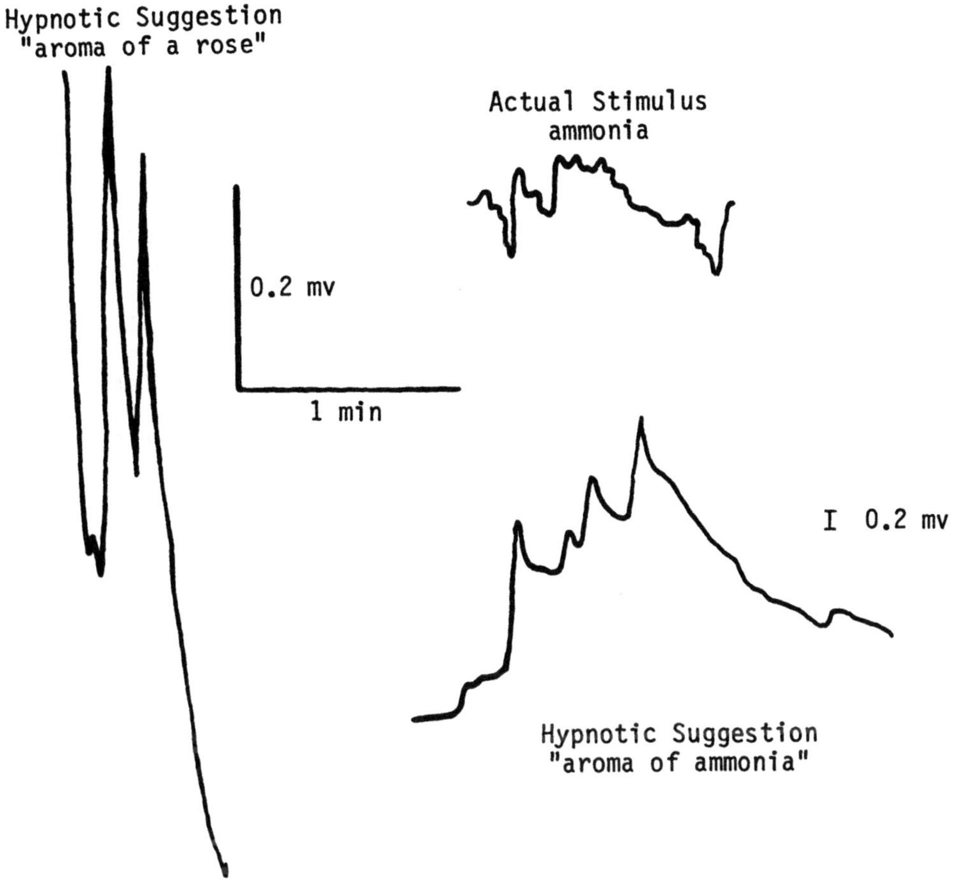

Fig. 2. The left-hand section of the figure shows an ISOP flare-up during an hypnotic suggestion of the hallucination of the aroma of a rose. When an actual strong odor (ammonium hydroxide) is presented in the waking state (top right-hand section), the response is hardly noticeable. The hypnotic suggestion of the smell of ammonium hydroxide also causes strong ISOP, shown in this figure (bottom right-hand section) on a reduced scale. The hallucination suggestion and the ISOP flare-up last about 2 - 3 minutes.

state; moreover, the presentation of a real object (similar to the suggested image) hardly causes any ISOP changes.

The left-hand part of Figure 2 displays an ISOP flare-up during the hypnotic suggestion of an olfactory hallucination, the aroma of a rose. When subjects are presented with an actual strong odor (ammonium hydroxide) in the waking state (top right-hand section), the response is hardly noticeable. However, the suggestion under hypnosis of the smell of ammonium hydroxide causes strong ISOP. The suggestion of hallucinations and the ISOP flare-up last about 2 to 3 minutes. If the suggestion is prolonged, exhaustion develops both in the experience of the image and in ISOP intensity.

In conclusion, the analysis of ISOP transformations makes it possible to examine in general form the basic mechanisms of cerebral functioning and leads to the observation that hypnosis in man is a special psychophysiological state which differs from both sleep and wakefulness. A specific feature of this state is a unique manner of absorbing and processing information which is characteristic neither of sleep nor of the waking state. A study of the ISOP pattern during hypnosis permits the objective determination of important relationships between the physiological state of the brain and simultaneous psychological processes.

REFERENCES

Aladjalova, N.A. Slow electrical processes in the brain. Edition of the USSR Academy of Sciences, Moscow, 1962.

Aladjalova, N.A., Rozhnov, V.E., & Kamenetsky, S.L. Hypnotically induced hallucinations and slow oscillations of electrical potentials in human brains. Conference on Psychiatry, Moscow, 1973.

A STUDY OF SELF-HYPNOSIS, WITH IMPLICATIONS FOR OTHER SELF-CONTROL PROCEDURES

John C. Ruch

Mills College, U.S.A.

Abstract: Self-hypnosis and the effects of prior hypnotic experience on self-hypnosis were investigated with hypnotically naive college students. Adaptations of conventional hypnotic scales were used to provide for group testing and to assess self-hypnotic performance. The question investigated was whether experience with conventional heterohypnosis would inhibit later self-hypnosis rather than enhance it, as is customarily believed. In testing this proposition, three groups of about 30 subjects each (final N = 88) were tested in four hypnotic sessions. One group had two initial heterohypnosis scales of a conventional type, one had similar scales phrased completely in the first person, and one had two initial experiences with untrained self-hypnosis. All three groups then had one session of self-hypnosis and one of conventional heterohypnosis.

Self-hypnosis offers a variety of possible advantages, e.g., in self-control, psychotherapy, and pain relief, and was known to such pioneers as James Braid (Waite, 1960). Yet researchers have only recently (e.g., Fromm, Litchman, & Brown, 1973; Shor & Easton, 1973) begun to develop standardized approaches for using, teaching, or measuring this phenomenon.

To a large extent, this relative neglect has been the result of ambiguity in defining self-hypnosis and the lack of quantitative measures of it. Self-hypnosis has been typically considered to be either a pallid imitation of heterohypnosis, or merely the result of it through post-hypnotic suggestion - even when the "hypnotist" has been present only in the form of a book of instructions. It is, thus, not surprising that most investigations have focused on heterohypnosis. Furthermore, even if one wished to study self-hypnosis, the measurement problems may have seemed insurmountable. But similar problems of definition and measurement have already been confronted for heterohypnosis. It has been defined as a convergent cluster of hypnotic behaviors and has been measured by a work sample of these: a standardized induction and the objective scoring of standardized items. The present study represents an attempt to define, measure, and examine the development of self-hypnosis in a similar way.

The key assumption in defining self-hypnosis for this study was that one need not - and could not - specify the conditions for heterohypnosis or self-hypnosis. Instead, hypnotic behaviors were assumed to fall on a continuum, ranging from the most authoritarian heterohypnosis to some unreachable "pure" self-hypnosis. Behaviors with minimal active guidance by a hypnotist working directly with a subject, particularly regarding an induction, could thus reasonably be termed self-hypnosis.

METHOD

The problem of measuring self-hypnosis was approached by minimal-input adaptations of heterohypnotic scales, specifically the Stanford Hypnotic Susceptibility Scales, Forms A and C (Weitzenhoffer & Hilgard, 1959, 1962). The Harvard Group Scale adaptation of Form A (Shor & Orne, 1962) was used, and similar group modifications were developed for Form C. Modifications for inducing and measuring self-hypnosis consisted of a new introduction, almost total elimination of the induction, and extensive shortening of the individual items. First, the new introduction modified subjects' expectations by defining the situation as self-hypnosis. Then, the induction was replaced by a very brief description of an eye-closure induction, followed by 15 minutes of silence. Finally, "thin" items were used, with the content reduced to a minimum (typically lasting 5 - 10 seconds). This eliminated the possibility that the lengthy suggestions of conventional items would act as secondary inductions.

The resulting "self-instructed" scales fall somewhat short of pure self-hypnosis, since they provide some situational definition and suggest particular items. They do not, however, provide the customary induction or lengthy item elaboration. This seemed as close to the self-hypnosis end of the heterohypnosis/self-hypnosis continuum as could be devised, while retaining consistent conditions and quantifiable scoring.

With the measures devised, self-hypnosis could then be investigated. A clinical observation provided the basis for the experimental variation. J.R. Hilgard had reported* that patients with demonstrated hypnotic ability in psychotherapy often failed at later self-hypnosis. This seemed to conflict with the traditional concept that self-hypnosis was created, or at least facilitated, by previous heterohypnosis. It was then hypothesized that the opposite might be true, i.e., that extensive heterohypnosis, with the hypnotist defined as the active agent and the subject as the passive one, might be inhibiting self-hypnosis, rather than training it. While this could be especially true in the context of repeated hypnotherapy, it was further hypothesized that the initial few experiences would be critical. Thus the first hypothesis to be tested was whether initial heterohypnosis seemed to inhibit later self-hypnosis, as would be implied if the self-hypnosis scores dropped below the heterohypnotic scores.

But self-hypnosis scores might perhaps never be expected to equal heterohypnotic ones; if these scores were lower, would it necessarily imply an inhibitory effect? Ideally, one would like to employ a procedure that provides some initial heterohypnotic experience, but that does not define the situation in the active hypnotist/passive subject manner hypothesized to be inhibitory. For a full comparison, of course, one would also wish to examine the self-hypnotic performance of subjects who have not received <u>any</u> prior heterohypnotic experience. Certainly, complete elimination of an induction procedure avoids the situational definition of a controlling hypnotist. But it also eliminates all other suggestions provided by a conventional induction, such as those for increasing relaxation and focusing attention, and these might be useful in teaching subjects how to become hypnotized.

A second set of modified scales was thus developed, in an attempt to retain the relaxation and other suggestions of the conventional induction, while at the same time shifting the definition of the situation so as to keep the subject an active participant. Again, a finding of J.R. Hilgard's (1970) provided a starting point. Some subjects whom she interviewed had reported that they incorporated the hypnotist's voice as if it were their own, and thus, in effect, behaved as if they were telling themselves what to do. It was hypothesized that such subjects might be better prepared for later self-hypnosis, on the grounds that they might more easily reproduce for themselves what had originally been suggested by the hypnotist. The second set of adapted scales was designed so as to maximize the possibility that the subjects would incorporate the hypnotist's suggestions and reuse them for later self-hypnosis.

---

* J.R. Hilgard, personal communication, 1970.

This involved two changes: the phrasing of the suggestions and the introduction used with them.

All phrasing, in both induction and individual items, was changed from the second person that we use in addressing others ("You are going to...") to the first person that we are more likely to use in giving ourselves suggestions ("I am going to..."). (Results of an informal questionnaire suggested that most people use first person in giving themselves directions). This provided all of the necessary suggestions for self-hypnosis in a form suited for self-hypnosis.

The next question was how to provide these suggestions to subjects. Shor, in his Inventory of Self-Hypnosis forms (Shor & Easton, 1973), has subjects read each step of the procedure and then attempt it. But the purpose of the present study was to investigate effects of heterohypnosis on later self-hypnosis. Thus, the first-person forms were treated as heterohypnotic ones and were administered to the subjects in the same way as the conventional forms. The introduction to the first-person forms, however, defined the situation somewhat differently. Subjects were told that they would be receiving a hypnotic measure, but that it would be phrased in the first person, as if the speaker were hypnotizing himself. Subjects were asked to follow the words and try to think of them as if they were their own, as if they were hypnotizing themselves, even though they knew it was someone else's voice giving them suggestions. Thus, although these forms are considered to be heterohypnotic, they may be thought of as being further from the heterohypnotic end of the heterohypnosis/self-hypnosis continuum than the conventional scales.

The experimental design is summarized in Table 1 (adapted from Ruch, 1975). Three groups of subjects - conventional, first-person, and self-instructed - received, as their first hypnotic experience, a variant of the Stanford Hypnotic Susceptibility Scale, Form A, on Day 1, followed by a similar variant of Form C on Day 2. Two experiences were used rather than one for several reasons: experience of researchers at the Stanford Laboratory suggested that most score changes were likely to be found between the first and subsequent measures; any effects of initial heterohypnotic experiences might be expected to be more notable with more experience; and the two scales together provided a wider range of items. To ensure that the primary comparison between groups was of induction types, each administration used the thin items designed for the self-instructed scales, and item 1 of Form A, which normally precedes induction, was deleted.

On Day 3, one week later, all groups received the self-instructed version of Form C of the Stanford Scale as the criterion measure of self-hypnosis. This was followed, on Day 4, by the standard

TABLE 1

Summary of Procedure: Experimental Groups by Days

Experimental Groups	Initial Learning Sessions (differ by groups)	
	Day 1: Form A variant	Day 2: Form C variant
Conventional (N = 28)	Conventional induction, thin items	Conventional induction, thin items
First-person (N = 29)	First-person induction, thin items	First-person induction, thin items
Self-instructed (N = 31)	Self-induction, thin items	Self-induction, thin items
Experimental Groups	**Self-Hypnosis Test (common to groups)**	**Conventional Hypnosis (common to groups)**
	Day 3: Self-instructed Form C	Day 4: Harvard Group Scale
Conventional (N = 28)	Self-induction, thin items	Conventional Induction, conventional items
First-person (N = 29)	Self-induction, thin items	Conventional induction, conventional items
Self-instructed (n = 31)	Self-induction, thin items	Conventional induction, conventional items

Harvard Group Scale, with conventional item elaboration. This Day 4 measure was, in effect, a pre-test given post; it was intended only for comparing the subjects' scores with established norms.

Volunteer undergraduates signed up on a sheet that requested subjects with no previous hypnotic experience, and were told not to discuss, read about, or practice hypnosis until the end of the experiment. They were then randomly assigned to the three groups. Each group occupied a separate room with a single experimenter, who introduced each session from a script and handled the scoring forms and required materials. The actual scales were administered by tape recordings played simultaneously in a central control room. All scales were self-scored by the subjects immediately after each session, in the same fashion as the conventional Harvard Group Scale. In order to note any subtle differences that might not show up in these objective scores, subjective scores were also obtained at the same time, with subjects ranking the experienced quality of each item on a 5-point scale. After Day 4 scoring was completed, an additional open-ended questionnaire was administered, seeking comments on various aspects of the procedures. The data were obtained in two separate cycles, using identical procedures.

Three formal hypotheses were proposed, based both on the reasoning described above and on pilot tests of the adapted scales.

(1) Self-hypnosis will correlate with heterohypnosis.
(2) Self-hypnosis effectiveness will approximate that of heterohypnosis.
(3) Self-hypnosis scores following conventional heterohypnosis will be depressed, as compared with those following first-person heterohypnosis.

RESULTS

The results may be considered in three sections, corresponding to the three hypotheses.

(1) Correlations of Self-Hypnosis and Heterohypnosis.

The first finding, one that was necessary before considering the others, was that the self-instructed forms yielded results comparable to the conventional ones. The results indicate that self-hypnosis performance, as defined in the present study, may be measured as adequately with self-hypnotic scales as heterohypnosis is with existing heterohypnotic scales. Since the relative effectiveness of naive self-hypnosis and heterohypnosis had not been previously established, comparing the Day 1 or 2 scores of the different groups would not necessarily tell us about the measures themselves. Two types of correlations do imply comparability of measures, however. Subjective scores were obtained via identical questionnaires for all scales. One indication of how well objective scores reflected subjective experience, for either self-hypnosis or heterohypnosis, is the correlation between the objective and the subjective scores. These correlations, as seen in Table 2, were high - all were above .70, with half above .90 - and were as high for the self-instructed scales and the self-instructed group as for their conventional equivalents.

A different correlation that also implies comparability of measures is that between scores on the self-instructed Form C of Day 3 and the fully conventional Harvard Group Scale of Day 4. As shown in Table 2, these correlated as highly, for all three groups, as do the Stanford Forms C and A from which they were adapted: .67 - .79 vs. the published .72 (Weitzenhoffer & Hilgard, 1962). (Table 2 provides day-to-day correlations for objective scores only; subjective scores showed similar values).

(2) Effectiveness of Self-Hypnosis.

Table 3 presents the mean objective scores for all days. (Since subjective scores yielded the same pattern, they are not presented). The equivalence of the mean scores of the conventional and the self-instructed groups on both Day 1 and Day 2 suggests that initial self-hypnosis was as effective as heterohypnosis, as hypothesized. These results were quite consistent; they occurred on both days, on both objective and subjective scores, and in an analysis of particular items passed. Even spontaneous reports of unusual subjective experiences were similar. Furthermore, although Table 3 shows only the combined data, the pattern of results was the same in both cycles of the experiment.

(3) Influences of Initial Hypnotic Experiences on Later Hypnotic Performances.

These effects were more complex than expected. They included not only the hypothesized inhibitory influence of heterohypnosis on self-hypnosis, but also an unexpected opposite influence.

First we may concentrate on the Day 3 results. As hypothesized, the conventional group's Day 3 self-hypnosis scores dropped significantly from the Day 2 heterohypnosis scores, while the first-person group's scores did not. Again, the pattern of results was consistent for objective and subjective scores and for individual items, and, again, similar results were obtained in each cycle of the experiment. Subjects in the conventional group also made significantly more unfavorable comments about their self-hypnosis experience.

The foregoing analyses complete the basic study. While the Harvard Group Scale administered to all groups on Day 4, could potentially demonstrate differential effects of the experimental

TABLE 2

Correlations between Objective and Subjective Scores and between Scores on Different Days

Days and Scales	Conventional Group	First-Person Group	Self-Instructed Group
Objective vs. Subjective Scores:			
Day 1 (Form A variant)	.82	.74	.80
Day 2 (Form C variant)	.77	.88	.90
Day 3 (self-instructed Form C)	.89	.92	.91
Day 4 (Harvard Group Scale)	.90	.92	.91
Objective Scores:			
Day 1 vs. Day 2	.57	.41	.60
Day 2 vs. Day 3	.62	.59	.61
Day 3 vs. Day 4	.71	.79	.67
Day 1 vs. Day 4	.70	.58	.61

(Adapted from the October, 1975 International Journal of Clinical and Experimental Hypnosis. Copyrighted by The Society for Clinical and Experimental Hypnosis, October, 1975).

TABLE 3

Mean Objective Scores[a]

Experimental Group	Day 1: Form A variant	Day 2: Form C variant	Day 3: Self-instructed Form C[b]	Day 4: Harvard Group Scale[c]
Conventional	6.18	5.29	4.04	5.29
First-person	6.34	4.72	4.69	5.03
Self-instructed	6.13	5.55	4.94	6.77

[a] Maximum possible score was 11 for Form A variants, including Day 4, and 12 for Form C variants. (Item 1 of Form A was deleted, since it precedes induction and thus is not appropriate for induction variations).

[b] Significant Day 2-to-Day 3 drop for conventional group only: $t = 2.78$, $p < .01$.

[c] Day 4 mean score for self-instructed group significantly higher than other two groups: $F = 3.26$, $df = 2, 85$; $p < .05$.

treatments, it was not expected to; measured hypnotic susceptibility is typically quite stable, even when attempts are made to increase it (e.g., Diamond, 1972; Kinney & Sachs, 1974). However, as shown in Table 3, the self-instructed group's Day 4 scores were significantly higher than those of the other two groups (6.77 vs. 5.29 and 5.03). This finding, while unexpected, was as consistent as the hypothesized findings; it was found in both objective and subjective scores, it was found across individual items, and it occurred in both cycles of the experiment. Such a consistent and significant finding deserves an explanation, even though any such explanation must necessarily be post hoc.

DISCUSSION

Now let us review these results and their implications. First of all, it has been shown to be feasible to measure self-hypnosis via group-administered and self-scored scales, with results comparable to similar heterohypnotic scales. A variety of questions about self-hypnosis can now be investigated with quantitative measures.

Second, initial untrained self-hypnosis is as effective, on both objective and subjective measures, as initial heterohypnosis. In considering the implications of this finding, one must differentiate between the results obtained in the present study and those resulting from what has been termed subject compliance, on the one hand, and waking or imagination suggestions, on the other. The present results cannot be attributed to compliance, since the instructions did not in any way demand compliance, and nothing in the data implies its presence. Instructions to the subjects were intentionally neutral, suggesting that self-hypnosis would be possible for some subjects, but that they might or might not experience it. Furthermore, the findings, including the correlations and spontaneous subjective experiences, suggest that the self-instructed subjects in fact had experiences comparable to those of the subjects in the conventional hypnosis group.

Nor should the self-instructed group be confused with a waking or an imagination group. Several studies (e.g., Barber & Glass, 1962; Hilgard & Tart, 1966; Ruch, Morgan, & Hilgard, 1973) have found that a conventional induction increases hypnotic responsiveness compared to such groups. But subjects in such groups are typically given neither the time for, nor the expectation of, self-induction. They may even be told that they will not be hypnotized. In the present study, where subjects were encouraged to provide a self-induction, and were given both the expectation that it could be successful and 15 minutes to do so, they experienced effects equivalent to those of conventional heterohypnosis.

On the other hand, these results should not be taken to imply that the experimental situation had no effect on these subjects. They were interested enough to volunteer for an experiment in self-hypnosis, and then demonstrated a capability for it, yet they had not previously tried it. Subject-expectation regarding self-hypnosis may be important here. Subjects later reported a mixture of expectations: partly that they would not be successful, and partly that, if they were somehow successful, they would lose control. Thus, it is probable that the experimental situation was important in aiding the initial self-hypnosis, by overcoming these negative expectations through sanctioning self-hypnosis, rather than by training it. On these grounds, many more people may be presumed to be able to hypnotize themselves than in fact do; their expectations about the nature of self-hypnosis apparently prevent them from attempting it.

Self-hypnotic performance was inhibited by two initial experiences with conventional heterohypnosis scales, but not by experiences with the same two scales phrased in the first person. This finding not only supports the hypothesis that heterohypnotic experience may inhibit, rather than train, self-hypnosis, but suggests that it is the expectations engendered by the situations and phraseology of the procedures that are critical. Both conventional and first-person groups heard over 15 minutes of similarly detailed suggestions, but these apparently inhibited later self-hypnosis only when they occurred in the conventional context of active hypnotist and passive subject.

These results suggest both that initial heterohypnotic experiences may inhibit later self-hypnotic ones, and that they need not do so. In light of the significant self-hypnosis performance drop after only two experiences of conventional heterohypnosis, it is not surprising that extensive heterohypnosis in therapy may leave patients unable to do self-hypnosis. Training may in fact take place, but may be negative, i.e., patients may be trained to be passive and to be unable to actively hypnotize themselves. The lack of such inhibition for the first-person group, on the other hand, suggests that it may be avoided by relatively minor changes in procedure. A hypnotherapist who positively sanctions the concept of self-hypnosis and actively involves the patient from the beginning in a cooperative form of heterohypnosis may avoid such negative training.

Finally, we may consider the Day 4 results, wherein the self-instructed group showed significant enhancement with conventional heterohypnosis. Subjects' comments suggested that this enhancement resulted from a facilitative interaction of the two different procedures, when given in the self-hetero sequence. The self-instructed procedures, by firmly placing the burden of hypnosis on the subject from the beginning, apparently required an active involved concentration in the attempt to become hypnotized. This active involvement was then supplemented by the conventional procedure, with subjects continuing to be active, yet drawing upon the heterohypnotic procedure for aid as necessary.

Note that the suggested effects are nearly the opposite of those seen in the conventional group, who received the same two types of experience,but in the hetero-self sequence. These subjects later commented that their initial experiences - listening passively sively and following instructions - left them confused, uncertain, and even a bit resentful when they were asked to hypnotize themselves on Day 3.

Note, also, that the Day 4 enhancement effect was not seen for the first-person group. This procedure sanctioned self-hypnosis, but did not demand the same degree of autonomy as in the case of the self-instructed group. Furthermore, the change in phrasing from first person to second person was reported to be confusing by some subjects (one of whom reported changing "you" to "I" as he listened to the conventional Harvard Group Scale, because it seemed more natural).

The unexpected finding on Day 4 is, thus, that initial untrained self-hypnosis is not only possible, but may even facilitate later heterohypnotic performance, apparently by involving the subject initially as an active partner in the process. At the same time, it suggests that not all procedures that facilitate self-hypnosis will necessarily yield this result; the first-person scales did not inhibit self-hypnosis as did the conventional ones, but neither did they facilitate later conventional heterohypnosis, as did initial self-hypnosis.

What do these findings, taken as a whole, tell us about hypnotic phenomena? When the Day 4 finding is added to that of Day 3, the two are seen to be complementary, and together they constitute a pattern directly opposite to what is traditionally believed; not only does initial conventional heterohypnosis inhibit rather than enhance later self-hypnosis, but initial self-hypnosis enhances later heterohypnosis. This inversion of conventional expectations suggests a similar inversion in the conceptualization of hypnotic phenomena. In such a reconceptualization, self-hypnosis is the primary phenomenon, with heterohypnosis secondary, in effect a form of guided self-hypnosis. The hypnotist is not a controller, but a coach, guide, or instructor, who does not create the phenomena but, rather helps the subjects to discover, develop, and use their potential.

Such a reconceptualization is not so extreme a change as it might seem. In fact, it represents only a further step in a long-continuing trend. Early considerations of the behavior now called hypnosis were very much oriented to authoritarian manipulation, beginning with the Mesmerists. Later psychological explanations retained a similar orientation. Although this has gradually shifted toward cooperation between subject and hypnotist, the hypnotist is still presumed to have the most influence.

These results suggest that this trend may be pushed a bit further - at least far enough for the subject to be recognized as the important contributor and the hypnotist as the secondary one. In addition to being more accurate, such a reconceptualization would lend itself more readily to a unified account of hetero-hypnotic procedures, self-hypnosis, and autogenic training (Schultz & Luthe, 1959), and perhaps even to other altered states, e.g., accidental trance states, meditation states, and self-induced states in drama exercises, religious rites, and athletics.

REFERENCES

Barber, T.X., & Glass, L.B. Significant factors in hypnotic behavior. Journal of Abnormal and Social Psychology, 1962, 64, 222-228.

Diamond, M.J. The use of observationally-presented information to modify hypnotic susceptibility. Journal of Abnormal Psychology, 1972, 79, 174-180.

Fromm, E., Litchman, J., & Brown, D. Similarities and differences between hetero-hypnosis and self-hypnosis: A phenomenological study. Paper presented at the meeting of the Society for Clinical and Experimental Hypnosis, Newport Beach, California, December, 1973.

Hilgard, E.R., & Tart, C.T. Responsiveness to suggestions following waking and imagination instructions and following induction of hypnosis. Journal of Abnormal Psychology, 1966, 71, 196-208.

Hilgard, J.R. Personality and hypnosis: A study of imaginative involvement. Chicago: University of Chicago Press, 1970.

Kinney, J.M., & Sachs, L.B. Increasing hypnotic susceptibility. Journal of Abnormal Psychology, 1974, 83, 145-150.

Ruch, J.C. Self-hypnosis: The result of heterohypnosis or vice-versa? International Journal of Clinical and Experimental Hypnosis, 1975, 23, 282-304.

Ruch, J.C. Morgan, A.H., & Hilgard, E.R. Brief reports: Behavioral predictions for hypnotic responsiveness scores when obtained with and without prior induction procedures. Journal of Abnormal Psychology, 1973, 82, 543-546.

Schultz, J.H., & Luthe, W. Autogenic training: A psychophysiological approach to psychotherapy. New York: Grune and Stratton, 1959.

Shor, R.E., & Easton, R.D. A preliminary report on research comparing self- and hetero-hypnosis. American Journal of Clinical Hypnosis, 1973, 16, 37-44.

Shor, R.E., & Orne, E.C. Harvard Group Scale of Hypnotic Susceptibility, Form A. Palo Alto, California: Consulting Psychologists Press, 1962.

Waite, A.E. (editor) Braid on hypnotism. (Re-issue of 1889 edition) New York: Julian Press, 1960.

Weitzenhoffer, A.M., & Hilgard, E.R. Stanford Hypnotic Susceptibility Scale, Forms A and B. Palo Alto, California: Consulting Psychologists Press, 1959.

Weitzenhoffer, A.M., & Hilgard, E.R. Stanford Hypnotic Susceptibility Scale, Form C. Palo Alto, California: Consulting Psychologists Press, 1962.

III: Clinical Perspectives and Reports

THE COMBINATION OF HYPNOSIS AND BEHAVIORAL METHODS IN PSYCHOTHERAPY

Edward Dengrove

West Allenhurst, New Jersey, U.S.A.

Abstract: The fields of behavior therapy and hypnotherapy share much in common. However, behavior therapists tend to neglect hypnosis, feeling that there is no use for it in their particular approach to treatment; while hypnotherapists, who have used behavioral techniques for many years, have done so unsystematically and without full knowledge of the potential of these techniques.

In treating phobias, for example, a basic approach in behavior therapy involves gradual contact with the feared object, situation, or feeling, motivating the patient to make contact on a regular basis, and assisting him to reduce fear by whatever means the therapist finds successful. Exposure to the phobic scene is not always easy or possible. Hypnosis can produce conditions most like real life and can make treatment easier by relaxing the patient, easing the path to visual imagery, and providing techniques which aid in the management of more difficult patients.

This sharing of knowledge and related techniques contributes greatly to the improvement of the patient and the satisfaction of the therapist.

Hypnotherapy and behavior therapy share much in common. However, behavior therapists have tended to neglect hypnosis, stating that there is no need for it in their particular approach to treatment, while hypnotherapists, who have used behavioral techniques for ages past, have done so without organization or full knowledge of their potential.

One of the comments made by observers of systematic desensitization, one form of behavioral psychotherapy, is that it bears a similarity to hypnosis. Ullman and Krasner (1969) stated that if hypnosis is defined as role enactment, there is much overlap between hypnosis and systematic desensitization: both are potential forms of social influence and, if used to alter behavior directly, of behavior therapy. Horowitz (1970) found a positive relationship between improvement and his subjects' self-report of hypnotic depth. On the other hand, Cautela (1966a, 1966b) analyzed the relationship between both the hypnotic induction procedure and suggestibility to the desensitization process and concluded that these variables are not significant aspects of the desensitization process.

The many studies that have evaluated the role of suggestion in behavior therapy (both suggestion under hypnosis and instructions for therapeutic change in the absence of hypnosis) (Litvak, 1970; McGlynn, Mealiea, & Nawas, 1969; Borkovec, 1973; Oliveau, Agras, Leitenberg, Moore, & Wright, 1969; Kazdin, 1973; Woody, 1973; Woody & Schauble, 1969; Kohn, 1955; Paul, 1966; Lang, 1969; Lang, Lazovik, & Reynolds, 1965; Marks, Gelder, & Edwards, 1968) have obtained contradictory findings: some have supported the possible role of hypnotic suggestion and autosuggestion, while others have obtained no significant correlation between suggestion and therapeutic outcome in behavior therapy. There is a tendency in the behavioral literature to confuse suggestibility with hypnosis. In evaluating these contradictory findings, however, one must keep in mind that increased suggestibility is not hypnosis, but only one of its features, arising at least in part as a consequence of the changes in the state of the hypnotized person (Hilgard, 1965). Nevertheless, it is convenient to study hypnosis in terms of alterations in suggestibility, regardless of how these changes come about.

Though not indispensable, hypnosis does have an important role in the practice of behavior therapy. When properly used, it adds leverage to treatment and shortens treatment time. In treating phobias, for example, a basic approach in behavior therapy involves contact with the feared object, situation or feeling. Using a graduated approach, the patient is motivated to make contact on a regular basis, and is assisted in reducing the fear by whatever means the therapist finds successful. Exposure to the phobic scene is not always easy or possible. Hypnosis can produce conditions most like real life and can make treatment easier by relaxing the patient, easing the path to visual imagery, and providing techniques that aid in the management of the more difficult patient.

In my experience, relaxation induced by hypnosis can be quite deep and satisfactory. Barber and Hahn (1963) insist that hypnosis (a 20-minute "hypnotic induction procedure" consisting of suggestions of relaxation, drowsiness, and sleep) is no more effective in the production of relaxation than merely the instruction to sit quietly, as indicated by physiological criteria. Paul (1969b) compared relaxation training and hypnosis (induction patterned after Kline's visual imagery technique, with an eye fixation induction emphasizing suggestions of heaviness, drowsiness, sleep and relaxation, directed to the subject's image of herself, and followed by a test challenge for arm immobilization). His conclusion was that, in general, while both methods were effective in reducing subjective reports of tension-distress, progressive relaxation training was more effective than hypnotic suggestion in producing desired physiological changes even within a single session. However, one must keep in mind other features that form part of the hypnotic state and that are useful in systematic desensitization, chiefly the altered suggestibility of the subject, or, as Meares (1960) terms it, the "lack of criticality," which provides an added bonus to therapy.

Besides the usual suggestions to relax, there are numerous "tricks of the trade" that are available through hypnosis. Lazarus (1963) has the patient simulate a state of sensory deprivation and finds it highly useful in treating pervasive free-floating anxiety. Weitzenhoffer (1957) and Lazarus (1958) also use autohypnosis to reduce a feeling of panic to one of calmness. Patients are taught relaxation at home by autosuggestion. Weitzenhoffer details another sensorimotor method, in which the individual is hypnotized without his awareness (the postural sway can be considered a form of sensorimotor induction). Under hypnosis, suggestions are made to the effect that, in response to a signal from the therapist, the patient will enter a more deeply relaxed state in the next session in a much shorter time. In no way is the patient pressured.

When there is difficulty in visualizing the next step in a hierarchy (a list of stimuli to which the patient reacts with anxiety, arranged from the least disturbing to the most frightening), hypnotic vivification can intensify the visual image. A statement given in the hypnotic trance, such as "When I touch your shoulder, you will visualize it with ease and comfort," will often nudge the patient along gently. Schubot (1967) found that hypnotic susceptibility and vividness of hypnotic imagery were positively related to reduction of fear in highly anxious subjects. In another study, Paul (1969a) found that relaxation induced through brief relaxation training or through hypnotic suggestion inhibits the physiological response to stressful imagery, and that hypnotic treatment resulted in significant reduction in physiological systems not under direct voluntary control.

Time distortion techniques may be used for desensitization. One can project a patient into the future and have him live through an anxious situation as if it were happening in the present, but in a relaxed manner. On awakening, he can be left with the feeling that he has been through all of this before and has progressed adequately.

The induction of dreams by hypnosis, particularly if they are repetitive, is a useful desensitization device with graduated responses. Patients are given tasks to perform in the "dream state" and suggestions are paced to the progress of the patient, or the patient may be told to set the pace himself.

Tart (1965, 1966) casts doubt on the notion that most hypnotic dreams are dream-like. However, experiments reveal that posthypnotic suggestions may affect the content of dreams at night, often quite markedly. The patient may be instructed under hypnosis to dream of doing those very things he fears most, but with ease and pleasure. Barber, Walker, and Hahn (1973) gave presleep suggestions to hypnotic and nonhypnotic subjects and found that these suggestions were equally effective in altering the contents of nocturnal dreams when they were given with or without a hypnotic induction procedure. However, these suggestions had the greatest effect on dreams when they were given authoritatively to the hypnotic subjects and permissively to the nonhypnotic subjects.

By associating new and pleasant stimuli with old responses, it is possible to diminish general anxiety. At the conclusion of a session, posthypnotic suggestions to the effect that the patient will continue to feel relaxed and will carry out that which he performed in the session, can be most helpful. For example, a patient of mine feared she might hurt her infant son with a knife. She was told to visualize herself cutting bread in front of her child, but to see the baby happy and laughing, and to visualize herself quite pleased with her son posthypnotically. This proved most helpful to her.

Erickson (1966) employs posthypnotic suggestions to the effect that the patient will experience panic episodes, but that they will be brief and last only seconds, and that the patient will be amazed at how shortlived the feeling is.

Aversive stimuli produced through hypnosis have been used to eliminate unwanted behavior for years. Typical, perhaps, is the posthypnotic suggestion used to modify a patient's smoking habit. Under hypnosis it is suggested to the patient that he view rat dung rubbed into the tobacco used to prepare the cigarette which he then puts into his mouth, lights up and inhales deeply. This produces intense nausea. Cautela (1966a) employs a similar technique which he calls covert sensitization and which is used to produce aversion to certain foods, alcohol, tobacco, or sexual deviation. The scenes and responses may be vivified with hypnosis.

Feamster and Brown (1963) successfully used aversive treatment through hypnosis to control excessive drinking. A somnambulistic trance was achieved and the patient was instructed to relive his worst hangover whenever he smelled, tasted, looked at, or even thought of alcoholic beverages. After recovery from the hangover, he was instructed to feel hungry, to eat a satisfying meal, and to achieve relaxation by pressing together his left index finger and thumb. Brief reinforcement was required. Other authors (Miller, 1959; Abrams, 1964) have used hypnotically induced conditioned aversion techniques successfully in the treatment of alcoholism.

When aversive conditioning is employed, basic principles must be strictly adhered to (Franks, 1966). The creative use of hypnosis makes it possible for the behavior therapist to satisfy the basic requirement for aversive conditioning in a manner not easily achieved by any other technique. Some of the examples cited above illustrate this point and suggest some of the ways by which appropriately chosen posthypnotic suggestions can be employed in the context of conditioning therapy. Behavior therapists are noted for their ingenuity, but hypnotherapists have long shown a more extensive inventiveness because of the extra leverage of hypnosis.

In recent years, a wide range of behavior therapies have been developed. Only systematic desensitization and aversive conditioning have been discussed in the present paper. These and other methods are effective without employing any hypnotic techniques; however, many outstanding therapists report hypnosis to be an extremely useful adjunct in their practice. It would seem that there are many situations where some of the special characteristics of hypnosis can be employed to great advantage in a behavior therapy setting. The exciting possibilities inherent in the combination of hypnosis and behavior therapies have barely been tapped.

REFERENCES

Abrams, S. An evaluation of hypnosis in the treatment of alcoholics. American Journal of Psychiatry, 1964, 120, 1160-1165.

Barber, T.X., & Hahn, K.W. Hypnotic induction and "relaxation": an experimental study. Archives of General Psychiatry, 1963, 8, 295-300.

Barber, T.X., Walker,P.C., & Hahn, K.W. Effects of hypnotic induction and suggestions on nocturnal dreaming and thinking. Journal of Abnormal Psychology, 1973, 82, 414-427.

Borkovec, T.D. The effects of instructional suggestion and physiological cues on analogue fear. Behavior Therapy, 1973, 4, 185-192.

Cautela, J.R. Desensitization factors in the hypnotic treatment of phobias. Journal of Psychology, 1966a, 64, 277-288.

Cautela, J.R. Hypnosis and behavior therapy. Behavior Research and Therapy, 1966b, 4, 219-224.

Erickson, M.H. Experiential knowledge of hypnotic phenomena employed for hypnotherapy. American Journal of Clinical Hypnosis, 1966, 8, 299-309.

Feamster, J.H., & Brown, J.E. Hypnotic aversion to alcohol: Three-year follow-up of one patient. American Journal of Clinical Hypnosis, 1963, 6, 164-166.

Franks, C.M. Conditioning and conditioned aversion therapies in the treatment of the alcoholic. International Journal of Addiction, 1966, 1, 61-98.

Hilgard, E.R. The experience of hypnosis. New York: Harcourt, Brace and World, 1965.

Horowitz, S.L. Strategies within hypnosis for reducing phobic behavior. Journal of Abnormal Psychology, 1970, 75, 104-112.

Kazdin, A.E. The effect of suggestion and pretesting on avoidance reduction in fearful subjects. Journal of Behavior Therapy and Experimental Psychiatry, 1973, 4, 213-221.

Kohn, H.B. Suggestion relaxation as a technique for inducing hypnosis. Journal of Psychology, 1955, 40, 203-208.

Lang, P.J. The mechanics of desensitization and the laboratory study of human fear. In C.M. Franks (editor), Behavior therapy: Appraisal and status. New York: McGraw-Hill, 1969.

Lang, P.J., Lazovik, A.D., & Reynolds, D.J. Desensitization, suggestibility and pseudotherapy. Journal of Abnormal and Social Psychology, 1965, 70, 395-402.

Lazarus, A.A. Some clinical applications of autohypnosis. Medical Proceedings, 1958, 14, 848-850.

Lazarus, A.A. Sensory deprivation under hypnosis in the treatment of pervasive ("free floating") anxiety: A preliminary impression. South African Medical Journal, 1963, 27, 136-139.

Litvak, S.B. Hypnosis and the desensitization behavior therapies. Psychological Reports, 1970, 27, 787-794.

Marks, I.M., Gelder, M.G., & Edwards, G. Hypnosis and desensitization for phobias: A controlled prospective trial. British Journal of Psychiatry, 1968, 114, 1263-1274.

McGlynn, F.D., Mealiea, W.L., & Nawas, M.M. Systematic desensitization of snake avoidance under two conditions of suggestion. Psychological Reports, 1969, 25, 220-222.

Meares, A.A. A system of medical hypnosis. Philadelphia: Saunders, 1960. Reissued 1972 by The Julian Press, New York.

Miller, M.M. Treatment of chronic alcoholics by hypnotic aversion. Journal of the American Medical Association, 1959, 171, 1492-1495.

Oliveau, D.C., Agras, W.S., Leitenberg, H., Moore, R.C., & Wright, D.E. Systematic desensitization, therapeutically oriented instructions, and selective positive reinforcement. Behavior Research and Therapy, 1969, 7, 27-34.

Paul, G.L. Insight vs. desensitization in psychotherapy: An experiment in anxiety reduction. Stanford: Stanford University Press, 1966.

Paul, G.L. Inhibition of physiological response to stressful imagery by relaxation training and hypnotically suggested relaxation. Behavior Research and Therapy, 1969a, 7, 249-256.

Paul, G.L. Physiological effects of relaxation training and hypnotic suggestion. Journal of Abnormal Psychology, 1969b, 74, 425-437.

Schubot, E.O. The influence of hypnotic and muscular relaxation in systematic desensitization of phobias. Dissertation Abstracts, 1967, 27, 3681-3682.

Tart, C.T. The hypnotic dream: Methodological problems and a review of the literature. Psychological Bulletin, 1965, 63, 87-99.

Tart, C.T. Some effects of posthypnotic suggestion on the process of dreaming. International Journal of Clinical and Experimental Hypnosis, 1966, 14, 30-46.

Ullmann, L.P., & Krasner, L. A psychological approach to abnormal behavior. Englewood Cliffs: Prentice-Hall, 1969.

Weitzenhoffer, A.M. General techniques of hypnotism. New York: Grune and Stratton, 1957.

Woody, R.H. Clinical suggestion and systematic desensitization. American Journal of Clinical Hypnosis, 1973, 15, 250-257.

Woody, R.H., & Schauble, P.G. Desensitization of fear by video tapes. Journal of Clinical Psychology, 1969, 25, 102-103.

CLINICAL USE OF HYPNOSIS FOR ATTENUATION OF BURN DEPTH

Dabney M. Ewin

Tulane Medical School, U.S.A.

Abstract: This paper reviews the experimental work of Chapman, Goodell, and Wolff (1959) in which they demonstrated that the inflammatory reaction and tissue damage caused by a standard burn could be increased or decreased by hypnotic suggestion. Burn depth is ordinarily a function of the temperature of the causative agent and the length of time of the contact. These vary so much in accidental burns that it is rarely possible to estimate the expected depth, and consequently any attenuation of that depth by hypnosis tends to be speculative.

The author has had 18 years of experience with burns at a local aluminum plant, and when molten aluminum at 950 degrees centigrade spills, it invariably causes third degree burns requiring skin grafting unless the area is small. A man slipped and fell into a pot of molten aluminum up to his knee; he was a good hypnotic subject, developed only second degree burns, was out of the hospital in three weeks, and returned to work in two and a half months.

The purpose of this paper is 1) to review experimental work showing that in a standard thermal burn the depth and severity result not only from the heat applied, but also from the body's inflammatory reaction to the stimulus; and 2) to show that in the burned patient early hypnosis can prevent the body's inflammatory reaction and thus attenuate the depth and severity of the burn.

Anyone who has had a significant sunburn knows that at the time of leaving the sun there may be redness and some discomfort, but it is only later that inflammation occurs, with the serious symptoms of burning pain, tenderness, swelling, fever, and blistering. Very little morbidity would ensue if the inflammatory reaction could be aborted and the process arrested at the time the stimulus is withdrawn. Augmenting Delboeuf's (1877) experiment, Chapman, Goodell, and Wolff (1959a) have done experiments demonstrating that the degree of inflammatory response and tissue damage to a standard burn can be augmented or diminished by hypnotic suggestion as well as by thermoregulatory reflexes induced by immersing the feet in hot or cold water.

But what of the patient whose burn is severe and deep, and who has what we call a third degree or full-thickness burn? Can he be helped? Brauer and Spira (1966) did a remarkable experiment showing that in a full-thickness burn the destruction of all skin elements does not occur immediately. A standard and reproducible full-thickness burn was applied to young pigs (whose skin most nearly resembles human skin in laboratory studies) and the burned area was excised and transferred as a free skin graft to a viable bed where the response of the body favored acceptance like that which occurs with any skin graft. Of 53 burn skin to normal beds there was an estimated 73% take, while 23 grafts of normal skin to the same burn beds had an 80% take and 18 normal skin to normal beds had 98% take. They noted that a delay of hours before removal of the burn graft materially influenced graft survival in the new bed. This correlates with the evidence of Chapman, Goodell, and Wolff (1959a, 1959b) that the bradykinin-like substance associated with the inflammatory response is released within the first two hours of injury.

Entin and Baxter (1950) using human volunteers plotted a graph showing temperature-time relations for different degrees of thermal injury at temperatures up to 110 degrees Centigrade. Coagulation of skin occurs with two second exposure at 110 degrees Centigrade. No studies are available going as high as 950 degrees Centigrade.

CASE REPORT

R.G., 28 year old white male anode worker in an aluminum plant slipped and fell on August 22, 1974, with his right leg going down into molten aluminum at 950 degrees Centigrade (approximately 1750 degrees Fahrenheit). He was holding on to a stud and extricated himself quickly. First-aid attendants at the plant applied ice packs immediately and transported him in the plant ambulance directly to the emergency room where he was met by the author. The outer layers of skin were cooked brown and peeling, while the inner layers were blanched white with no apparent blood supply. He had very little pain, and pin-prick testing produced no blood and only an occasional response of sensation. With the example of how a thought produces a blush and dilates all the blood vessels in the face, his attention was directed to the idea that what he thought about could affect the healing of his burn. He was receptive to learning how to do this and went easily into trance with a simple request that he close his eyes and focus his attention entirely on what I was saying. He had had 50 mg. of meperidine (Demerol) and the ice packs were still in place. He was given suggestions that his right leg was cool and comfortable, and he readily acknowledged that this was how he felt and that it was a pleasant sensation. He was then given the suggestion that his mind would lock itself to this feeling so that his leg would continue to feel cool and comfortable day and night until it healed. He was asked to let his index finger rise to signal when he had a sense of certainty that he could accomplish this, and when he did the trance was terminated.

A photograph (Figure 1) was taken and the burns dressed with cyclomethycaine (Surfacaine) ointment and Vaseline gauze pressure dressings. No topical antibiotic or systemic antibiotic was given. The following morning (21 hours post burn) his blood count showed 9300 white cells, with 70% segmented neutrophiles, 25% lymphocytes, and 5% monocytes. His temperature varied between 99 degrees and 100 degrees until his first dressing change on the sixth post burn day when there was a single spike to 102 degrees. There was no clinical infection, no odor, almost no drainage on the dressing, and no edema of the foot in spite of the circumferential burn. He required one to three tablets of propoxyphene, aspirin, phenacetin and caffeine (Darvon Compound 65) per day for relief, knowing that he could have meperidine if he requested it. On the 12th post burn day the dressings were removed and he was started on daily whirlpool baths which were too vigorous for the delicate epithelium and caused some subepithelial hemorrhage. The leg was photographed on the 13th day (Figure 2). He was ambulatory and discharged from the hospital on the 19th post burn day and returned to work on November 4, 1974, ten and a half weeks post burn. The skin on the leg healed without scar tissue formation, with regrowth of hair, and with some permanent bronzing of the skin still present 22 months later (Figure 3). The patient returned to his same job, and had been promoted to foreman.

DISCUSSION

There are an estimated two million burns annually in the United States (Salisbury & Pruitt, 1976); it is possible that a great deal of morbidity could be alleviated by early hypnosis. Since both brain and skin have the same ectodermal origin in the embryo and the skin is the most highly innervated organ in the body, it is not surprising that the central nervous system exerts a profound control over physiological responses in the skin.

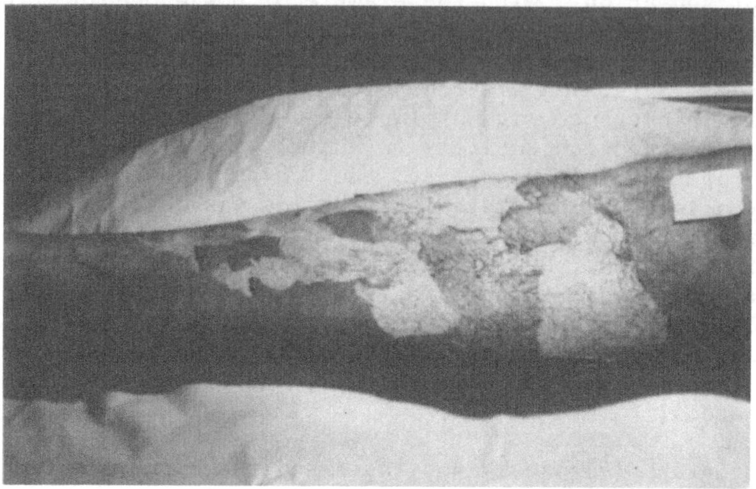

Fig. 1. Day of burn. Circumferential burn from shoetop to knee.

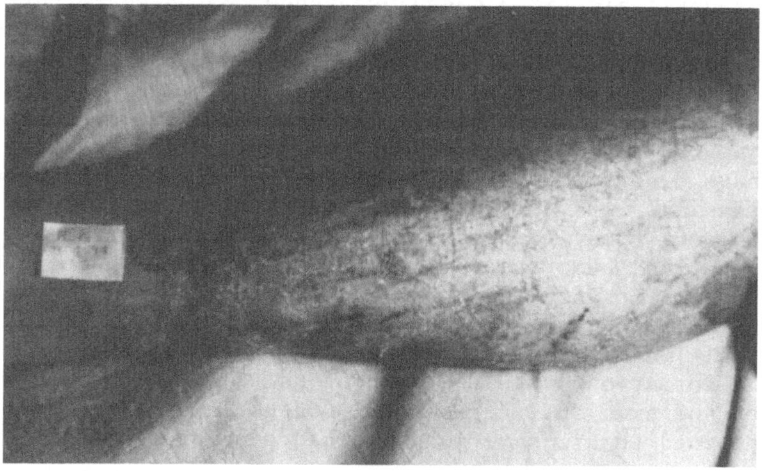

Fig. 2. Thirteen days post burn. Healing without infection.

Reporting their experiences, Chapman, Goodell, and Wolff (1959b) conclude "that the subject's perceptions and attitudes may be relevant to neural activities that engender or enhance inflammatory reactions." There are multiple reports of hypnotic recollections of a previous burn (Ullman, 1947; Bellis, 1966; Johnson & Barber, 1976) causing acute inflammation and/or blister formation at the

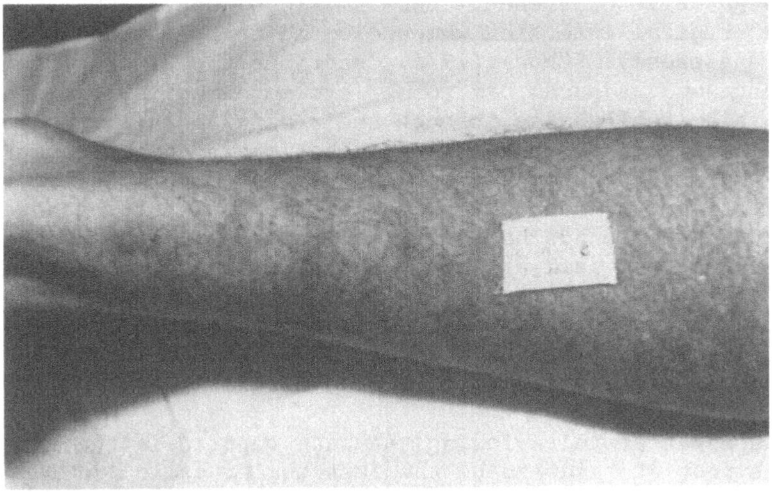

Fig. 3. Twenty-two months post burn. Skin bronzed, healed without scar tissue and with regrowth of hair.

site of the earlier trauma. This author has observed the same phenomenon on several occasions. Since every burned patient has had the experience of a burn, it is thus possible for his mind to maintain and enhance the inflammatory reaction by thinking about it. One of the most damaging emotions is guilt (Cheek, 1962; Ewin, 1973), and if present it must be removed before a patient will accept good suggestions for healing.

The patient should not only avoid harmful thoughts, he should develop a positive, optimistic attitude. Artz is quoted (Dahinterová, 1967) as drawing attention to the finding "that the well motivated, secure individual did extremely well after even the most severe burn injury whereas individuals without these resources had considerable difficulty adjusting to the result of a massive injury." A number of clinical reports describe burn patients, who, on a pitiful, hopeless, downhill course, experienced a dramatic shift with rapid healing after being hypnotized and encouraged to be optimistic (Crasilneck, Stirman, Wilson, McCranie, & Fogelman, 1955; Cheek, 1962; Bernstein, 1965; Dahinterová, 1967; LaBaw, 1973; Schafer, 1975).

Infection will deepen a second degree burn to third degree requiring a skin graft where primary healing might have occurred. The effect of hypnosis on infection is perplexing; the individual in trance maight be viewed as analogous to trees in a dormant state, the cyst form of the amoeba, and the spore of the clostridium, which are resistant to assaults that would easily overwhelm them in their active, vegetative existence. Esdaile (1850) had a 50% mortality rate from surgical infection which dropped to 5% when he began using hypnotic anesthesia. Chong (1976) describes the Hindu firewalkers of Singapore on Thaipusam Day going into somnambulistic trance, piercing thin steel shafts through their skin and silver pins through the tongue and cheeks, and walking on hot coals across a pit 20 by 30 feet. He says, "Curiously enough, with no aseptic preparation of the steel shafts and needles no case of sepsis or tetanus of the multiple puncture wounds has ever been reported. None of the fire-walkers suffer from pain or burns, though as they walk across their feet may sink into the hot cinders up to their ankles." Schafer (1975) notes that in the patients whom he hypnotized on the Burn Unit of Orange County Medical Center "There was no infection of any burns;" he then attributes this to good surgical care.

It is apparent in reviewing the case reports in the literature that the hypnotist tends to be the last healer called in, and then only in desperation. The author found only one patient treated *early*, namely, Case 3 of Crasilneck, Stirman, Wilson, McCranie, & Fogelman (1955). "A 32-year-old non-white man was admitted to the hospital with a mixed superficial and deep dermal burn over 35% of the body surface. He was subjected to hypnosis after arriving at the hospital about *four hours after the injury*. No narcotics were required during the acute phase of injury or at any time during his 18 days of hospitalization. Complete alleviation of pain was obtained with hypnosis in this man throughout his hospital course." This case is quoted in its entirety because it describes the usual course of these patients in the experience of the author as treating surgeon and hypnotist. An occasional patient will laugh at the whole idea and have a poor response, as did some of Schafer's patients (1975). It should be noted that the work of Chapman, Goodell, and Wolff (1959a) showed that icing a burn holds the inflammatory process in check for several hours. Since icing is now standard emergency room care in the United States, there is ample time to call for the assistance of a qualified hypnotist if the primary physician is not skilled in the technique of hypnosis.

SUMMARY

(1) In burns, there is no substitute for prevention; but once a burn has occurred, nothing could be more desirable than limiting its depth.

(2) Experimental work shows that this can be done with *early* hypnosis, and in the author's clinical experience these patients heal rapidly with increased resistance to infection, with very little pain, and with an optimistic expectation of early return to normal activity.

(3) It is emphasized that the suggestion "cool and comfortable," or suggestions of anesthesia, are effective; the word "normal" is to be avoided because in experimental studies these subjects did develop a "normal" burn.

(4) A case is reported of a young man whose leg was immersed in molten aluminum at 950 degrees Centigrade; he was hypnotized within 30 minutes, developed only a second degree burn, and although antibiotics were not used had no infection. He was discharged from the hospital on the nineteenth day and healed without scar tissue formation on the leg.

REFERENCES

Artz, C.P. Quoted in Dahinterová, 1967. See below in this Reference list.

Bellis, J.M. Hypnotic pseudo-sunburn. The American Journal of Clinical Hypnosis, 1966, 8, 310-312.

Bernstein, N.R. Observations on the use of hypnosis with burned children on a pediatric ward. International Journal of Clinical and Experimental Hypnosis, 1965, 13, 1-10.

Brauer, R.O., & Spira, M. Full-thickness burns as source for donor graft in the pig. Plastic and Reconstructive Surgery, 1966, 37, 21-30.

Chapman, L.F., Goodell, H., & Wolff, H.G. Augmentation of the inflammatory reaction by activity of the central nervous system. Archives of Neurology, 1959a, 1, 557-572.

Chapman, L.F., Goodell, H., & Wolff, H.G. Changes in tissue vulnerability induced during hypnotic suggestion. Journal of Psychosomatic Research, 1959b, 4, 99-105.

Cheek, D.B. Ideomotor questioning for investigation of subconscious "pain" and target organ vulnerability. American Journal of Clinical Hypnosis, 1962, 5, 30-41.

Chong, T.M. Cultural-religious trance states in Singapore. In J.G. Watkins (chairman) Symposium - Hypnosis throughout the world. Presented at the 7th International Congress of Hypnosis and Psychosomatic Medicine, July, 1976, Philadelphia, U.S.A.

Crasilneck, H.B., Stirman, J.A., Wilson, B.J., McCranie, E.J., & Fogelman, M.J. Use of hypnosis in the management of patient with burns. Journal of the American Medical Association, 1955, 158, 103-106.

Dahinterová, J. Some experiences with the use of hypnosis in the treatment of burns. International Journal of Clinical and Experimental Hypnosis, 1967, 15, 49-53.

Delboeuf, J. De L'origine des effets curatifs de l'hypnotisme. Bulletin de L'Académie royale de Belgique, 1877. In Bernheim, H. Hypnosis and suggestion in psychotherapy. New York: Jason Aronson, Inc., 1973.

Entin, M.A., & Baxter, H. Experimental and clinical study of histopathology and pathogenesis of graduated thermal burns in man and their clinical implication. Plastic and Reconstructive Surgery, 1950, 6, 352-373.

Esdaile, J. Mesmerism in India and its practical application in surgery and medicine. London: Longman's Green & Co., 1850. Reissued under title, Hypnosis in medicine and surgery. New York: Julian Press, 1957.

Ewin, D.M. Hypnosis in industrial practice. Journal of Occupational Medicine, 1973, 15, 586-589.

Johnson, R.F.Q., & Barber, T.X. Hypnotic suggestions for blister formation: Subjective and physiological effects. The American Journal of Clinical Hypnosis, 1976, 18, 172-180.

LaBaw, W.L. Adjunctive trance therapy with severly burned children. International Journal of Child Psychotherapy, 1973, 2, 80-92.

Salisbury, R.E., & Pruitt, B.A. Burns of the upper extremity. Philadelphia, W.B. Saunders Co., 1976.

Schafer, D.W. Hypnosis use on a burn unit. International Journal of Clinical and Experimental Hypnosis, 1975, 23, 1-14.

Ullman M. Herpes simplex and second degree burn induced under hypnosis. American Journal of Psychiatry, 1947, 103, 828-830.

COMPLICATIONS ARISING FROM HYPNOSIS FOR ENTERTAINMENT

H. Clagett Harding

Portland, Oregon, U.S.A.

Abstract: There is increasing interest in obtaining or retaining legislation banning the use of hypnosis for entertainment purposes. Successful implementation of that interest demands data acceptable to the courts or legislatures justifying action to protect the public. A search of the English publications led to retrieval of only two documented cases of damage allegedly precipitated by hypnosis for entertainment; yet frequent newspaper (hearsay) reports indicate such incidents are not uncommon.

This paper includes a case summary of physical damage arising from participation in a demonstration for entertainment.

Cooperation of all professionals in calling attention to such incidents should result in adequate source material to allow the governing bodies, courts, and professionals to arrive at reasonable conclusions.

CASE SUMMARY

E.S. a 24 year old, previously healthy female, attending a hypnosis performance March, 1975, went into a hypnotic state while a member of the audience. Her response came to the attention of the entertainer who ordered her to the stage and proceeded to suspend her with her head on one chair and her feet on another. He then stood on her abdomen.

Immediately after the performance, she had neck and back pain of enough severity to cause her to seek help in the hospital emergency room, and from her physician the next day. She was hospitalized for seven days. Since the injury, she has had x-rays, lumbar puncture, and orthopedic, neurologic, and psychiatric consultations. Treatments included analgesics, muscle relaxants, and physiotherapy.

Headaches, backaches, and nerve conduction disturbances had persisted unabated for six months at the time of this report.

Virtually every serious hypnotherapist has a built-in aversion to hypnosis for entertainment purposes. Such therapists find it difficult to accept exhibition of a subject principally for amusement; they feel this exhibition involves exploitation and exposure to substantial risks without reasonable gain for the subject or the audience.

Orne (1965), in discussing the dangers of hypnosis as found in treatment situations versus experimental studies, drew attention to the need for taking into account the context in which the hypnosis is employed, and for distinguishing between episodic and non-episodic situations. His conclusions are verified by the study of Levitt and Hershman (1963), who reported that 27% of trained physicians or dentists witnessed undesirable after-effects among patients in therapeutic (non-episodic) situations. Hilgard (1974) reported that 15% of experimental (episodic) subjects experienced lingering, undesirable effects in excess of one hour, and some for several days. It is reasonable to assume that therapeutic hypnosis, a non-episodic or continued relationship, has potential for a larger percentage of undesirable responses than is found in the assumed episodic stage experience; however, since a common method for enticing subjects to the stage is an implied or overt offer to help with problems of smoking, obesity, stuttering, or other habits, the stage performance assumes more of a non-episodic quality than is commonly believed.

Stimulated by newspaper reports of damage, or by various interested organizations, eight of the United States (Kansas, Minnesota, Nebraska, New Jersey, Oregon, South Dakota, Virginia, and Wyoming), three provinces of Australia (Tasmania, Victoria, and South Australia), and the province of Quebec, Canada, have enacted restrictive or prohibitive legislation regarding the public exhibition of hypnotized persons. In addition, Marcuse (1964) reported that ten major countries, and numerous municipalities have enacted various means of restriction.

Organizations other than government bodies taking similar formal action include a number of religious groups: the Catholic Church, the Church of the Seventh Day Adventists, and the Christian Science Church. The U.S. Air Force has banned stage hypnosis from all its installations, and the National Broadcasting Company has a restrictive code which requires review and approval of scripts containing hypnotic episodes. Most treatment oriented professional organizations have adopted resolutions or regulations denouncing the entertainment aspects of hypnosis: the American Medical Association (1958), the American Society of Clinical Hypnosis, the American Psychiatric Association (1961), the Society for Clinical and Experimental Hypnosis, and the American Psychological Association (1953).

Once protective legislation is achieved, it still requires surveillance. A law was repealed in Japan during the post World War II period, and another in Oregon in 1970. In the latter instance, quick action by interested organizations resulted in a re-enactment in 1972. This law was then attacked on constitutional grounds and trial was held in January, 1975, with judgment resulting in favor of the law (Carey v. Horton, 1975). In preparation for that litigation, a survey of the literature was fruitless. In discussing dangers, almost all authors condemn stage hypnosis and cite time-worn hypothetical examples. Erickson (1962) reported "about a score" of back injuries possibly due to stage demonstrations, but did not include any case reports of damage. In Rosen's reports of damage (1957, 1960), there is only a single sentence relating to injury arising from stage hypnosis. Kost (1965) and West (1965) reported the only cases of untoward effects from entertainment hypnosis found in the English literature.

A survey of published monographs was only slightly more rewarding. Marcuse (1964) listed eight cases which resulted in the passage of the British Hypnotism Act of 1952. In 1969, he listed two cases from his personal experience (Marcuse, 1969). Such case reports are crucial to documenting support for legislative authority to protect the public. Feeling that the reported cases were inadequate in number and detail, the author requested that colleagues communicate their experiences to him. Protocols on six additional cases were received in this manner. J. Schultz (1922) reported 100 cases in a German language monograph. The above-mentioned cases are but the tip of the iceberg. All of us should report cases coming to our attention to the national associations mentioned above, or to authors interested in the subject. A series of cases could, and should lead to success in obtaining legislative support for preventing this damaging use of hypnosis. Documentation of the need for public protection is essential for the passage of legislation. According to Committee Reports of the California Legislature (1965), a valiant effort in the California Assembly by several organizations failed because the supporters did not document a single case of injury.

In the opinion of the author, the greatest damage from stage hypnosis is not necessarily to those who act as subjects, but to members of the audience. A large percentage of any audience, despite the entertainer's brief "educational remarks regarding safety, leaves the performance convinced: 1) that the hypnotist does indeed have total control, since to them the stage actions speak louder than words; 2) that hypnosis is instantaneous; 3) that those incapable of responding are stupid; 4) that the hypnosis patient is unaware of any unsuggested perceptions; 5) that amnesia is the rule; and 6) that the hypnotist could make the subject carry out any act, even against his moral code. Overcoming these blocks to therapy increases the cost to the patient in time, money, effort, and suffering.

Many practicing clinicians have received calls for assistance from patients who were once hypnotized and then felt that the "influence" was still being exerted. Most therapists who have had a year or more of experience have had patients for whom hypnosis is the treatment of choice, who refuse the therapy because of a previous untoward or unpleasant experience. Restricting the use of hypnosis to the clinical, educational, or experimental setting is therefore appropriate and desirable.

Authorities should be reminded that bedlam was once a place for the amusement of the public, and that nitrous oxide inhalation was a popular parlor game at the turn of the century. Individuals exposed to this anesthetic engaged in compulsive laughter and related absurd kinds of behavior. Stage hypnosis is being used at this time in an analogous fashion. In prohibiting stage performances of hypnosis, we can and should also similarly seek to prevent the misrepresentation of hypnosis on television and on the screen. It is likely that plays dealing with the theme of Svengali (duMaurier 1894) are responsible for the same kind of damage to the viewer as that resulting from observing stage hypnosis. In the past, the National Broadcasting Company has taken an enlightened position on this matter, which should be emulated.

Collecting carefully documented instances of damage caused wittingly or unwittingly to either the subject or the observer of stage hypnosis, will surely serve to provide the impetus for more widespread and sorely needed restraints on this anachronistic use of a therapeutic modality for entertainment.

REFERENCES

American Medical Association Report of Council on Mental Health. Journal of the American Medical Association, 1958, 168, 186-187.

American Psychiatric Association. Position statement. Washington, D.C.: American Psychiatric Association, 1961.

American Psychological Association. Ethical standards of psychologists. APA 1333. Washington, D.C.: American Psychological Association, 1953.

California Legislature. California Interim Committee Reports. 1963-1965, Vol. 9 #26. North Highlands, CA: California State Printer, 1966.

Carey v. Horton. Docket #73-4122, Lane County, Oregon. Feb. 27, 1975.

duMaurier, G. Trilby: a novel. New York: Harper and Brothers Publishers, 1894.

Erickson, M.H. Stage hypnotists back syndrome. American Journal of Clinical Hypnosis, 1962, 5, 141-142.

Hilgard, J.R. Sequelae to hypnosis. International Journal of Clinical and Experimental Hypnosis, 1974, 22, 281-298.

Kost, P.F. Dangers of hypnosis. International Journal of Clinical and Experimental Hypnosis, 1965, 13, 220-225.

Levitt, E.E., & Hershman, S. The clinical practice of hypnosis in the United States: A preliminary survey. International Journal of Clinical and Experimental Hypnosis, 1963, 11, 55-65.

Marcuse, F.L. Hypnosis throughout the world. Springfield, Ill: Charles C. Thomas, 1964.

Marcuse, F.L. Hypnosis: Fact and fiction. Baltimore, Md: Penguin Books, Inc., 1969, Pp. 169-170.

Orne, M.T. Undesirable effects of hypnosis: The determinants and management. International Journal of Clinical and Experimental Hypnosis, 1965, 13, 226-237.

Rosen, H. Hypnosis and self-hypnosis in medical practice. Maryland Medical Journal, 1957, 6, 297-299.

Rosen, H. Hypnosis: Applications and misapplications. Journal of the American Medical Association, 1960, 172, 683-687.

Schultz, J. Gesundheitsschädigungen nach Hypnose. Halle: C. Marbold, 1922.

West, L.J. Dangers of hypnosis. Journal of the American Medical Association, 1965, 192, 95-98.

UTILIZING THE PHASES OF THE BREATHING RHYTHM IN HYPNOSIS

Beata Jencks

Murray, Utah, U.S.A.

Abstract: Skills in hypnotherapy and self-hypnosis can be improved by observing the breathing pattern. Moreover the appropriate breathing phases can be utilized to evoke and enhance special effects.

The normal breathing rhythm varies according to the demands of a situation, and the relaxed swinging of the diaphragm is inhibited by fear, fright, anxiety, concentration, and unhealthy breathing habits. The influence of the mind on the action of the diaphragm is also observed in the response to suggestions. The accepted suggestion of sleep produces a breathing rhythm similar to that during sleep. The accepted suggestion of exercise initiates faster, deeper breathing. Conversely, modifying the breathing rhythm purposely initiates intended changes in sensations, emotions, and actions.

In general, long, slow, deep exhalations bring about relaxation with the accompanying sensations of sinking, widening, opening up, and softening; the feelings of comfort, heaviness, warmth, and moisture; and the moods of patience and calmness. Inhalations evoke invigoration, tension, or levitation; and they are related to the feelings of lightness, coolness, and dryness, and to the moods of courage, determination, and exhilaration. The actions of the breathing phases are evoked by paying attention to them differentially. If the effect to be attained is "cool and moist," suggestions can be superimposed during both inhalation and exhalation respectively. The repetition of suggestions in phase with the breathing rhythm has an additional hypnotic deepening effect.

From the experiences of the majority of the author's students and patients, a table has been constructed which lists additional sensations, feelings, and images which are predominantly related to the respective breathing phases. Often the states experienced with inhalation are diametrically opposite to those experienced with exhalation, for instance: tension with inhalation, to relaxation with exhalation; or the feeling of warmth with exhalation, to the feeling of coolness with inhalation.

Suggestions made during the inappropriate breathing phase may counteract the suggested response. By coordinating repeated suggestions of deep relaxation with inhalation phases only, the author succeeded in arousing anxiety in experimental subjects.

Utilization of the breathing phases is especially indicated for subjects who are unwilling, or seem unable, to enter a hypnotic state.

Illustrative case histories are presented.

The phases of a relaxed breathing rhythm (Jencks, 1977b) are a tension-reducing, long, slow exhalation, followed by a patient pause of relaxed emptiness until the need for oxygen finally prompts a passive inhalation. During the latter the diaphragm contracts automatically, acting like a piston which moves downward and forward, creating a space in the chest cavity to be filled by the expanding lungs. This expansion reduces the air pressure, and the outside air enters the lungs passively through the respiratory passages which are normally in free communication with the outside air.

The phases of a tense breathing rhythm are a forced inhalation which usually employs the chest muscles maximally, followed by a tense pause of retention, until excess tension or tension for too long forces an explosive exhalation.

In addition to the breathing phases the length of respirations, repetitive rhythms, real or imagined breathing pathways, and "locks" or tense contractions at certain places in the body play a role in the use of breathing. For evoking certain patterns the imagination is very useful.

Methodical Uses of the Breathing Rhythm

Breathing techniques and therapies, depending on their purpose, use different combinations of the described aspects of breathing. Yogic breathing (Vishnudevananda, 1960) makes much use of retention, rhythms, and locks. Relaxation therapies emphasize exhalations or use "pumping" of the breath with a following deep exhalation. In Schultz's Standard Autogenic Training (Schultz & Luthe, 1969; Jencks, 1973b, 1977a) the fourth exercise is concentration on the formula "It breathes me." This passive concentration on the breathing rhythm in a deeply relaxed, self-hypnotic state further relaxes the breathing rhythm and deepens the hypnotic state even more. In Fuchs' Functional Relaxation (1949/50; 1974), longer, slower exhalations are encouraged by the use of imagery (Jencks, 1970a, 1970b) or by very slight pressure on the patient's body with the therapist's hand (Jencks, 1970c). In Jencks' (1974) method, use is made of the imagination, especially with respect to imagined pathways (see Figure 1) and to the different feelings, actions, and images related to the phases of the breathing rhythm (see Table 1). This table has been constructed on the basis of the experiences of the majority of the author's students and patients. Often the states of feeling elicited by the images connected with inhalations are diametrically opposite to those connected with exhalations, as for instance, tension with inhalation to relaxation with exhalation, or the feeling of warmth with exhalation to the feeling of coolness with inhalation.

The inhale-hold-exhale breathing pattern, used during inductions for relaxation or "going down," is the most frequent use of breathing in hypnosis. Also frequently used is the coupling of levitation suggestions with inhalation. However, all repetitive breathing patterns spontaneously induce a hypnotic state.

The practitioner of hypnosis must observe the subject's breathing and give further suggestions on the basis of what is observed and of what is intended. If the subject's breathing rhythm is very relaxed, suggestions of general relaxation are superfluous and may even be irritating to the subject. If the rhythm is tense or excited, attention should be paid to this and suggestions structured accordingly.

Often, not enough attention is paid to the wording of suggestions with respect to inhalations and exhalations. Hypnotic subjects can be very literal in their reactions, and if the practitioner suggests that the subject "breathe deeply," there is no way of predicting whether the subject will interpret this to mean the inhalation, the exhalation, or both, or if the ambiguous instruction will confuse the subject.

TABLE 1

Physical, Physiological, and Psychological Feelings, Actions, and Images Related to the Breathing Rhythm

	Exhalation	Inhalation	Holding the Breath
Physical and Physiological	Relaxation	Increase of tension	Maintenance or increase of tension
	Calmness	Stimulation	Restlessness
	Heaviness	Lightness	Unstable equilibrium
	Warmth	Coolness	Variability
	Darkness	Brightness	Variability
	Softness	Hardness	Rigidity
	Moisture	Dryness	
	Weakness, weariness	Strength, invigoration, refreshment	Momentary conservation of strength
Psychological	Patience, endurance	Speed, being startled	Anxiety, oppression
	Contemplation	Ready attention	Strained attention
	Equanimity	Courage	Cowardice or Determination
	Deep thought, concentration	Openmindedness, creativity	Closed-mindedness
	Introversion	Extroversion	
	Boredom	Excitement	Keen interest
	Satisfaction	Curiosity	Uncertainty
	Depression	Cheerfulness	Nervous tension
	Comfort	Exhilaration	Uneasiness
	Generosity	Greed	Stinginess

(Continuation of Table 1)

	Exhalation	Inhalation	Holding the Breath
	Relax, release, let go, loosen	Tense, bind, tighten grasp	Hold on
	Release pressure	Increase pressure	Maintain or increase pressure
	Stream or flow out	Stream or flow in	Congestion
	Liquefy	Solidify	Maintain consistency
	Expand, widen, open	Contract, narrow, close	Dimension unchanged
Actions	Sink, descend	Ascend, levitate, rise	Maintain level
	Fall asleep	Wake up	
	Lengthen	Shorten	Maintain length
	Move or Swing forward, strike, kick, punch, reach out	Move, draw, or swing backward, haul in	Stop, stand or hold still
	Send, give help, offer	Receive, take, demand	Keep, interrupt
	Laugh, sigh, giggle	Sob, gasp	Smile, frown
	Soothe	Irritate	Compress

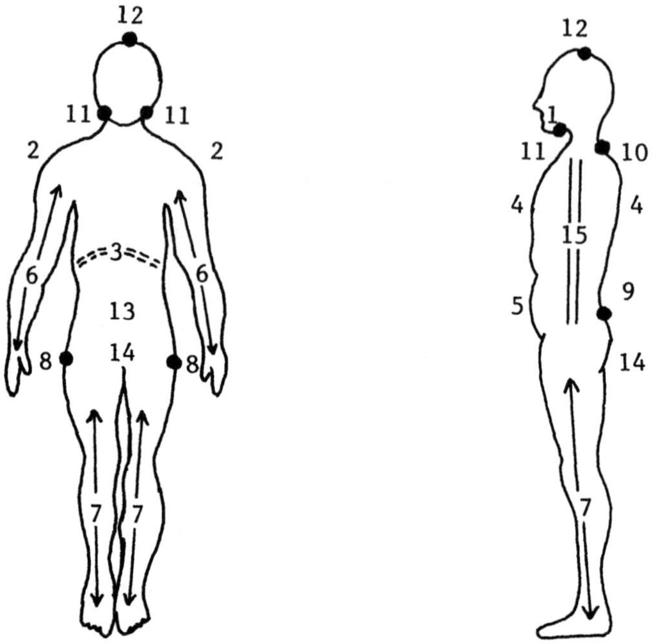

Fig. 1. Real and imagined breathing pathways and movements. 1) Through nose, mouth, and throat; 2) raising the shoulders; 3) raising and lowering the diaphragm; 4) expanding and contracting the ribcage; 5) expanding and pulling in the abdomen; 6) through the arms; 7) through the legs; 8) through the hips; 9) through the small of the back; 10) through the back of the lower neck; 11) through two holes under the chin, to the right and left of the throat; 12) through the crown of the head; 13) filling an abdominal reservoir; 14) by means of a pump at the anus or crotch; 15) up and down a tube from the throat to the pelvis.

Suggestions made during inappropriate breathing phases may counteract the suggested responses. The author has succeeded in making experimental subjects very confused by timing suggestions for the induction of deep relaxation with inhalation phases only, while instructing the subjects during the exhalation phases to let their mind "go blank." Responses reported included the inability to cooperate in spite of good will, hyperventilation, tension, and anxiety. When, on the other hand, suggestions for the induction of relaxation are timed to coincide with the exhalation phases of the subjects, they invariably induce deeper relaxation.

Use of the Breathing Rhythm in Conjunction with Suggestions

In general, long, slow, deep exhalations are conducive to relaxation with the accompanying sensations of sinking, widening, opening up, and softening; feelings of comfort, heaviness, warmth, and moisture; and moods of patience and calmness. Inhalations evoke invigoration, tension, or levitation; feelings of lightness, coolness, and dryness; and moods of courage, determination, and exhilaration. Suggestions can be given during inhalations that, for instance, tension is disregarded while nothing but "courage" is "inhaled."

Suggestive formulas can be constructed which give attention differentially to both respiratory phases. If, for example, the effect to be attained is "cool and moist," suggestions can be timed to coincide appropriately with inhalations and exhalations. Examples of self-suggestion formulas for use with the breathing phases are given in Table 2.

The normal breathing rhythm varies in accordance with the physical and emotional requirements of a situation, but the action of the diaphragm can also be greatly influenced by responses to suggestions. The accepted suggestion of sleep results in a breathing rhythm similar to that during sleep. The accepted suggestion of exercising initiates faster, deeper breathing. The suggestions of stress or fright may halt the rhythm or make it irregular.

Fear, fright, anxiety, concentration, and unhealthy breathing habits inhibit the relaxed swinging of the diaphragm. This is especially obvious in psychosomatic and neurotic patients, but irregularities in the normal breathing rhythm can be observed in any person during stress. Inappropriate reactions to daily stresses can be reduced by purposely modifying the breathing rhythm.

Therapeutic Uses

The respiratory phases can be used in connection with hypnosis for many therapeutic purposes (Jencks, 1973a). However, use of the respiratory phases is also highly effective with patients who are unwilling, or seem unable to enter a "hypnotic state." Finally, practitioners of hypnosis should be aware that hypnosis is often induced unintentionally during therapy and in everyday situations.

Following are examples of the use of the respiration in connection with hypnosis:

<u>Unintentional hypnosis by abdominal rhythmic breathing</u>: A twenty-four year old nurse had severe breathing difficulties during

TABLE 2

Self-Suggestion Formulas for Use with the Breathing Phases

For Relaxation:
Body relaxed (EX)*, mind alert (IN)*
Relaxed (EX) and easy (IN)

To Ease the Respiration:
Breath streams calm and free (EX), limbs are light (IN)
Breath streams into small of back (IN), slowly out through legs (EX)

For Concentration:
Concentrated on task (IN), yet relaxed and steady (EX)

For Motivation:
When the going gets tough (IN), the tough get going (EX)
(Note: some athletes like reverse breathing phases for this)

For Invigoration:
Awake and aware (IN), I blow away all tiredness (EX)
Sweep out slag (EX), fresh air in (IN)!
Exhilarated and excited (IN), but body steady (EX)

For Strength and Endurance:
I am a mountain (IN) of endurance (EX)
Endless endurance (EX), solid strength (IN)

For Competition:
Compete intensely (IN) with relaxed control of body (EX)
Compete calm (EX), cool (IN), collected (EX) and competitive (IN)!

To Reduce Anxiety:
Fear flows out (EX), courage comes in (IN)

To Reduce Eye Discomfort:
Eyes cool (IN) and relaxed (EX)
Eyelids light (IN) and soft(EX)
Moisture on eyeballs (EX), eyelids float (IN)

To Ease a Sore Throat:
Throat wide and moist (EX), coolness on forehead (IN)

* EX means during exhalation, IN means during inhalation

the abating stage of a miliary tuberculosis. She was wheezing, could not "breathe through," and was so sensitive to atmospheric conditions that, when a strong wind blew against the window of her hospital room, she had to turn around for relief with her head to the foot of the bed, in order to lie "with the wind" instead of against it.

Before her illness the patient had been an ardent swimmer with good vital capacity. With some knowledge of artificial respiration, she invented the following in order to ease her breathing. She would lie on her back and concentrate on nothing but the muscles of the abdomen, moving them rhythmically up and down, completely disregarding her chest and breathing pathways. She would do this especially in the evenings when the lights were out. By doing this she would soon slip into a very deep sleep from which she awakened rather refreshed in the morning. Meanwhile her roommate, who was distressed by the nurse's incessant loud wheezing, spent so many disturbed nights that she finally requested a transfer to another room.

When the nurse learned many years later about formal hypnosis, she interpreted her good nights of sleep during her illness as deep trance states which were instrumental in her recovery before the era of chemotherapy for tuberculosis.

<u>Changing the breathing of a "hypnotic failure:"</u> A fifty-eight year old woman, although diagnosed as a "hypnotic failure" by three hypnotists, wanted to " learn hypnosis to combat emotional, mental and physical disorders and overcome those conditions that make me susceptible to sickness." Specifically she reported nervous tension, tingling and numbness in limbs, itching skin, some thyroid and/or adrenal dysfunction, insomnia, and high blood pressure for the last ten years; she also complained of inefficiency in working and concentrating, anxiety, worries, and since childhood occasional colitis due to emotional upsets, largely involving feelings of inferiority and depression resulting from the treatment given her by her mother and her sister.

After a short investigatory talk, the patient, who was sitting primly on the edge of a wooden rocking chair, was asked to sit back comfortably and close her eyes. An anxious look appeared on her face but she complied. As she closed her eyes she inhaled, held her breath, and grasped the arms of the rocking chair tightly while the anxious look on her face increased. She was told, "That is fine. Now open your eyes and come back into the room." She opened her eyes and relaxed somewhat. The following conversation ensued. "Did you notice what you did with your breathing when you closed your eyes?" "No...?" "I wonder what was going on within you after you closed your eyes." "Oh, the same as always when they try to hypnotize me. You know, they never succeeded. I always go backward or fall backward as soon as I close my eyes. It even happens at night now when I close my eyes to go to sleep. It is terrible. And now it happened again." "Allright. We will do it now once more. But this time I want you to observe what you do with your breathing. Work very gently and observe your breathing. Ready? Close your eyes again and tell me what you are doing with your breathing." She complied. "I...I...I stopped breathing!" "Are you going backward?" "Yes, a little, but not as much as before." After this she was told to open her eyes which she had kept closed while she answered. Then, in order to train her sensory awareness she was instructed to inhale and stop her breathing while her eyes were open, and observe what feelings this evoked. After repeating this a few times she recognized that inhalation and holding her breath caused her to have feelings of going backward. Exhalation with open eyes could give her the feeling of going forward, but not every time she tried it. During exhalation with closed eyes she learned at least "to stand still." Next, she was told to practice moving forward with closed eyes during exhalation and to disregard her inhalation or to use various images to "hold on to" during inhalation. The rest of the therapy hour was spent on teaching her relaxation, anxiety reducing, and posture exercises as described in Table 3. The following week she reported that she had been able, for the first time in years, to close her eyes without the fear of feeling that she was going backward.

The patient was seen twice during the first month and monthly thereafter for a total of seven therapy sessions. During these she learned other exercises using exhalation to reduce anxiety and inhalation for ego-strengthening and enhancing vigor. She was an extremely good hypnotic subject, and was taught to use self-induced hypnotic states for positive suggestions and enjoyable imagery as a substitute for her previously self-reproaching, self-punishing, and self-deprecatory daydreaming.

Two years after termination of therapy the patient reported upon inquiry; "Things are going just beautifully! Sometimes I still remember all those troubles with my mother and my sister, but whenever I get tense I sit or lie down and have that flower open up in my chest, or I reach for that golden rope and pull myself up. And then I have all those nice forgiving feelings, and I forgive them all and can be rid of all that tension." She did not mention her numerous complaints but emphasized only how well she felt and how thankful she was for "those exercises."

Two cases of asthma. The following two cases are contrasted here because of similar complaints and treatment, yet vastly different immediate reactions and long-term results. It is also interesting to compare the reactions of the woman in the previous case history with those of the woman of similar age in this report.

TABLE 3

Examples of Jencks' Respiration Exercises

Long Breath: for relaxation and a slower breathing rhythm imagine that the inhaled air enters at the fingertips, goes up the arms into the shoulders and chest, and then, during exhalation, down through the trunk into the legs and leisurely out at the toes. Repeat a few times.

Warm Shower: to counteract tension in the shoulder and neck region, imagine water from a warm shower streaming pleasantly over the back of the head, shoulders, and neck. Feel the warmth and relaxation during exhalations.

Imagined Pathways: for easing the breathing or relieving pressures, imagine that the breathed air streams in and out easily at any of the places shown in Figure 1, or at any additional ones where relief is needed. Asthma patients found relief by "breathing through the small of the back;" tension headaches may be relieved by "inhaling or exhaling through the top of the head or the temples;" and "breathing through the holes under the chin" opened up the sinuses.

Opening Flower: to counteract anxiety and feelings of tightness in throat, chest, or abdomen, imagine during exhalations a flower bud opening at the tight place, as in a time lapse film. Repeat and feel the opening for several exhalations.

Bellows: to ease the breathing or to increase the vital capacity, breathe as if the flanks were bellows which draw air in and push it out. Imagine that the air streams in and out freely through the flanks.

Golden Thread and Clothes Hanger: for a well aligned posture with an alive yet relaxed feeling, imagine a golden, energizing thread all the way up the spine and through the crown of the head. Imagine being held from above by this thread, so that straightness is achieved effortlessly. Imagine during inhalations that the thread is pulled from above and invigoration streams into the spine from below. Imagine during exhalations that the tissues of the shoulder region are relaxedly draped over the shoulder blades or over a suspended clothes hanger.

Toad: for ego-strengthening, inhale and imagine blowing yourself up to an enormous size, like a toad. Stay this size in your imagination while you relax during exhalations.

At about the same time a 59-year-old woman and a 16-year-old girl were referred with the major complaint of asthma. Both patients also complained of nervousness, tingling sensations, headaches, inability to relax, and dissatisfaction with the home situation. In addition the woman complained of digestive troubles, insomnia, inefficiency, anxiety, and depression; and the girl of cramps during menstruation, skin rashes, swelling of extremities, bad hayfever, multiple food allergies, and biting her nails to the quick.

One important difference between the two was that the woman maintained and demonstrated that her asthma was due to emotional causes, while the girl maintained that hers was due to physical factors like dust, smoke, foods, cold, climbing, etc.

Both were seen at approximately weekly intervals and offered similar exercises (see Table 3 for examples), and were also taught to "breathe mainly through imagined pathways" (see Figure 1). The sequence of the introduction of different exercises varied according to the needs expressed during successive therapeutic conversations. The girl was an excellent hypnotic subject; the woman was good, but her cooperation varied. The concept of hypnosis was never discussed with the woman, and with the girl only during later therapy sessions.

The great difference between the two patients seemed to be with respect to cooperation. When the exercises were introduced in the office both were able to cooperate and execute them easily. The girl would then practice at home and apply them as needed. The woman did not practice at home nor use them in emergencies.

The girl suffered no asthma attack while in the office; occasionally she had the sniffles, possibly due to cigarette smoke in the waiting room. However, initially, she did report several asthma attacks every week, usually due to inhalants. She was progressively better able to cope with these, and they diminished in number. Her nailbiting and other complaints also decreased. She continued for a total of twelve sessions, with a course of Standard Autogenic Training added during the last six.

When the older patient could be distracted from her self-consciousness and lured into being interested in something, her wheezing would abate and she would seem quite normal with respect to her breathing and other reactions. However, as soon as something reminded her of her "troubles," she appeared to be a "very sick" person. This was especially related to difficulties with her husband and to her attempts to obtain an early retirement for Social Security benefits. After seven treatment sessions she discontinued therapy because she felt "too sick to do those exercises." About the same time she was admitted to hospital for investigation.

Five years after termination of therapy, reports upon inquiry are as follows:

The woman is on church welfare, and has a breathing machine at home which she uses several times a week, sometimes several times a day. Her husband divorced her to marry another woman and was killed six weeks later. Emotional upsets determine how she feels. She added, "I got hooked on cortisol. They don't want me to be on it, but I got hooked. I get it in pills now. I took it even when I saw you but did not know it. They gave it to me in shots then. No, I do not do your exercises. I have forgotten them and do not need them. I am with those doctors at the hospital now and I do what they tell me."

The girl, now a young woman, differed entirely. She is at age 20 a junior in college with a double major in German and drama, is married, and has a daughter. She often gets only four hours of sleep. Her daily medication is one tablet of chlorpheniramine (Chlortrimeton) which she increases when necessary during hayfever time and when she is exposed to smoke-laden or other allergy-producing situations. She still, approximately once a month, has an asthma attack for which "I breathe through that imagined hole in the small of my back and take one asthma tablet. I need your exercises most before the medication works, or if I am exposed to something I did not expect and have a reaction." She still uses many of the exercises she learned and has modified and applied them according to need, for instance: to alleviate tension or pain during menstruation she induces warmth in the pelvic region; when her legs are swollen from standing too long during rehearsals she induces coolness in her feet; after a knee operation she induced warmth in the scar region for comfort and greater mobility; she relieves headaches by inducing coolness on the forehead; and if she has insufficient sleep she uses fifteen to twenty minutes during the day to "sink into a very deep sleep and wake up fully refreshed."

REFERENCES

Fuchs, M. Über Atemtherapie und entspannende Körperarbeit. Psyche, 1949/50, 3, 538-548.

Fuchs, M. Funktionelle Entspannung. Stuttgart: Hippokrates Verlag, 1974.

Jencks, B. Self-rhythmization. Part I. Instructing a person in the basic concepts. A teaching film. Salt Lake City: University of Utah, 1970a.

Jencks, B. Self-rhythmization. Part II. Instructing a group in finding and adjusting self-rhythms. A teaching film. Salt Lake City: University of Utah, 1970b.

Jencks, B. Self-rhythmization. Part III. Self-rhythmization therapy with a psychosomatic patient. A teaching film. Salt Lake City: University of Utah, 1970c.

Jencks, B. Ausgewählte individuelle psychophysiologische Kombinations-therapie (AKT). In H. Binder (editor), Zwanzig Jahre praktische und klinische Psychotherapie. Munchen: J.H. Lehmanns Verlag, 1973a. Pp. 131-149.

Jencks, B. Exercise manual for J.H. Schultz's standard autogenic training. Salt Lake City: Jencks, 1973b.

Jencks, B. Respiration for relaxation, invigoration, and special accomplishment. Salt Lake City: Jencks, 1974.

Jencks, B. Autogenic training. Psychotherapy Bulletin, 1977a, 10, 17-22.

Jencks, B. Your body: biofeedback at its best. Chicago: Nelson-Hall, 1977b.

Schultz, J.H., & Luthe, W. Autogenic methods. New York: Grune and Stratton, 1969.

Vishnudevananda, Swami. The complete illustrated book of yoga. New York: The Julian Press, 1960.

DYNAMIC RELATION OF THE SECONDARY PERSONALITY INDUCED BY HYPNOSIS TO THE PRESENT PERSONALITY

Reima Kampman and Reijo Hirvenoja

University of Oulu, Finland

Abstract: Multiple personality induced by hypnosis has been studied relatively little in the world literature. In the present study efforts were made to find a dynamic relation between the present personality and the induced multiple personalities. Two carefully selected subjects underwent hypnotization at intervals of about seven years. The findings support the idea that the experiences of the present personality are reflected in the multiple personalities, both in the form of realistic details and as emotional experiences. The recall of a song is an outstanding example of how very detailed information can be stored in our mind, and how it can be retrieved in deep hypnosis without any idea of it whatsoever in the conscious mind.

Secondary personality induced by hypnosis has attracted very little scientific research. It is a general opinion, however, that such a secondary personality results from a subconscious dissociative reaction evoked by hypnosis, which cannot be accounted for by the conscious acting of the subject (Harriman 1942, 1943). Zolik (1958) stated that it is very difficult to find a dynamic connection between the present personality and the fantasy of previous existence created in hypnosis (secondary personality). According to Zolik (1962), the phenomenon of secondary personality probably offers a means of examining unconscious mechanisms. In hypnosis it is possible to project such material that is disturbing to the conscious ego, and attach it to a previous life. Then part of rejected emotional experience becomes in a way decathected and neutralized.

A real sensation associated with the phenomenon of secondary personalities was created by a book of Bernstein, "The Search for Bridey Murphy," published in 1956 (Bernstein, 1956). Many people regarded the book as evidence of the reincarnation theory. The book provoked heated debates among scientists on the origin of the phenomenon.

Kampman and Hirvenoja (1972) examined the incidence of secondary personality induced by hypnosis in the normal population. They observed that about seven per cent of volunteering subjects could produce secondary personalities when in deep hypnotic trance. Kampman (1973) compared two groups of subjects with each other; one group was able to create secondary personalities in deep hypnosis, and the other was able to enter a deep hypnotic state but unable to create secondary personalities. He observed that those capable of creating multiple personalities were healthier and more adaptable than those incapable of doing so. He assumed that the suggestion to enter a time preceding birth would create a very stressful situation for the subject. In deep hypnosis the subject would, in a way, have to re-evaluate the basic values of security: what comes after death, and before birth. He assumed that if the basic sense of safety of the subject is weak and the integrity of the ego defective, the deep fears of death and unconscious guilts trying to reach consciousness will be dealt with by means of religious belief (whatever the religion is); the subject will therefore not be able to create a secondary personality. If the personality of the subject is free from conflicts, he is able to follow the hypnotist's suggestion unconsciously, and will create a suitable secondary personality for the situation using his conscious or unconscious store of data.

Case Reports

Subject #1. The subject was a 15-year-old girl who was hypnotized in 1968 and age-regressed to a time preceding her birth. She said she was a girl aged seven years, whose name was Milina Bostojevski. She said she was living in the year 1780. She gave an accurate description of the conditions in which she lived, of her attitudes, feelings, etc. She was living in a time of war and told about the disasters caused by war. When the subject was age-regressed further she again presented a new personality. Thus, a total of five different secondary personalities were found in this subject in the course of the examination. She underwent similar experiments about one month later. The secondary personalities were identical to the previous ones.

An attempt to induce secondary personalities in the above-mentioned subject was renewed seven years later. She again entered a deep hypnotic state. She formed several secondary personalities, but to the author's surprise they were all entirely different from the previous ones. One of the secondary personalities was a boy of seven, who lived at the base of a big mountain. He said he was Aitmatov's son. The boy used vivid fantasy play: stones and stumps were animals who were his playmates; his father was the captain of a river craft; and the boy saw little of his father who sailed on the lake Issykjokul. The secondary personality was transferred with the help of a suggestion to the moment of death when he watched the fish swimming in the river, and how they moved freely along the river. He wanted to become a fish and swim to the lake Issykjokul to join his father. He suddenly felt he was a fish, jumped in, and was drowned.

When the hypnosis was terminated, the subject remembered nothing of what she had said. In the following hypnotic session, she was given the suggestion that she could remember the origin of the story of the little boy. The subject remembered that she had read a book called "Valkoinen laiva" (The White Ship) recording a similar story about a boy who was drowned in the same way as the boy in her narrative. The name of the lake was the same, and the author's name was Aitmatov. It is quite evident that the subject had acquired both the details and the emotional life of the secondary personality from the book she had read.

Subject #2. The second subject, a 19-year-old girl, had also been hypnotized seven years earlier. She had then produced eight secondary personalities in all. One of them was a young lady called Dorothy who lived in England in the 13th century and had been daughter to an inn-keeper. She gave a very explicit account of the contemporary happenings using names of places amazingly correctly, reporting distances in miles, etc. While she was in Dorothy's personality she sang a song which she called "the summer song." She sang it in English. The language she used was later recognized by a student with high honors in the English language as being Middle English. After termination of hypnosis, the subject had no memory at all of having heard the words or the melody of the song before. Another secondary personality developed by her was a young, blind Chinese girl called Ving Lei, who died when falling from a steep cliff.

The subject was rehypnotized seven years later. She was again able to enter a deep hypnotic state and created four new secondary personalities. However, the previous secondary personalities persisted. One of the new secondary personalities was a girl whose name was Karin Bergström. She had died at the age of seven in an air raid. She remembered accurately the day the bomb fell, as well as her home address at the time. She also gave the name and occupation of her parents. She had died in the year 1939.

In the investigation efforts were made to elucidate the connections between the reports of these secondary personalities and the present personality. The subject was encouraged in deep hypnosis to associate the experiences of the secondary personality to the emotional world and experiences of the present personality. Probably the most astonishing detail was the song that the subject had sung seven years earlier. During the later hypnotic experiment she was age-regressed to a moment when her present personality had perhaps seen the words of the song or heard it. She then went back in time to the age of 13, when she once, by chance, took a book from the shelves in the library. The name of the book was "Musiikin vaiheet" (The Phases of Music). She did not read it but ran through the pages. In hypnosis she was able to recall the authors of the book who were Benjamin Britten and Imago Holst. Furthermore, she could remember accurately where the song had appeared in the book. Later, when the data were checked by the author, it appeared that the original song was not Middle English but modernized medieval English, just as it was in the book.

A suggestion was also given to the subject that she relive in her emotional life a moment in her present personality like the one she experienced as the Chinese girl Ving Lei when she fell from the cliff. The subject then went back to the age of four, to a moment when she had been left alone in a dark room. She had been afraid, and had fallen from the upper level of the bunk-bed in which she had been sleeping.

The identification data on Karin Bergström who died in an air raid in 1939 were easily checked in the population register. The inquiry proved that neither she nor her relatives died in the raid. The subject was age-regressed by means of hypnotic suggestion, to the moment when she first obtained her information. She went back in time to when she was a little girl turning over the leaves of a patriotic book with pictures of just this address, and the picture of a seven-year-old girl who had died with her mother on the day of the air raid. From the book she had taken the exact date of the raid and the addresses where the bombs had fallen.

DISCUSSION

Secondary personality induced by hypnosis has been studied relatively little in the world literature. It has been found difficult to establish a dynamic relation between the narratives of the secondary personalities and the present personality (Zolik 1958).

In the present study, two carefully selected subjects underwent hypnosis at intervals of about seven years. In the case of one of the subjects the secondary personalities had completely changed and the other subject produced four new secondary personalities besides the previous ones. In addition, efforts were made to find a dynamic relationship between the present personality and the secondary personalities. The observations supported the idea that the experiences of the present personality were reflected in the secondary personalities, both in the form of realistic details and as emotional experiences. The recording of a song from a book by merely turning over the leaves of the book at the age of 13, is an outstanding example of how very detailed information can be stored in our brain without any idea whatever of it in the conscious mind, and how it can be retrieved in deep hypnosis. Kris (1934) presented his conception of hypnosis as regression in the service of the ego. It appears that producing multiple personalities in healthy subjects in deep trance is a healthy, progressive procedure, dealing with unconscious knowledge in a creative way. The suggestion of regression to a time preceding birth allows more freedom for the fantasy, and the subject is also able to project feelings previously repressed. In connection with spontaneous secondary personalities it can be clearly observed that the characteristics of secondary personalities very much reflect the features rejected by the present personality. Producing multiple personalities might be a sort of psychic mechanism that the subject can utilize when striving progressively for greater adaptation and satisfaction. On the other hand, the ability to create secondary personalities spontaneously might be a regressive defence mechanism against an insurpassable intrapsychic conflict. It is remarkable that in connection with both spontaneous and hypnotically-induced multiple personalities the subject preserves his sense of reality. He is not psychotic and can differentiate between his outer and inner world.

In schizophrenia patients frequently have delusional fantasies and hallucinate that they are powerful princes and kings. In these cases, however, the fantasies are indefinite and not integrated functional personalities as in the case of secondary personalities. It can be assumed that in psychoses the trauma to the self-esteem of patients is so extensive that they have to develop grandiose and potent alteregos to compensate for their deep feelings of inferiority.

REFERENCES

Bernstein, M. The search for Bridey Murphy. Garden City, New York: Doubleday, 1956.

Harriman, P.L. The experimental induction of a multiple personality. Psychiatry, 1942, 5, 179-186.

Harriman, P.L. A new approach to multiple personalities. American Journal of Orthopsychiatry, 1943, 13, 638-643.

Kampman, R. Hypnotically induced multiple personality: An experimental study. Acta Universitatis Ouluensis, Series D, Medica No. 6, 1973, Psychiat. No. 3, 7-116.

Kampman, R., & Hirvenoja, R. Research of latent multiple personality phenomenon using hypnosis, projective tests and clinical interview. In D. Langen (editor), Hypnose und Psychosomatische Medizin. Stuttgart: Hippokrates Verlag, 1972. Pp. 106-109.

Kris, E. Psychoanalytic explorations in art. New York: Basic Books, 1934.

Zolik, E.S. An experimental investigation of the psychodynamic implications of the hypnotic "previous existence" fantasy. Journal of Clinical Psychology, 1958, 14, 179-183.

Zolik, E.S. "Reincarnation" phenomena in hypnotic states. International Journal of Parapsychology, 1962, 4, 66-75.

MULTIPLE PERSONALITY: PSYCHODYNAMIC ISSUES AND CLINICAL ILLUSTRATIONS

Milton V. Kline

Institute for Research in Hypnosis, New York
and
Florida Institute of Technology, U.S.A.

Abstract: After a brief history of multiple personality, a number of psychodynamic issues are considered, and a variety of partial states of the self are distinguished. Particular attention is given to the role of hypnotherapy in the development and treatment of multiple personality. Several cases treated by the author are presented in some detail.

Multiple personality is generally considered to be a dissociative personality alteration which affects the patient's state of consciousness and identity. It generally falls within the diagnostic category of hysterical neurosis. There may, however, be some exceptions to this where we find hysterical overlays in an otherwise borderline or psychotic patient. For the most part, dissociative alterations which lead to the development of multiple personalities make use of varying degrees of amnesia, somnambulism, and fugue.

The dynamic and somewhat dramatic history of multiple personality is closely associated with the work of Morton Prince (1929), although there are historical references to much earlier accounts. The most intensive studies were undertaken by Prince. He attempted to deal with dissociation as an aspect of personality dynamics within the framework of a concept of coconsciousness and unconsciousness. He felt strongly that a firm understanding of psychopathology and hypnosis was important in the evolution of the mechanisms of multiple personality. In the attempt to delineate what he referred to as the disintegrative personality, Prince grouped together such phenomena as hypnosis, sleep, dreams, and somnambulism, relating them to motivational factors in the dissociative process which could give rise to alterations of character and to the eventual development, in specific instances, of hallucinations, fixed ideas, amnesia, and related mental mechanisms.

One might differentiate between the presence of double personality and multiple personality, simply according to the number of persons represented. Perhaps a more correct term is dissociated or disintegrated personality, since each secondary personality represents a part of a whole self. Presumably, no one secondary personality preserves the whole ego state or psychological life of the individual.

The choice of altered identity states as an aspect of adaptive defense, in contrast to the utilization of other defense mechanisms, is clearly representative of the cultural, social, and intellectual climate within which the individual exists. It is less fashionable at the present time, and perhaps less useful in an adaptive sense, to develop a multiple personality than it was in past generations.

In reviewing the literature of classic cases of multiple personality, it is clear that all make use of dissociative mechanisms or automatisms which lead to the acting out of unconsciously organized ego states with the evolution of an identity meaningful and useful to that acting out process.

In more fully developed forms, secondary personalities are not unlike those encountered in the "trance states" of mediums and the spontaneously evolving personalities of "reincarnated selves."* In such cases, the secondary personality does not have a completely independent existence but comes out of its repressed state only under special conditions when the subject goes into trance. There is a natural relatedness between multiple personalities, reincarnated selves, and spontaneous trance states (cf. Kline, 1956), and those behavioral characteristics symptomatically represented by amnesia, somnambulism and fugue.

Prince (1929, p. XV), in describing his own interest in multiple personality, wrote: "There is no more fruitful material for the study of the mechanisms and processes of personality than in cases of this sort where there is a disintegration of the normally integrated structural holds and the reassembling of the component elements into new composite holds." Prince (1929) observed in his experimental-clinical studies that different hypnotic states may be distinguished

---

* Identities, such as Bridey Murphy, that sometimes emerge when a hypnotized person is asked to describe earlier and still earlier experiences. (Kline, 1956).

in the same individual and that one might find different and independent systems of memories in each. It is not uncommon at the present time to find certain somatic symptoms linked with rather autonomous systems of memory in individuals who do not display multiple personality but whose overall functioning reveals an hysterical overlay.

Fluctuations and alterations in ego states produce varying characteristics of hypnotic behavior during the course of hypnoanalysis. It is not uncommon for different aspects of regressed behavior to appear during different phases of hypnosis (cf. Kline, 1976) and for the hypnotic state itself to be significantly altered both in depth and intensity.

Prince (1929, p. 19) refers to a case reported by C. Lawe Dickenson of a hypnotized woman who narrated a dream-like fabrication of a highly imaginative character. On one occasion, through the imaginary intervention of the spirit of a fictitious person who supposedly had lived in the time of Richard the Second, she gave a great many details about the Earl and Countess of Salisbury, about other personages of the time, and about the manners and customs of that age. The personages referred to, the details given in connection with them, and especially their geneological foundations, were found on examination to be correct to a degree that would not have been possible without an extensive amount of historical research. After coming out of the hypnotic trance, the subject was completely ignorant about how she could have obtained this knowledge, and could not recall ever having read any book that contained the information she had given. From her automatic writing, however, it was discovered that the information could be found in a book entitled "The Countess Maude" which had been read to her by an aunt when she was a young child.

Meyers (1954) and others have described the manner in which hypnosis and other trance states may facilitate the emergence of reincarnated personalities which, upon careful observation, often appear to be dual or multiple personalities. It would seem that the evolution of multiple personality is dynamically related to the need to act out or to express some aspect of the self which has not been adequately integrated into the total identity. The primary motivation must be sought in the conflicts, dissatisfactions, and inadequacies of the patient's lifestyle. In a simplistic sense, the development of separate states of personal identity or the splitting off of various aspects of the ego into somewhat autonomous and spontaneously generated personalities is not unlike the imaginative process found in the fantasies of children, the daydreams of adolescents, and the wishful thoughts of adults. Sometimes the patients will identify with personalities that they encounter during the course of reading, watching television, or observing a motion picture.

A clinical case of the author's that illustrates this process involved a 22-year-old man who was seen in psychotherapy for a severe case of stuttering that had been present since the age of four. Despite prior psychoanalysis, speech therapy, and behavior modification, he manifested a serious impairment of speech. During hypnosis, he was encouraged to visualize himself and to feel himself participating in those activities that produced anxiety related to speech. A form of assertive training was utilized with the hypnosis to permit him to develop an increased sense of self-mastery, and he was able to utilize this along with self-hypnosis to achieve considerable improvement in his speech. He found that it was possible for him to concentrate better on many tasks and to participate more in certain experiences involving his own association with others when utilizing self-hypnosis. There still remained, however, a distinct impairment, particularly at times of social pressure. He therefore developed the procedure of using self-hypnosis while reading and while watching television or movies. During one of these occasions, he saw the film "The French Connection" in which Gene Hackman portrayed the role of an aggressive uninhibited police officer. The patient identified with Hackman during the film and for one month following this he strengthened the image of Hackman via self-hypnosis. He was even able to produce an excellent simulation of Hackman's speech. When utilizing this personality, there was no visible evidence of stuttering. When the identification became weaker and was not specifically reinforced, his speech reverted to its previous level of difficulty. He has continued to strengthen this image, and his speech has often been flawless.

In some multiple personalities, the induced secondary self has no awareness of the primary self and the primary personality has no awareness of the secondary personality. In other instances, the primary personality may be aware of the existence of the secondary one but may not be in a position to communicate with it. A number of variations of this process are possible depending upon the nature of ego functioning in the individual and the meaningfulness of the altered state of personality that has been created.

In encountering a secondary personality during the course of hypnoanalysis, it is usually possible to find (or to create) additional secondary personalities so that one may evolve a variety of ego states ranging from five to ten or more. It would appear that these may be artifacts of the psychotherapeutic and hypnotic processes. With a patient who manifests a dissociative reaction, it is quite possible to elucidate other states of the self under hypnosis which contain components of the whole ego but which assume autonomous and distinct qualities expressive of various underlying motivational and emotional needs. Some personalities may take on various components of the ego, while others may take on characteristics of the id, and still others, of the super ego. A variety of combinations is possible depending upon the regressive and hypnotic capability of the patient and the techniques of therapy that are utilized (cf. Kline, 1958). While all of this may take place within the hypnotic process, it may also be observed in non-hypnotic but dissociating experiences that are frequently found in some of the newer psychotherapies.

In the following case of the author's, a secondary personality emerged spontaneously. The patient was a 26-year-old married woman, highly intelligent, with an ambition for recognition and worldly success. The only child of a Jewish family, she was strongly motivated to move up the social and economic ladder to a prestigious marriage. She was employed as a school teacher. She was referred by her family physician when she appeared to be confused and disoriented and was actively hallucinating.

During my first session with her, she displayed extreme anxiety about what was happening in her life, as well as much anger toward her husband and parents. She and her husband had been heroin addicts until about one year before her referral for therapy, and since that time both had been on a Methadone program. The patient had married a young man with little formal education and a rather limited income. Shortly after the marriage, he had inherited twenty-five thousand dollars which was used for the purchase of heroin during the period of addiction. During our initial consultation, she indicated that she was in serious legal difficulties because she had been apprehended for issuing checks under an assumed name and for stealing vast amounts of clothing and jewelry from department stores in the city. The name she used on the checks, for which there was no actual account, was different from her own; she identified this person as a young woman named Alice.

Alice was known to the patient and was admired by her. She described her as someone who enjoyed spending time in museums, going to the theatre and ballet, and visiting department stores. She knew that Alice at times moved into her life, but she had no control over her. Alice, on the other hand appeared to have no memory or awareness of the primary personality.

Alice appeared easily during the course of hypnoanalysis. She described herself as the same age as the patient but dramatically different in appearance, personality, and background. The patient was obese, haphazard about her physical appearance, and spoke in a loud, assertive, and somewhat frivolous manner. Alice described herself as thin, extremely well-dressed, and spoke in a distinctly cultivated manner. Alice did not have a job of her own, but indicated that she was very well educated and was married to one of the most prominent attorneys in New York. Since he was so busy, they had relatively little time to spend together, but he would meet her for lunch in the more elegant restaurants in the city and was always interested in the purchases she had made. She indicated that she had a very large wardrobe and that this was necessitated by the fact that her husband had to attend many social and professional affairs to which it was essential that she accompany him.

During the course of hypnoanalysis, it became clear that, from adolescence on, the patient had engaged in a good deal of fantasy and that several images of her self had been shaped during this time. She would project aspects of her self in relation to sexual strivings, social goals, and social recognition. The seeds for the development of a variety of secondary personalities were uncovered with little difficulty, and it appeared that it would be possible to shape them into different ego states with minimal suggestion. However, it was decided not to pursue this approach therapeutically, but rather to work primarily with Alice and to give Alice a more appreciative and realistic understanding of the difficulties that she had been creating for the patient.

Within a six-month period, much of this goal was achieved and Alice indicated a willingness to be of help to the patient and to give up her somewhat autonomous existence. This led to an increasingly realistic approach to living on the part of the patient, including a reappraisal of her marriage and the desire to work towards a constructive change in her husband's vocational and economic difficulties. In this respect, she proved to be supportive and helpful. She also realized the role which her own personality had played in her legal difficulties, and approached the indictment constructively. There was an equitable resolution of the charges.*

At this juncture, Alice and the patient were able to communicate more effectively. With the reintegration of Alice into the primary personality, the patient focused upon the relationship with her parents and, for the first time, was able to delineate the true sources of her conflict. Clarification of these factors in her life coincided with her detoxification from the Methodone, primarily through the use of self-hypnosis.

The spontaneous development of multiple personality as a defense against a conflict that cannot be resolved on any other basis, is clearly indicative of a form of psychopathology that may lead to increasing disorientation, acting out, and serious behavioral consequences. This type of dissociative reaction should therefore be carefully and intensively treated.

---

* The court accepted a full report of her emotional illness and a prison sentence was avoided on the condition that she continue in treatment.

It is not unlikely that, within the framework of many depressive reactions, as well as of borderline disorders, there may be found the dynamics for the elucidation of multiple personalities which have been rigidly repressed and kept in check by ego defenses. In these instances, it would be of value to permit the repressed selves to emerge during therapy and to deal with them with the goal of ultimate reintegration. Very often their emergence will lead spontaneously to a remission of the presenting symptoms.

In an instance that illustrates this circumstance, a 24-year-old psychiatric nurse was seen for symptoms of depression accompanied by the excessive use of alcohol. During the initial session, she displayed an inability to perform a variety of motor and verbal tasks. Under hypnosis, a secondary personality emerged and indicated that she disliked the patient very much and that, while she was aware of the patient, the patient was unaware of her. The implication was that the patient was on the verge of becoming more aware and she appeared to be telling me that this was something I should know.

The secondary personality, who preferred not to have a name at first but later referred to herself as Maria, was vivacious and outgoing to the point of impulsiveness, and indicated that the sexual inhibitions and repressions of the patient were attributes that she personally scorned and she had no use for. Maria, who had been allowed to emerge only very rarely, was sexually promiscuous and would use every opportunity to become involved in sexual affairs.

As therapy progressed, it became apparent that the patient had experienced during the past year short fugue states that were, in fact, periods of somnambulism. In addition to the secondary personality described as Maria, two additional personalities were uncovered eventually which constituted strong departures from the strict religious mores and inhibitions of the patient herself. As the multiple personalities were permitted to have greater existence within the therapeutic framework, the patient's depression lifted, and she became more outgoing and capable of undertaking those tasks and activities which before had seemed impossible.

In this case, it was clear that the suppression of the multiple personalities, as well as of the ego strivings and needs contained within them, had produced the symptoms of depression. In some phases of therapy with this patient, the elucidated personality was permitted to have increased existence outside the therapeutic framework, with the understanding that she would always indicate the extent of her anticipated activities, and that she would maintain some contact with the patient herself.

This proved to be an effective means of beginning the slow process of integration. Over a period of several years, this very complex and seriously disturbed young woman was able to integrate the various phases of her own unconscious strivings into one increasingly acceptable self. In this role, she made major changes in her life including a divorce and remarriage, became a supportive and effective mother, and changed her career to correspond with her own aspirations and needs.

In this instance, the proliferation of multiple personalities was clearly adaptive, both in terms of the presenting symptoms and the eventual reintegration. Like so many patients within this classification, it was clear that she had lapsed into spontaneous trance-states at various times during her life.

During the course of therapy with patients in which hypnosis has not necessarily been used, I have found a tendency towards dissociative reactions when patients have been exposed to such quasi-therapeutic procedures as certain types of encounter groups, emotional intensification, imagery, and out-of-body experiences. In such circumstances, dissociative reactions are likely to occur in individuals with precarious or fragile personality structures, who may begin to show disintegrative characteristics.

The development of multiple personality is not unrelated to the capacity for the creative development of individual needs and the expression of unexpressed qualities of the self. This process, in individuals capable of constructive unconscious cognition and adaptive fantasy, may lead to an enlargement of the parameters of their own identity. On the other hand, in individuals with underlying hysterical mechanisms, unstructured dissociative activities may lead ultimately to the development of characteristics of multiple personality. Multiple personality may, then, be viewed as an extension of an individual's need for an enriched and enlarged sense of self where that need has been denied creative expression.

REFERENCES

Kline, M.V. A scientific report on the search for Bridey Murphy. New York: Julian Press, 1956.

Kline, M.V. Freud and hypnosis. New York: Julian Press, 1958.

Kline, M.V. Emotional flooding: A technique in sensory hypnoanalysis. In P. Olsen (editor), Emotional flooding. New York: Human Sciences Press, 1976.

Meyers, F.W.H. Human personality and its survival of bodily death, Vol. I and II. New York: Langmans, Green and Co., 1954.

Prince, M. The unconscious. New York: The MacMillan Company, 1929.

SIMILARITIES AND DISSIMILARITIES BETWEEN HYPNOSIS AND BEHAVIOR THERAPY*

William S. Kroger

University of California, Los Angeles, U.S.A.

Abstract: Hypnosis can potentiate behavior therapy by making the therapeutic experience more vivid and realistic. Hypnotherapists should be alerted to covert conditioning procedures to facilitate this approach.

Both hypnotic and behavior techniques make use of expectancies, demand characteristics, and reinforcement principles. "Shaping" or "successive approximation" is similar to the steps of "working through" a problem, the method used by hypnotherapists. Both personalize their approach stressing "homework" between sessions. Both use aversive techniques, counterconditioning (reconditioning in the hypnosis literature), positive reinforcements, and self-reinforcement. Thought stopping is similar to autosuggestions for interrupting a stimulus-response pattern. Both use modeling, via fantasy evocation in hypnosis and with in vivo techniques during behavior therapy.

There are, however, some basic differences. Behavior therapy attempts to change and sustain behavior with reinforcement; thus, attitude change follows. Hypnotherapists traditionally attempt to change attitudes assuming behavioral change will follow. Many also attempt to give "insight" into the "cause." Behavior therapists are not interested in exploring the past.

---

* Kroger, W.S., & Fezler, W.D. Hypnosis and behavior modification: Imagery conditioning. Philadelphia, J.B. Lippincott, 1976, pp. 76-80.

A second difference between hypnotherapy and behavior therapy is that hypnotherapy is more permissive, while behavior therapists are more directive; the focus is on the target behaviors to be changed. Ignored are psychodynamic or hypnoanalytic techniques such as interpretation of the transference and dreams, nature of resistances, and uncovering of memories. Directive suggestions, desensitization, and assertive training are also used.

A unique and ingenious contribution by behavior therapy is the hierarchy used for desensitization. Time distortion, glove anesthesia, age regression, and sensory recall via imagery are the unique contributions made by hypnotherapy.

There are several important areas where hypnosis and behavior therapy cross-fertilize. Unfortunately this interaction has been ignored until recently. Some leaders in the behavior school are conversant with current sophisticated hypnotic techniques and are incorporating these in a multi-modal approach (Lazarus, 1971). As greater knowledge of hypnosis is disseminated, behavior therapists are becoming increasingly aware that some of their techniques have been employed by hypnotherapists for years. The latter have used these techniques intuitively in conjunction with learning theory in a manner unmistakenly recognized as behavior therapy. A basic similarity is that both approaches utilize relaxation. It is axiomatic that relaxation and anxiety are incompatible responses and cannot co-exist at the same time in the same person. Therefore, inasumch as most psychologic problems are associated with anxiety, it is difficult to assess how much of the result obtained with either hypnosis or behavior therapy is due to these modalities or the combination of relaxation plus non-specific placebo effects.

Therapists of both schools have become aware that hypnosis can potentiate the precise techniques employed by behavior therapists, thus making the therapeutic experience more vivid and realistic (Barrios, 1973; Astor, 1973; Dengrove, 1975; Cautela, 1975; Kroger, 1975). When experiences are revivified imaginally under hypnosis, they closely approximate the effects achieved by "in vivo" desensitization.

Unique and ingenious contributions made by behavior therapists are observational learning or "modeling" and the successive approximation or step by step progression called a hierarchy. This is referred to by behavior therapists as systematic desensitization. Some investigators (Fuchs, Hoch, Paldi, Abramovici, Brandes, Timor-Tritsch, & Kleinhaus, 1973) have employed hypnodesensitization. Under hypnosis the patient can be confronted with a hierarchy of anxiety-provoking stimuli until eventually even the strongest of these fails to evoke any degree of anxiety in him. Stated another way, it appears that hypnosis raises the anxiety tolerance level. On the other hand, hypnotherapists should be alerted to covert conditioning procedures to facilitate their approach (Cautela 1975).

SIMILARITIES

Therapists in both schools make use of expectancies, demand characteristics, and reinforcement principles. Both reinforce their patients' efforts with praise. Also, both maximize the probability of patient success by not demanding too much too soon. The hypnotherapist may suggest to his patient that a desired feeling such as anesthesia is just beginning to develop and is growing. It may happen this session or at home in practice; no demand is made for immediate production of a given response. The same tactic of shaping, or successive approximation is used by the behaviorist. He may desensitize a patient to stage fright, for example, by first having him see himself in front of one person in a living room, then among a small group of friends in a meeting room, and finally in front of an audience in an auditorium.

Those using these therapies personalize their approach. The patient is not forced into a procedural mold; if one method fails, others are available. In both approaches current situations are of major concern. Both therapies also stress "homework" between treatment sessions. In hypnotherapy this involves practice in self-hypnosis and the use of auto-suggestions. In behavior therapy, homework assignments might consist of overt behavior practice such as saying "no" to certain demands at work or ignoring a spouse's complaining. Some similarities also exist in techniques of operant conditioning used by behavior therapists and the double bind strategies employed by hypnotherapists.

The hypnobehavioral model accepts the tenets of both schools of thought. Attitude change leads to behavioral change and behavioral change leads to attitude change. However, an attempt is made to change both attitude and behavior <u>in conjunction</u>. It is not necessary to work on only one in the hope that the other will follow; both are dealt with directly and simultaneously. If, for example, an individual is driven to smoke through anxiety caused by a nagging spouse, the couple is counseled not only in an attempt to produce attitude changes toward each other, but is also given instructions for eliminating the smoking behavior by aversive techniques utilized under hypnosis.

Hypnotherapists encourage free expression by the patient. They are directive to the point of encouraging recall of positive feeling states so that the patient can "turn them on" as he needs them. Hypnotic recall of past trauma might provide insight or understanding and serve to desensitize the patient to his fears. While the behaviorist and hypnobehaviorist are relatively directive, they are not authoritarian. Like the traditional psychotherapist, they constantly seek clarification and patients' feedback.

Both behavior modifiers and hypnotherapists are similar in that they take a history, and attempt to identify the original cause or causes of the disorder, reduce anxiety, ccrrect misconceptions, and outline objectives. They both also might extend therapy to the family and other significant figures in the patient's life.

Aversion Therapy and Hypnotherapy

Weitzenhoffer (1972) was puzzled by the omission in the behavior literature of the use of hypnosis with aversive techniques. Its use dates back to the late nineteenth century or earlier, during which nicotinism, morphinism, and alcoholism were thus treated in Europe. Commonly, hypnotic suggestions ranging from moderate disgust to nausea and vomiting were associated with the patient's contact with the addictive substance. Use of this type of hypnotic aversion therapy has been described (Kroger, 1970; Hershman, 1955, 1956; Erickson, 1954; Wolberg, 1948; Feamster & Brown, 1963; Von Dedenroth, 1964a, 1964b; Kroger & Fezler, 1976).

Counterconditioning and Hypnotherapy

Counterconditioning is a modification technique which is also found in the hypnosis literature but under different labels. Wolberg (1948) gives two of the earliest accounts of hypnosis applied in the context of counterconditioning (he called it *reconditioning*). One patient experienced an intense dislike for orange juice while another experienced profound unease and discomfort in the presence of people. Treatment for both patients consisted of hypnotically inducing fantasies in which the problem stimulus (oranges, people) was experienced in association with hypnotically induced feelings of pleasure, happiness, relaxation, and peace. Erickson (1955) used hypnosis to countercondition the behavior of two patients with cosmetic problems caused by dental defects by associating positive feelings with these defects. Kroger and Freed (1951) used hypnosis to countercondition the response to itching associated with pruritus vulvae.

Positive Reinforcement and Hypnotherapy

Hypnotherapists have also made use of the behaviorist's principles of positive reinforcement in their treatment. Hershman (1955, 1956) and Kroger (1970) used hypnosis to help their patients associate pleasant, positive feelings with the desired behavior (abstinence from smoking, consuming less food, and eating only the right foods). Von Dedenroth (1964a, 1964b) and Kroger (1967) describe a treatment for smoking where, through hypnotic suggestions, various good feelings are associated with a particular sequence of activities in which smoking is prohibited.

Miscellaneous Techniques

Other behavioral techniques have hypnotherapeutic analogues. "Thought stopping" closely resembles a hypnotic procedure used by Ludwig, Lyle, and Miller (1964) for treating drug addicts. In this case, complex posthypnotic suggestions were employed to evoke hallucinations which acted as automatic thought-stoppers. The hallucinations were triggered by thoughts of using drugs. Another instance of thought-stopping in hypnotherapy is described by Spiegel (1970) in the treatment of smokers. The smoker reaffirms his commitment to maintaining good health whenever he feels the urge to smoke.

Self-reinforcement as an active agent is an important factor in many hypnotherapeutic procedures. Meyer and Tilker (1969) gave their patients with character disorders posthypnotic suggestions to reward their own appropriate actions by strong, immediate self-approval. A modeling technique was used by Ludwig, Lyle, and Miller (1964) in an attempt to cure drug addiction. Hypnotized drug addicts were repeatedly instructed to "watch" a television show in fantasy in which the hero overcame his desire for drugs.

DIFFERENCES BETWEEN BEHAVIOR THERAPY AND TRADITIONAL HYPNOTHERAPY

The behavior therapist focuses on that which is observable and measurable. He is on the qui vive for specific situations where maladaptive response does or does not occur. Furthermore he is more interested in the modification of the presenting behavior that requires changing than in searching for psychodynamic factors.

The behavioral approach pays special attention to systematic manipulation of the environmental determinants and behavioral variables related to the maladaptive functioning. The behavior therapist, where possible, attempts to identify the initial problem and to assess the behaviors requiring change, and formulates a program for change. He also can present evidence of change by offering charts of the patient's progress. He is not only concerned with the problem behaviors but with the consequences. He will try to determine under what circumstances the faulty behavior occurs. He also makes full use of conditioning and learning theory, believing that a faulty behavior is unadaptive and can be unlearned.

In contrast to hypnotherapy, behavior therapy also permits the testing of clinical hypotheses by the systematic manipulation of behavioral and environmental variables thought to be related to the patient's problem behavior. The principal goal is to change and modify the behavior.

On the other hand many hypnotherapists are interested in the psychodynamics responsible for a symptom. They often make use of hypnoanalytical techniques as well as ideomotor signaling, time distortion (condensation and expansion), glove anesthesia, age regression and revivification, negative and positive hallucinations, and automatic writing. These have no counterparts in behavior therapy.

Symptom utilization techniques used by directive hypnotherapists, such as symptom substitution, symptom intensification, symptom transformation, and symptom amelioration have been described in the behavior therapy literature but not conceptually integrated into behavior therapy per se.

There are other dissimilarities between behavior therapy and hypnotherapy as well as some basic operational differences. The primary focus of behavior modification is to change and sustain behavior with reinforcement; attitude change will naturally follow. Traditionally, hypnotherapists attempt attitude change first and assume that behavioral change will follow. The behaviorists claim "you are what you do," and if you can change the behavior you will in time come to feel the role you are playing. The school of psychodynamic psychotherapy which many hypnotherapists have followed, argues that one must first develop insight before any lasting change can take place. For instance, clinicians following that school believe that another symptom will manifest itself in place of the phobia if a patient is helped to rid himself of his phobic behavior without first resolving the underlying conflicts. There is no concrete evidence that such symptom substitution does occur.

Another basic difference is found in the therapeutic relationship. Historically the behavior therapist has been less permissive. While the hypnotherapist in an attempt to maximize free expression is receptive and interested in everything said by the patient, the behaviorist pays little attention to the patient's discussion of historical information. Verbalized feelings of hopelessness or despair ("sick talk") are ignored. Moss and Bremer (1973) state that as the behavior therapist's primary focus is on the development of assets, talk of liabilities is minimized. Approval is made deliberately contingent rather than unconditional.

Use of guided imagination, fantasy evocation, and sensory imagery conditioning are used by hypnotists and behavior therapists. Kroger and Fezler (1976) have combined the two therapies into a hypnobehavioral model. These authors advocate the use of standardized images tailored for specific clinical entities. When these images are employed under hypnosis they are experienced with greater vividness. However, it should be emphasized that all forms of covert conditioning involve images of one type or another.

COMMENTS

American psychiatry is currently experiencing an identity crisis. It is riding off vigorously in all directions and has been splintered by many disparate groups claiming effectiveness for their particular school of psychotherapy. It has been estimated that the placebo effect in psychotherapy is around 65%. It is apparent that the conviction that cure will occur, in many instances leads to cure; and psychologically ill people are cured in the manner by which they expect to be cured! Solutions will ultimately be provided by the data of scientific investigation. The biomedical engineers and neuropharmacologists will soon overtake us with their findings. As Norbert Wiener prophetically once said "Psychology is like a tapeworm. It is losing more and more of its segments to mathematics."

It is possible that both hypnosis and behavior therapy will fall into the category of phenomena of conviction, once better criteria of cure are developed, and when more rigid assessment of various therapies becomes available. Both rely heavily on demand characteristics, the effects of implicit or explicit cues, role playing, and expectancies. A hypnobehaviorist purposefully and knowingly uses both hypnosis and behavior techniques in conjunction. If he has been using one technique (hypnosis) and borrowing from the other without realizing what he has been doing, he cannot be truly classified as a hypnobehaviorist. The behavior modifier has to know how to apply the precise technique used in behavior modification.

Treatment, in any type of psychotherapy, is a mutual endeavor in which the rapport or strength of the interpersonal relationship is one of the important elements. Belief, confidence, and conviction that the method will work are also important factors. The universality of suggestion in any type of psychotherapy is well recognized. Thigpen and Cleckley (1964), in a discussion of psychoanalysis, hypnosis, and faith healing, and the role of the latter in the conditioning therapies suggest:

> If we learn that we are working chiefly through the imperfectly understood but powerful effects of faith, let us admit it to be so, use it with more insight, and seek better and more straightforward means of application.

REFERENCES

Astor, M.H. Hypnosis and behavior modification combined with psychanalytic psychotherapy. International Journal of Clinical and Experimental Hypnosis, 1973, 21, 18-24.

Barrios, A.A. Posthypnotic suggestion as higher-order conditioning: A methodological and experimental analysis. International Journal of Clinical and Experimental Hypnosis, 1973, 21, 32-50.

Cautela, J.R. The use of covert conditioning in hypnotherapy. International Journal of Clinical and Experimental Hypnosis, 1975, 23, 15-27.

Dengrove, E. Hypnosis and behavior therapy. Springfield: Charles C. Thomas, 1975.

Erickson, M.H. Indirect hypnotic therapy of an enuretic couple. International Journal of Clinical and Experimental Hypnosis, 1954, 2, 171-174.

Feamster, J.H., & Brown, J.E. Hypnotic aversion to alcohol: Three-year follow-up on one patient. American Journal of Clinical Hypnosis, 1963, 6, 164-166.

Fuchs, K., Hoch, Z., Paldi, E., Abramovici, H., Brandes, J.M., Timor-Tritsch, I., & Kleinhaus, M. Hypno-desensitization therapy of vaginismus: Part I "in vitro" method. Part II "in vivo" method. International Journal of Clinical and Experimental Hypnosis, 1973, 21, 144-156.

Hershman, S. Hypnosis in the treatment of obesity. International Journal of Clinical and Experimental Hypnosis, 1955, 3, 136-139.

Hershman, S. Hypnosis and excessive smoking. International Journal of Clinical and Experimental Hypnosis, 1956, 4, 24-29.

Kroger, W.S. Thanks, doctor, I've stopped smoking. Springfield: Charles C. Thomas, 1967.

Kroger, W.S. Comprehensive management of obesity. American Journal of Clinical Hypnosis, 1970, 12, 165-176.

Kroger, W.S. Behavior modification and hypnotic conditioning. In E. Dengrove, (editor), Hypnosis and behavior therapy. Springfield: Charles C. Thomas, 1975, Pp. 379-388.

Kroger, W.S., & Fezler, W.D. Hypnosis and behavior modification: Imagery conditioning. Philadelphia: J.B. Lippincott, 1976.

Kroger, W.S., & Freed, S.C. Psychosomatic gynecology: Including problems of obstetrical care. Philadelphia: W.B. Saunders, 1951.

Lazarus, A. Behavior therapy and beyond. New York: McGraw-Hill, 1971.

Ludwig, A.M., Lyle, W.H., & Miller, J.S. Group hypnotherapy techniques with drug addicts. International Journal of Clinical and Experimental Hypnosis, 1964, 12, 53-66.

Meyer, R.G., & Tilker, H.A. The clinical use of direct hypnotic suggestion: A traditional technique in the light of current approaches. International Journal of Clinical and Experimental Hypnosis, 1969, 17, 81-88.

Spiegel, H. A single-treatment method to stop smoking using ancillary self-hypnosis. International Journal of Clinical and Experimental Hypnosis, 1970, 18, 235-250.

Thigpen, C.H., & Cleckley, H.M. Some reflections on psychoanalysis, hypnosis, and faith healing in the conditioning therapies. In J.S. Wolpe, A. Salter, & L.J. Reyna (editors), The conditioning therapies: The challenge of psychotherapy. New York: Holt, Rinehart, and Winston, 1964.

Von Dedenroth, T.E. The use of hypnosis with "tobaccomaniacs." American Journal of Clinical Hypnosis, 1964a, 6, 326-331.

Von Dedenroth, T.E. Further help for the "tobaccomaniacs." American Journal of Clinical Hypnosis, 1964b, 6, 332-336.

Weitzenhoffer, A.M. Behavior therapeutic techniques and hypnotherapeutic methods. American Journal of Clinical Hypnosis, 1972, 15, 71-82.

Wolberg, L.R. The principles of hypnotherapy: Medical hypnosis, Vol. 1. New York: Grune and Stratton, 1948.

HYPNOSIS IN THE CONTEXT OF BEHAVIOR THERAPY

Arnold A. Lazarus and Robert A. Karlin

Rutgers University, U.S.A.

Abstract: Behavior therapy, while retaining a primary allegiance to principles of scientific rigor, is no longer bound to narrow stimulus-response theories as in the early 1960's. Its purview now encompasses human responses that stem from internal as well as external sources. No longer is it necessary to reject or play down the significance of "cognitions," "imagery," or related covert processes. Hypnosis, which had long been recognized as a useful way of facilitating behavioral change directly, is now also seen as helpful in altering internal events that, in turn, indirectly bring about desired behavioral change. Furthermore, besides affecting cognitive, memory and perceptual processes, hypnosis is presented as a powerful placebo. Given the specific expectancies and various demand characteristics of the hypnotic context, hypnosis can facilitate a wide range of behavioral techniques. The present paper briefly discusses the impact of hypnosis across various modalities - behavior, affect, sensation, imagery, cognition, and interpersonal relationships. There is some discussion of trance-specific effects in terms of graphic imagery, and in the general areas of pain control and amnesia.

Hypnosis is probably one of the oldest of the major forces in secular psychotherapy, and formalized behavior therapy is probably the youngest. There are some interesting similarities between the two, however, that are not immediately obvious. One major similarity is the amount of misunderstanding and misinterpretation that both have engendered.

Extremely misleading stereotypes about behavior therapy abound. The range extends from those who view behavioral approaches to clinical problems with benevolent amusement as naive, simplistic, mechanistic, superficial - of marginal value in reducing minor symptoms - to the Orwellian alarmists who see behavior therapy as dangerously manipulative, Machiavellian, coercive and dehumanizing. Since its formal inception as a distinctive scientific and clinical discipline some 20 years ago, behavior therapy has undergone tremendous growth. This proliferation of ideas has led behavior therapy to mean different things to different individuals. Yet most behavior therapists would subscribe to the notion that a behavioral orientation presupposes a close adherence to a combination of social and cognitive learning theories and stringent scientific methods which are systematically applied to the clinical scene. Whenever possible, the behavior therapist adapts the findings and methodology of the laboratory scientist to the complex and less structured world of the clinic and the natural environment.

In short, while behavior therapy owes a certain historical allegiance to M and M's, shocked cats and salivating dogs, it needs to be stressed that over the past five or six years, behavior therapy has assumed a conceptual sophistication that differs markedly from the constraints of the stimulus-response models of the early sixties. There is no longer an eschewal of "cognitive processes," or "private events." A new and progressive behavioral genre emphasizes the importance of various mediating constructs and deals with "internal events," yet without recourse to any superfluous superstructures or mentalistic forces. As Lazarus and Wilson (1976) point out: "To be truly dynamic, behavior modification must somehow combine scientific rigor with an open-minded spirit of inquiry which holds nothing sacrosanct, which has no disciples, and which is ever open to self-correction on the basis of empirically derived data."

While behavior therapy is wide open to clinical experimentation, its practitioners avoid techniques that have no demonstrable empirical support. Methods based purely on inference, speculation, hearsay, fanciful notions, or emotional appeal, have no place in the data-based orientation of behavior therapy. Practicing clinicians, however, need to proceed outside the boundaries of behavior therapy and behavioral techniques from time to time. It has become clear that there are many useful "nonbehavioral" techniques and strategies, and it is a serious error to equate <u>any</u> effective method with "behavior therapy."

Prior to the late 1960's behavior therapists who came to hypnosis did so with considerable misgivings. Sutcliffe (1960) and Barber (1969) outlined some of the fundamentals of the skeptical point of view about hypnosis. Their work paralleled the views expounded by many of those who operated from a behavioral framework as well. That is, until recently, hypnosis was seen as a combination of folie à deux and placebo, useful for patients who believed in it and wanted it, but possessing few if any special or intrinsic qualities.

Further, early behavior therapists, eager to differentiate their techniques from those of other schools, were eager to point out that hypnosis played little part in the effectiveness of their procedures. Lang and his colleagues (Lang, Lazovik, & Reynolds, 1965; Lang, 1969) showed that success using desensitization procedures was unrelated to the patient's hypnotizability. This finding made it difficult to dismiss desensitization as "mere hypnosis." Likewise Paul (1969) demonstrated that progressive relaxation could be more effective than hypnotic suggestion. However, with the growth of well-controlled studies on the specific effects of hypnosis and the increasing willingness of behavior therapists to consider internal mediating events, it seems possible that behavior therapy and hypnosis can provide some useful insights and techniques for each other (cf. Dengrove, 1976).

During the past few years the concept of multimodal behavior therapy has evolved (Lazarus, 1973a, 1976). This orientation emphasizes how specific problems in specific areas of functioning (modalities) are affected by specific treatments. The present paper considers hypnosis in light of both its specific and non-specific effects in each of these modalities. Why consider both specific and non-specific effects? We would stress that as practicing clinicians we are as interested in what our patients expect hypnosis to do to them as we are in trance-specific effects.

Hypnosis as an Effective Placebo

Hypnosis has such strong placebo effects that it is possible for a therapist to specify some of the results of using hypnosis with a cooperative patient almost independently of that patient's trance capacity. The reasons for this are simple. For example, hypnosis may induce relaxation not because of any demonstrable quality of trance per se, but because patients believe that when hypnotized, they will fully relax. Therefore, one can use either auto- or heterohypnosis to relax patients relatively quickly without a formal training procedure. Further, we should not dismiss the fact that hypnosis can be a placebo in the broadest sense of the word. Lazarus (1973b), in a clinical study, showed that clients who believe that hypnosis will facilitate therapeutic progress often possess a self-fulfilling prophesy that enhances positive outcomes. Clients who requested hypnosis and received a standard relaxation sequence that substituted the word "hypnosis" for "relaxation" wherever possible, showed more subjective and objective improvements than those who received ordinary relaxation training. Additional clients who had not specifically requested either hypnosis or relaxation showed no differences when treated by either or both methods.

The importance of these kinds of placebo effects cannot be overestimated. Behavior therapy researchers have become very aware of the difficulties involved in producing effects greater than those generated by attention placebo conditions. A study by Steinmark and Borkovec (1974) clearly illustrated how much ingenuity is involved when separating active treatments from placebo effects.

Park and Covi (1965) have demonstrated how, even when patients are aware that they are receiving placebos, these treatments may still have positive effects, even in long-term and serious psychological disorders. The problem, then, often is to maximize the effectiveness of our placebos (Fish, 1973). Goldstein's (1971) significant work on effort and attraction in psychotherapy stands out in this area.

For therapeutic effectiveness, it is vital that a placebo be perceived as powerful. Evans (1974) recently noted that psychopharmacological placebos given in place of analgesics are more potent when patients think they are powerful drugs rather than weak drugs. He estimated that when a placebo took the place of aspirin it provided slightly more than half the pain relief of aspirin. However, when placebos were given in place of morphine, patients reported slightly more than half the analgesic effects found with <u>morphine</u>. Thus, when a placebo is presented as a powerful agent it is more effective. It cannot be overemphasized that hypnosis is a powerful placebo. Some patients believe hypnosis to be a highly efficacious procedure in the treatment of many conditions. Thus, despite the fact that there is little or no evidence that hypnosis is more effective than waking agreement in producing posthypnotic compliance, hypnosis may nonetheless produce such compliance in a clinical population because patients strongly believe that it should do so.

Let us examine another parallel between hypnosis and behavior therapy. Many behavior therapy procedures which we now have good reason to consider ineffective (such as the use of hand shockers with alcoholics) produced very good results when originally developed. Our strong belief in the animal model produced faith in techniques derived from animal analogues (Orne 1975). It must be remembered that many procedures work in psychotherapy not because of the reasons their advocates claim, but rather because of the faith and confidence that their advocates communicate. While it is our role as scientists to debunk fallacious rationales, it is our duty as practitioners to use our own and our patient's enthusiasms, within reason.

THE BASIC ID

As outpatient behavior therapy has broadened over the years, it has increasingly moved away from simplistic animal models. Narrow band behavior therapy has given way to broad-spectrum behavior therapy. The significance of cognitive processes and the subtle range of interpersonal relationships are now well within the purview of behavior therapy (Mahoney, 1974; Goldfried & Davison, 1976). More recently we have become interested in the full range of the individual's activities which have been studied in non-patient populations by experimental psychologists. These include maladaptive behaviors, negative emotions, unpleasant sensations, intrusive images, faulty cognitions, interpersonal shortcomings, and biochemical imbalances.

In addition to maladaptive responses, we are also concerned with the client's <u>deficits</u> across each modality - the <u>absence</u> of useful behaviors, pleasant feelings, good sensations. Thus, the major assessment framwork examines responses within each modality that are best <u>decreased</u>, as well as those that are best <u>increased</u>.

The model employed may be viewed as "actualization," "growth," or "educational" rather than as one based upon disease analogies, medicine, or pathology. Everyone can benefit from a change in behavior that eliminates unwanted or surplus reactions while stepping up the frequency, duration, and intensity of useful, creative, fulfilling responses. Similarly, the control or absence of unpleasant emotions coupled with an increase in positive feelings is a most worthy goal. In the sensory modality, while applying techniques to eliminate negative sensations (ranging from terrifying pain to mild but chronic muscular tension), the growth-enhancing elements concern precise ways of deriving more pleasure and meaning from each of our senses. Imagery refers to the wide range of "mental pictures" which ultimately coalesce in a series of "self-images" which we try to make overridingly positive rather than negative. Faulty assumptions and irrational cognitions clearly undermine our day-to-day living, and are replaced by as many reality-oriented, factual, and rational assumptions as can be mustered. And good, close, and rewarding interpersonal relationships call for specific skills and an elaborate series of prosocial interactions which everyone would do well to cultivate.

We have referred to behavior, affect, sensation, imagery, cognition, and interpersonal processes. These specific dimensions are all interactive and yet sufficiently discrete to preserve their own locus of control. But there is a non-psychological modality that cannot be ignored. Neurological and biochemical factors influence behavior, affective responses, sensations, images, cognitions, and interpersonal responses. If we subsume these organic or physiological processes under the term "Drugs," as a generic symbol for this biological substrate, a useful acronym emerges. The first letter taken from Behavior, Affect, Sensation, Imagery, Cognition, Interpersonal, and Drugs spells BASIC ID. The mnemonic advantages of this acronym are extremely useful. It serves as a constant compass to orient therapists towards the client's entire network of interactive modalities.

Let us look at how hypnosis can be useful in treating problems in each of these modalities.

Behavior

There is no evidence to date that any specific effects of hypnosis can change behavior directly except in the most limited sense. While in the moderate to high hypnotizable population, post-hypnotic suggestion can produce some automatic compliance for a relatively short period of time, there are no indications that such effects last more than two weeks in and of themselves (Gaunitz, Unestahl, & Berglund, 1975). Nor are there any data of which we are aware to suggest that one can elicit more behavioral compliance through post-hypnotic suggestion than by simply having someone in the waking state agree to do something. If anything, the reverse is true (Orne, 1971). Simple agreements between an experimenter and a subject result in more compliance than post-hypnotic suggestion.

However, some people believe that if they are told in trance not to smoke any more, they will not do so, and for them it works (Spiegel, 1970). We all realize that the treatment chosen should be compatible with the beliefs and needs of the individual patient. In this context, the effective and creative use of post-hypnotic suggestions to achieve significant behavior change is almost unlimited. Many years ago, Lazarus (1958) stressed the importance of autohypnosis as a post-hypnotic variant for inducing more permanent changes. In behavior therapy, post-hypnotic suggestions are primarily employed to assist clients in carrying out various homework assignments - to behave more assertively, to cut down on cigarette smoking, to reduce overeating, to start exercising, to increase prosocial interaction, etc. In short, hypnosis can facilitate the behavior therapist's attempts to systematically increase a patient's range of prosocial, positive, adaptive behaviors, while reducing or extinguishing negative, surplus or maladaptive responses.

Affect

Turning to emotions, or affect, hypnosis in the behavioral context is once again most useful because of its placebo effects. Since patients believe hypnosis is necessarily tranquilizing, we frequently employ it for anxiety-relief conditioning. Lazarus (1971) described the method as follows:

> The patient relaxes on a comfortable reclining chair or on a well-upholstered couch or bed, and is given repeated suggestions to feel more and more relaxed, pleasantly warm and heavy, drowsy and sleepy, calm and peaceful. Ever more deep and satisfying levels of calm and serenity are suggested over and over. This procedure continues for about 10 to 15 minutes, or until it is obvious (from psychophysiological measurement or direct observation) that the patient is profoundly relaxed and calm. The patient is then requested to think about the words "calmly relaxed" over and over, and to associate these verbal cues with the ongoing physiological and psychological states of tranquility. The patient is then informed that in tension or anxiety-producing situations, he/she will find the words "calmly relaxed" capable of relieving anxiety if uttered subvocally several times. (pp. 225-226).

When "hypnosis" is specifically added it is because the patient believes that trance is a relaxing experience. Thus the self-defeating effort some patients expend in trying to relax is avoided. Karlin and McKeon (1976) describe a case treated in this fashion. A 29 year-old single woman was taught to induce relaxation using autohypnosis. A long history of anxiety attacks, antisocial phobias, and test anxiety was immediately relieved when this procedure was used. Instead of a vicious cycle of negative sensations, fears, irrational cognitions, interpersonal clumsiness, and frightening images, the patient was able to substitute a one minute period in "trance" using the phrase "calm," as well as images of pleasant scenes. Treatment in other modalities was then able to proceed apace.

In the affective modality, the use of hypnosis can facilitate a wide range of techniques that serve to elicit and modify specific feelings and emotions. For example, hypnotic abreaction, regression, hypnotic dream induction, and time projection are well-known "hypnotherapy" techniques that were described long before the advent of "behavior therapy." As Dengrove (1976) points out, these techniques can play an important role in the practice of behavior therapy.

Sensation

The sensory modality is one area where specific rather than nonspecific effects of hypnosis become evident. Here the most obvious example is the case of pain control. The ability of highly hypnotizable subjects to maintain control of pain is well supported by both anecdotal and experimental data (McGlashan, Evans, & Orne,

1969; Garrett & Wallace, 1975). For the behavior therapist, pain control may be an end in itself, or a necessary intermediate step in the creation of a therapeutic relationship. In the latter case, a patient may be unable or unwilling to take part in an exploration of maladaptive interpersonal relationships or irrational cognitions when experiencing severe and chronic pain. As well as making direct suggestions about pain, the behavior therapist will very carefully explore all the other modalities. Even if pain is organically based, it will produce a series of changes in behavior, affect, cognitions, and interpersonal relationships. Behaviors of significant others in the environment will often reinforce the patient's pain-related behaviors and thus maintain higher degrees of discomfort than necessary (Fordyce, 1976). Pain control clinics have emerged in which pain is treated essentially as an operant. It is assumed that if one can eliminate the functional reinforcement for pain-related behavior, pain itself will be ameliorated. Similarly, medications in such clinics are given on the basis of reinforcement theory. (When heightened pain is rewarded by medication which relieves the pain, the sensations of pain are reinforced. This seems to produce high levels of reported pain and the need for higher dosages of medication). Reinforcement theory predicts, and pain clinics often find, that when medication is given on a fixed schedule, patients experience less pain. When hypnosis is used, a patient's ability to directly ameliorate pain is added to the standard behavioral treatment and a powerful combination is formed.

Hypnosis has also proved useful in heightening *pleasant* sensations. The enhancement of sensory input has been particularly helpful in the treatment of certain sexual disorders as well as in some depressive reactions. By increasing the awareness of sensual pleasure, non-orgasmic women have reported impressive breakthroughs. They were instructed, under hypnosis, to relax and to experience an ever-greater awareness of relevant tactile pleasures. In one case, the use of "stimulus words" was employed. The client would think the words "sexy feelings" subvocally during foreplay and reported a transfer of relaxation and subjective enjoyment. It is not clear that these effects were due to the "hypnosis," per se, although the latter may have facilitated the therapeutic process.

Similarly, certain people complaining of depression were hypnotized and told to recapture various bodily pleasures. For example, one man who complained of physical and emotional numbness was hypnotized and was taken through a series of events that had previously been positively reinforcing. He pictured himself sequentially taking a warm shower, eating ice cream, driving in an open sportscar, smoking an imported cigar, etc. For the first 15 or 20 minutes, he protested that no pleasures were experienced, but constant bombardment in imagination of the subjectively pleasant stimuli eventually took effect. It has been our experience that as soon as any pleasurable stimuli are observed and owned by a depressed individual, the chances of disrupting the web of depressive affect through other interventions are significantly increased.

It will be noted how several modalities may be combined in order to potentiate various positive effects. Thus in the forementioned situation, imagery was clearly invoked as an integral part of a basic sensory objective.

Imagery

In the imagery dimension we can again utilize specific abilities available in trance to capture lucid and realistic images, to revivify experiences, and even to produce hallucinations in the highly hypnotizable. Vivid imagery combined with positive suggestion is an exceedingly potent therapeutic mixture. In addition to enhancing various basic hypnotic procedures (e.g., age regression, time projection, abreaction, induced hallucinations), distinct and graphic imagery can facilitate many behavior therapy techniques (e.g., desensitization, aversion training, covert rehearsal techniques, sexual retraining, and various self-control and self-reinforcement processes).

The use of imagery procedures is limited only by the constraints of the therapist's own imagination. Through the use of imagery, patients can be taken into the past, into the future, onto other worlds, and into remote galaxies. They can shrink to the size of atoms, or become ten feet, indeed ten thousand feet, tall.

Cognition

In the cognitive modality, hypnosis is most useful in creating selective amnesias in relatively high hypnotizables (cf. Evans & Thorn, 1966). Let us describe a case which elucidates this point. In susceptible clients we have found the therapeutic use of hypnotic amnesia expecially useful in facilitating new adaptive approach responses. For example, a stumbling block was reached when treating a 24 year-old female school teacher who had been away from work following a traumatic incident. While teaching a ninth grade class, she became ill and fainted. Upon regaining consciousness, she felt extremely embarrassed. In addition she experienced a tension at the back of her neck that immediately radiated to her arms and legs so that she felt paralyzed. Thereafter, whenever she faced a class, she would experience the mounting tension and feared that she would faint and become permanently paralyzed.

While therapy focused upon several interrelated problems - her marriage, her perfectionism, her poor self-concept, and her basic unassertiveness - she remained unable and unwilling to return to work, despite constant protestations that she desired to resume teaching. Desensitization was ineffective because she reported "not being able to get the image of fainting and paralysis out of my mind." Consequently, she was tested for hypnotizability and proved to be highly hypnotizable. Under hypnosis she was told that when next standing in front of a class, she would be unable to recall the fainting and paralysis fears, and she would remain calm and unruffled. The amnesia suggestions were repeated several times. Thereafter, a series of in vivo desensitization procedures proved completely effective. (She was required to stand in front of an empty classroom for longer and longer periods of time; next a few students were present; and finally, an actual lesson was given to a class). While she described the amnesia as partially effective - "I never actually forgot what had happened to me but somehow it no longer bothered me so much!" - she was enabled to eliminate her phobic avoidance reactions and to resume her full-time teaching.

Interpersonal Relationships

The interpersonal modality presents a different problem. As discussed above, we can assign patients homework and reinforce those assignments with post-hypnotic suggestions. When the homework includes being assertive or non-competitive or the like, it is clearly relevant to the interpersonal modality. But the interpersonal dimension is of importance to the hypnotherapist for another reason. There are patients for whom hypnosis is not appropriate, or for whom there are specific points in treatment when hypnosis is contraindicated. For example, in an aforementioned case, hypnotic anxiety-relief training allowed a patient to recover rather quickly from severe and debilitating anxiety attacks. However, as treatment continued, inspection of the interpersonal modality revealed that the patient was ascribing change to the therapist rather than to herself because of the very ease and efficacy of the hypnotic procedure. Thus, when the time came to confront emotional issues concerning her mother, she was encouraged to use a technique which required her to expend a great deal of effort rather than rely on hypnotic procedures. Hypnosis was contraindicated at this time in this particular case because it would have allowed her to continue to ascribe change to the therapist's efforts, not to her own.

Drugs

Finally let us briefly touch on hypnosis and medication. We have found that hypnosis, both in pain control and as an anti-anxiety agent, is useful in decreasing the required amounts of medication. Expecially in the case of pain control, a combined program of hypnosis, behaviorally oriented training, and medication has proved effective.

At present psychotherapy is still an art form. The behavior therapy movement has attempted to bring some order out of the chaos; to cast some scientific light into the morass. In some ways we have been simplifiers, cutting through a heavy overlay of superstition and formalism. As a result, we have been seen as needlessly simplistic, and justifiably so. But we believe those days are gone. Multimodal behavior therapy attempts to look at all aspects of a person. Further, unlike earlier therapists, we refuse to be trapped in a linear causal model. All seven modalities covered by the BASIC ID form a multivariate system in which diverse and interactive patterns can be identified.

At best, hypnosis provides us with a tool, a wedge, a way in. At the very least it provides us with another gimmick, another prop which can add to the placebo effects of the therapeutic context. In either event, it is clear that hypnosis can play a significant role in the armamentarium of the behavior therapist.

REFERENCES

Barber, T.X. Hypnosis: A scientific approach. New York: Van Nostrand Reinhold, 1969.

Dengrove, E. Hypnosis and behavior therapy. Springflied, Illinois: Thomas, 1976.

Evans, F. The placebo response in pain reduction. In J. Bonica (editor), Advances in neurology, 4, pain. New York: Raven, 1974. Pp. 289-296.

Evans, F., & Thorn, W. Two types of posthypnotic amnesia: Recall amnesia and source amnesia. International Journal of Clinical and Experimental Hypnosis, 1966, 14, 162-179.

Fish, J.M. Placebo therapy. San Francisco: Jossey-Bass, 1973.

Fordyce, W.E. Behavioral concepts in chronic pain and illness. In P.O. Davidson (editor), The behavioral management of anxiety, depression and pain. New York: Brunner/Mazel, 1976. Pp. 147-188.

Garrett, J., & Wallace, B. A novel test of hypnotic anesthesia. International Journal of Clinical and Experimental Hypnosis, 1975, 23, 139-147.

Gaunitz, S., Unestahl, L., & Berglund, B. A posthypnotically released emotion as a modifier of behavior. International Journal of Clinical and Experimental Hypnosis, 1975, 23, 120-129.

Goldfried, M.R., & Davison, G.C. Clinical behavior therapy. New York: Holt, Rinehart and Winston, 1976.

Goldstein, A.P. Psychotherapeutic attraction. New York: Pergamon, 1971.

Karlin, R.A., & McKeon, P. The use of hypnosis in multimodal therapy. In A. Lazarus (editor), Multimodal behavior therapy. New York: Springer, 1976. Pp. 133-148.

Lang, P.J. The mechanics of desensitization and the laboratory study of human fear. In C.M. Franks (editor), Behavior therapy: Appraisal and status. New York: McGraw-Hill, 1969. Pp. 160-191.

Lang, P.J., Lazovik, A.D., & Reynolds, D.J. Desensitization, suggestibility and pseudotherapy. Journal of Abnormal Psychology, 1965, 70, 395-402.

Lazarus, A.A. Some clinical applications of autohypnosis. Medical Proceedings, 1958, 14, 848-850.

Lazarus, A.A. Behavior therapy and beyond. New York: McGraw Hill, 1971.

Lazarus, A.A. Multimodal behavior therapy: Treating the "BASIC ID." Journal of Nervous and Mental Disease, 1973a, 156, 404-411.

Lazarus, A.A. "Hypnosis" as a facilitator in behavior therapy. International Journal of Clinical and Experimental Hypnosis, 1973b, 21, 25-31.

Lazarus, A.A. Multimodal behavior therapy. New York: Springer, 1976.

Lazarus, A.A., & Wilson, G.T. Behavior modification: Clinical and experimental perspectives. In B.B. Wolman (editor), The therapist's handbook. New York: Van Nostrand Reinhold, 1976. Pp. 117-162.

Mahoney, M.J. Cognition and behavior modification. Cambridge, Mass: Ballinger, 1974.

McGlashan, T., Evans, F., & Orne, M. The nature of hypnotic analgesia and placebo response to experimental pain. Psychosomatic Medicine, 1969, 31, 227-246.

Orne, M.T. Hypnosis, motivation, and the ecological validity of the psychological experiment. In W. Arnold and M. Page (editors), Nebraska symposium on motivation: 1970. Lincoln: University of Nebraska Press, 1971. Pp. 187-265.

Orne, M.T. Psychotherapy in contemporary America: Its development and context. In D.X. Freedman and J.E. Dyrud (editors), American handbook of psychiatry, 5, Treatment. New York: Basic Books, 1975, Pp. 3-33.

Park, L., & Covi, L. Nonblind placebo trial: An exploration of neurotic patients' responses to placebo when its inert content is disclosed. Archives of General Psychiatry, 1965, 12, 336-345.

Paul, G.L. Physiological effects of relaxation training and hypnotic suggestion. Journal of Abnormal Psychology, 1969, 74, 425- 437.

Spiegel, H. Termination of smoking by a single treatment. Archives of Environmental Health, 1970, 20, 736-742.

Steinmark, S., & Borkovec, T. Active and placebo treatment effects on moderate insomnia under counterdemand and positive demand instructions. Journal of Abnormal Psychology, 1974, 83, 157-163.

Sutcliffe, J.P. "Credulous" and "sceptical" views of hypnotic phenomena: A review of certain evidence and methodology. International Journal of Clinical and Experimental Hypnosis, 1960, 8, 73-101.

THE USE OF HYPNOSIS IN THE TREATMENT OF IMPOTENCE

William Nuland

Scarsdale, New York, U.S.A.

Abstract: Secondary impotence typically develops following an instance where for one reason or another a man becomes temporarily unable to develop or maintain an erection. Such a situation often is experienced as extremely traumatic and easily leads to preoccupation resulting in progressively greater difficulties; these can ultimately lead to total sexual incapacity. Though there are other types of impotence, this form characterized by fear of failure is the kind of impotence most commonly seen in medical practice. Its treatment requires dealing with the fear as well as those aspects in the immediate environment which serve to maintain and exacerbate the fear as, for example, a deprecatory attitude on the part of the spouse. An approach based in part on a modification of Masters and Johnson's method and involving the use of hypnosis to facilitate imagery and relaxation will be described. These procedures require the cooperation of both the patient and his wife; given such cooperation, favorable therapeutic results can be anticipated.

What do we mean by impotence? It may be defined simply as an inability to execute the sexual act despite the presence of a conscious desire to do so. It may describe inability to obtain or maintain an erection, or inability to achieve an adequate orgasm.

Primary impotence is the disorder in which the patient never has been able to obtain potency. This paper is concerned with secondary impotence, (the condition in which a previously potent man loses his capability for erection) and particularly with cases where, for one reason or another, a man becomes temporarily unable to develop or maintain an erection. Such a situation often is experienced as extremely traumatic and easily leads to preoccupation resulting in progressively greater difficulties and eventually in total sexual incapacity. This type of impotence characterized by fear of failure is the form most commonly seen in medical practice.

Another very common condition known as selective impotence refers to the experience of men who are perfectly potent under certain circumstances yet quite impotent on other occasions. This might result from a variety of circumstances including excessive fatigue, excessive ingestion of alcohol, or impotence with certain sexual partners; it might reflect mental conflict, a fear of marital responsibilities, pressure of vocational adjustment, or other emotional stress. As a result of any of these situations the patient might experience an episode of acute impotence. At first he might merely be surprised, but his anxiety increases later if his wife is excited and expecting intercourse, and despite further sexual play his penis remains flaccid. Several nights later the experience is repeated. He then becomes so worried and upset by his poor sexual performance that he creates a cycle of pressure and demand on himself to perform with the fear and expectation of failure. This often develops into total sexual impotence, no longer selective, but occuring under all circumstances. Almost invariably these patients report they face each sexual encounter as a challenge and a performance at which they may not succeed. This fear of failure, of course, intensifies its likelihood. Some men fear being unable to have an erection and others fear being unable to maintain it. Some men respond to their fear of impotence by increasing the frequency of sexual activity; others by withdrawal from all attempts in fear of further failure and humiliation; and still others by seeking a sexual partner other than the wife. These last mentioned frequently discover that they are impotent also outside of the marriage, which may lead to the more serious consequences of guilt, severe depression, and even suicide.

The judgement of the wife may add to the problem of these individuals. Not recognizing the husband's real distress or the fact that the sexual disturbance as well as other depressive symptoms are out of his control, she may either criticize or minimize his distress.

The treatment of this form of impotence characterized by fear of failure requires dealing with the fear as well as those aspects in the immediate environment which serve to maintain and exacerbate it. The importance of information gained in the initial history taking must be stressed. It is important to distinguish between an impotence which is caused and then perpetuated by a transient performance anxiety, impotence which grows out of a deep neurosis, and impotence which stems from the interpersonal problems of the couple. Often the only treatment needed is reassurance, the correction of misconceptions, and sympathetic understanding. However, this paper deals with more severe cases where the impotence has been present for one year or more, and where treatment must needs last longer and be more ambitious in scope.

The therapeutic approach developed by Masters and Johnson is well documented (1970). While they advocate a male - female co-therapy team and employ an intensive seven days a week, two week format, it has been the author's experience that an approach based in part on a modification of Masters and Johnson's method will produce favorable results for the solo practitioner. It involves the use of hypnosis to induce relaxation and to facilitate imagery with such techniques as desensitization, hypnotic projection, and structural fantasy.

METHOD

Evaluation

Although in the management of the impotent patient the treatment of each case must be individualized, certain techniques are used consistently and will be described. Patients are usually seen at least twice a week at the outset. If the patient then requests additional sessions it must be the therapist who makes the decision. In the first session the patient is seen alone and a careful history of the sexual problem, its development, and duration is obtained. This should be discussed in as much detail as possible, the physician allowing for another interview if necessary. The patient is reassured and informed that his problem is a common every day occurrence for many men; that there is nothing drastic, unusual, or hopeless about it; and that it may be cured or changed given sufficient time, effort, and understanding. A warm approach, a friendly educational presentation, and a positive prognostic viewpoint whenever possible will provide better results. Treatment must be concerned with changing the patient's concept of himself as a failure; this in part, is achieved by adequate hypnotherapeutic manipulation.

A discussion and explanation of hypnosis is included in the initial interviews. Briefly, the patient is asked what he knows about hypnosis and whether he has any fears about unpleasant consequences. Fears are allayed and misconceptions clarified. Experience has shown that when more time is spent in the preliminary discussion, less difficulty is encountered in the induction procedure.

The partner with whom the patient is experiencing his impotence is then interviewed and encouraged to express her feelings. It is important to enlist the wife as a cooperative and understanding ally for the husband, placing responsibility on her as well as on him for working out the difficulties. Although there are situations in which the wife will not cooperate in the treatment because of her own intrapsychic or intrapersonal problems, discussion here is limited to instances in which there is an available cooperative partner. It is important to recommend joint sessions for the patient and his wife when the preliminary interviews reveal that the impotence is primiarily due to a disturbed interpersonal relationship. Both partners are encouraged to express and examine their feelings and interaction, and how these affect their sexual relationships.

In most cases conjoint interviews and techniques are less important after the initial session, and the therapy is then directed primarily at the patient; the cooperation of the wife is obtained so that she can participate later in situations of sexual closeness without expecting intercourse or exerting pressure toward it. The couple is asked to refrain from sexual activity until instructed otherwise. To avoid the constant strain it is important to eliminate the compulsive striving to sexual intercourse. This enables the couple to relax until coitus can be a more spontaneous interaction.

Treatment

Hypnosis and Imagery. The subsequent two or more sessions with the patient are devoted to the induction and deepening of hypnosis until deep relaxation and, if possible, hallucinations are obtained. The induction technique is simple and adapted to the patient's needs; the goal is not depth but relaxation. Direct suggestions are used to encourage self-confidence in his ability, ultimately, to achieve a normal, satisfying, sexual experience. Once the patient has been conditioned to enter hypnosis he is taught self-hypnosis for the purpose of promoting relaxation, and later for developing the sensory imagery necessary for conditioning. He is instructed to practice autohypnosis at home, primarily for producing relaxation. The rationale for this procedure is that the tensions which impede sexual performance can often be eased by muscular relaxation.

Patients who both fear and anticipate failure find themselves watching and monitoring their own performance while they are engaged in sexual activities; breaking this habit of self-observation represents one of the most crucial aspects of the therapy. In this approach, use is made of relaxation, desensitization, fantasy, and positive imagery to shape behavior toward the desired goal. In the subsequent sessions the patient, in the waking state, is asked to recall a sexual experience which he may remember as having been most successful. Then under hypnosis he is asked to relate this scene in great detail, to repeat it, and then to add any imaginary variations which may increase the stimulating action. In the recollection of this experience under hypnosis the patient is instructed to produce visual imagery as if he were watching a film. The imagery should be allowed to develop freely, but in each session in addition to direct suggestions under hypnosis, the scene previously described by him is repeated over and over again to the patient.

He is then instructed to use autohypnosis at home, first to relax and then to relive this successful experience as vividly as possible. When the patient feels that his fantasies are becoming less vivid he is to stop and relax by visualizing a pleasant, relaxing scene or by taking several deep breaths; he is then to resume the visualization. He should practice this technique twice daily when alone, usually in the morning and then shortly before going to sleep.

The number of sessions before proceeding to the next treatment phase are determined by the degree of sexual desire reported by the patient, and by the intensity of the erections which he describes he is capable of producing in the office or alone at home. Even when the patient has achieved adequate sexual desire and erection he is cautioned against attempting sexual intercourse at this time. This condition is imposed because even though most patients have been capable of erection and some have even gone on to successful intercourse early in the treatment, most patients attempting intercourse at this stage have lost the erection before penetration.

Systematic Desensitization. In the next few sessions systematic desensitization is introduced. While relaxed and under hypnosis, the patient is asked to imagine a series of progressively more intimate sexual encounters with his partner. For example, the first scene might simply be to imagine being kissed on the lips by his partner. This may elicit a small amount of anxiety. As he proceeds in the hierarchy, whenever the patient expresses any fears or anxieties, he is asked to relax and then to recall the sexual experience in which he was successful. The main purpose of the use of fantasy here is to reduce anxiety and inhibitions, rather than to stimulate. This procedure is followed for several sessions until the patient is able to visualize himself having a successful sexual experience with his partner without evoking any anxiety. It is expected that the success of this deconditioning procedure will carry over to the patient's real environment.

General Strategy. From this point in therapy, diversity of approach rather than uniformity is the rule. However, any approach must be designed to maintain an absence of pressure to perform. It is first necessary to eliminate the "anxiety impotence" reaction through the reassurance that the patient may attain an erection sometime after initial sexual contact. He is therefore instructed to ask his partner to participate on a few occasions in situations of great sexual closeness without expecting intercourse or exerting pressure toward it. The objective is to arrive at mutually acceptable experimentation that produces maximum anxiety free arousal. When assured of her cooperation, the patient might use self-hypnosis for relaxation purposes, and then while in the nude with his partner engage in foreplay without intercourse or orgasm as expected goals. Mutual stimulation should be leisurely and spontaneous and without obligation for either partner. He is to concentrate on enjoying bodily sensations and nothing else. The couple is encouraged to experiment sexually and to improve the variety and intensity of their stimulating caresses. As sexual tensions increase and the patient attains an erection, his partner should let it subside and then arouse him again into an erect state. Feeling free not to retain the erection relieves the performance anxiety and makes it easier to achieve a subsequent erection. When the patient has succeeded in maintaining a good erection for several sessions, the advisability of coitus is considered, but no specific time is indicated to the patient.

If the patient does not achieve an erection during foreplay, or if he is so anxious to sustain it that his concern interferes with his response to further stimulation, he is to relax himself by means of self-hypnosis and immerse himself in the sexual fantasy in which he was previously successful. Even when the period of abstinence is over, the patient is advised to avoid coitus until he can develop and maintain an erection for several minutes. He is instructed to stop at any point if negative feelings develop within him, and once again to use self hypnosis for further relaxation. In that way he knows he is under no obligation to succeed, and can relax and enjoy sexual stimulation. Once he is capable of maintaining an erection sufficient for penetration he may again immerse himself in the sexual fantasy.

Even after the patient has had successful penetration and orgasm, extensive foreplay is advised for future sexual encounters; he is advised never to attempt penetration unless he is firmly erect and sexually desirous. As anxiety diminishes and the patient's confidence returns, fantasy becomes less important and less of a crutch. The patient is instructed to come back for several further sessions, especially if the impotence shows any signs of recurring and before performance anxiety produces relapse.

Before ending this discussion the author would like to stress the fact that in his clinical experience, many patients treated for fear of performance failure have been sufficently depressed to warrant treatment with antidepressant drugs. Repeated sexual failure has brought on feelings of guilt, morbid thoughts, despair, and pessimism. Interpersonal problems are magnified and mishandled, and the patient often states that his partner is either unsympathetic or actively hostile. Conjoint therapy and hypnotherapy will be to no avail while the underlying state of depression remains unrecognized and untreated. For these reasons in some cases, treatment with antidepressant medication in addition to the approach described above has been beneficial.

Factors Affecting Results

Even when fear of performance failure has persisted for one year or more, favorable results can be anticipated by the solo practioner using this approach, given the cooperation of the patient and his partner. These results are based on experience with forty patients followed over a period of three years or more. Prognosis varies depending on the severity of the underlying problem. Obviously, the longer the patient has had the problem, and the more numerous the previous failures in treatment with other therapists, the less likely will be the success now. The prognosis is more favorable when the patient has had some previous satisfactory sexual experience, when a cooperative sexual partner is available, and when the circumstances accounting for the failure do not involve severe neurotic problems. However, it is important that serious underlying psychiatric illness be ruled out early in the evaluation, because a sexual problem can be the sign of a serious psychiatric disorder.

Finally it must be stressed that because impotence, no matter what the cause, invariably induces feelings of insecurity and anxiety, the approach described in this paper might be helpful in alleviating the distress associated with other forms of impotence. Furthermore, in the author's clinical experience, improvement in the symptoms of impotence does not necessarily require intensive psychotherapy but may be accomplished by briefer symptomatic behavior treatment.

REFERENCES

Masters, W.H., & Johnson, V.E. Human sexual inadequacy. Boston: Little, Brown and company, 1970.

PATIENTS' REACTIONS TO HYPNOSIS ON A BURN UNIT

Donald W. Schafer

University of California at Irvine, U.S.A.

Abstract: The adjunctive use of hypnosis in the treatment of 20 patients on a burn unit is described, including its effectiveness in paving the way toward positive transference, trust, support, and a generally psychotherapeutic environment. The author also discusses the reactions (both positive and negative) of patients and relatives to hypnosis, the attitude of the staff, countertransference on a burn unit, and the need to guard against omnipotent fantasies.

The effectiveness of hypnosis in providing anaesthesia and analgesia for burn patients on the Burn Unit of Orange County Medical Center (now the University of California Irvine Medical Center) has been reported previously (Schafer, 1975). Hypnosis was found to be a valuable adjunct to the treatment programs of two-thirds of the twenty patients involved in the study. As anticipated, the hypnotherapist was required to spend only two hours per week with patients in order to render adequate services.

This paper is intended as a review of the reactions of these 20 patients to the hypnosis; the reactions considered are those other than specific relief of pain. The hypnosis-burn project itself was initiated with five patients in 1969 as a pilot study to investigate the possibility of such an undertaking. Subsequently 15 additional patients were treated, providing the information necessary for a statistically valid analysis of the cases, an evaluation of the project (Schafer, 1975), and assessment in an independent setting of the work of Crasilneck, Stirman, Wilson, McCranie, and Fogelman (1955) regarding the management of patients in a burn unit through the use of hypnosis.

The Burn Unit consists of a relatively small ward with an average of six to eight patients. It is staffed by very dedicated personnel. The patients on this ward are different psychologically in many aspects from those on other hospital wards, in that they are healthy people in the middle of their active lives who suddenly find themselves in the hospital as a result of an unexpected thermal injury, unprepared for hospitalization, not knowing if they are going to live, not knowing how severely hurt they are, and worrying about whether they will ultimately have scars, be able to pay for their care, or be employable. In other words burn patients typically experience anxiety, guilt, and anger, and are beset by questions such as: "Why me?" and "Will my husband love me after I get out?"

Regressive Reactions

All bed patients regress. Burn patients, in particular, regress because of the unplanned transition from health to a hospital bed for a protracted period of time. The fact of regression is established; the symptoms of regression are specific for each patient based upon his personality characteristics and antecedent experiences. The author has personally observed various types of clinical pictures resulting from regression in burn patients. The following few case summaries are representative.

After a 37 year old woman who was receiving hypnosis for the relief of pain during dressing changes received a post-hypnotic suggestion, she became the best patient on the ward. In effect, she changed from her spoiled-child posture to becoming the "favorite child" of the chief nurse, but still related poorly to the other personnel. When the dynamics were explained to the chief nurse and the remaining staff, conditions improved, and the patient in reality became the best patient on the ward in the manner in which she must have been her mother's favorite child.

The next example is of a man in his late 20's described as "hospitalwise." He was a paraplegic who had previously had 20 to 30 operations to improve his disability. He seemed to enjoy playing the game of "let's you and him fight," and was highly skilled in setting the personnel against each other and against the patients. Although a somnambulist who experienced no pain after a brief introduction to hypnosis, he refused to utilize hypnosis while exercising his one remaining good hand which had been severely burned. This behavior was interpreted as his way of finally making himself as helpless as a child, so that the world would take care of him. There was some hint that he had unconsciously, but on purpose, initiated the thermal injury that brought him to the hospital.

The third example is that of a 21-year-old youth who can best be described as in near panic, with grossly exaggerated emotional responses. He was a somnambulist and had perfect results with hypnosis, but appeared to be very surprised when he experienced relief. He had been an exceptionally difficult patient prior to the hypnosis; he subsequently became a model patient as a result of the complete relief from his pain.

Reactions to the Offers of Hypnosis

In addition to these types of regressive responses, reactions to the offer of hypnosis were recorded among the patients on the Burn Unit. These patients were not specifically referred for hypnosis, but it was offered to them at some stage. Their reactions ranged from refusal through skepticism and acceptance, to an almost fervent desire for hypnosis. The initial reaction to the idea of hypnosis had no predictive value regarding the patient's ability to utilize it.

The refusals were often associated with religious reasons. For example, one family was burned in a car accident at an amusement park. The father suffered the least and was, therefore, not admitted as an inpatient on the Burn Unit. One of the girls burned was too young for hypnosis. The other child who was seven was an excellent subject, but was ostensibly prevented from using the hypnosis by the severity of her injuries. Although a somnambulist she would immediately waken the moment her dressings were touched. The mother, however, was a fair hypnosis subject who was helped by having her dressings changed while actually in person to person hypnosis. Because of the amount of time that would have been involved if all dressing changes were attended by the hypnotherapist, hypnosis was effected through the tape recording of a session. Her dressings were then changed with only mild discomfort. Later, however, after she had reached a point of maximum benefit her angered husband objected to the further use of hypnosis on religious grounds, claiming that he had not known hypnosis was to be included in the treatment. His objection might also have been related to his sense of guilt at having been the one least hurt in the accident, and to his sense of helplessness. Fortunately, the mother who was the only one who had been helped by hypnosis, had progressed so well that further hypnosis was unnecessary.

Another patient, a racecar driver, was burned while racing. He is the only patient whose initial reaction was "How much will it cost?" When assured that this was a research project and therefore would not add to his costs, his reply was "Well, might as well try it then." Although he could not go as far as somnambulism he responded well to hypnosis, and was able to utilize it for relief of pain during dressing changes.

Working with patients who are under the influence of narcotics is often difficult. However, if they are able to respond and are oriented, it is not impossible. The hypnotist should ensure, however, that he is not seen by the patients as someone who will deprive them of their narcotics or influence the pain medication in any way.

Factors Facilitating or Impeding Hypnosis

One of the more difficult experiences with hypnosis involved two middle aged male patients who were suffering from flash burns connected with boating. Both patients were seen individually. Both had been severely burned in terms of extent and pain, but the burns themselves were only second degree. Each man verbally accepted the idea of hypnosis, but both resisted becoming hypnotized to any usable extent and had to be considered failures. It is plausible that these men knew they would not die, that they would not be scarred, and that they would shortly be released from the hospital. Their resistance to hypnosis could have arisen out of a need to preserve their masculine self-esteem.

The factor impeding hypnosis most frequently was the panic state suffered especially by the younger patients - the children and adolescents. This occurred in the presence of the heavy use of narcotics administered to counteract both pain and panic. It is likely that the failures with adolescent patients reported by Dahinterová (1967) are related to this finding. Unfortunately time could not be spent in establishing the rapport necessary for successful hypnosis, with these younger patients. Bernstein (1965) found it helpful to combine hypnosis with psychotherapy in his work with burned children.

Skepticism on the part of patients never seemed to interfere with results as such, for there was no correlation between clinical results and such skepticism. The so called contagious aspects of hypnosis which are typically observed in similar situations were not apparent during this study. In fact, it did not seem that the hypnotic reaction of one patient affected that of any other. It is possible that this absence of hypnotic contagion can be attributed to the fact that each patient was suffering so profoundly, and was consequently so inner-oriented, as to be relatively insensivive to the behavior of other patients.

Attitudes of the Staff

Most of the doctors were cooperative, particularly the resident assigned to the burn ward at the beginning of the project, and the two successive service chiefs who were present during the entire project. Specifically, the enthusiasm of the personnel helped prepare the patients for hypnosis. Typically, the personnel related well to the author; almost all were inclined to disclose and discuss their own problems, and appreciated the explanations regarding the dynamics of their patients. One surgical resident, unable to comprehend that hypnosis might provide anaesthetic relief, very sadistically removed a dressing immediately after witnessing his patient enter hypnotic trance. It seemed as if his need to disprove the effectiveness of hypnosis temporarily pre-empted his concern for the patient's comfort.

Countertransference Reactions

There are a number of reasons for negative reactions: the appearance of a badly burned patient; the fact that the personnel is often in the presence of death and dying; the frequent downhill course of a patient, regardless of the care given him; and the painful lingering of the average patient who does die in the hospital. Moreover, during the first several days of hospitalization the patient is typically sufficiently conscious and alert to interact with personnel, making it harder on them should he die than if he had entered in an unconscious state.

The distressing appearance of burn patients not infrequently leads to attempts by interns to avoid a surgical assignment on the burn ward. The histories of the thermal injury, and the patients' own unfortunate contributions to some of their injuries, evoke critical and disdainful feelings in the caretakers, very difficult to suppress. These kinds of feelings and the consequent guilt and anger have to be endured and handled by the personnel.

In these situations therapists should also guard against their own feelings of omnipotence. Typically, on other wards, psychiatrists are regarded as are other members of the staff. On the Burn Unit, however, where there is usually little exposure to psychiatrists and even less psychiatric knowledge, fantasies of psychological omnipotence can by sustained by the psychiatrists, by other members of the staff, and by the patients. The author found it necessary to fight continually against such fantasies because the personnel needed to see him as a miracle worker.

General Observations

From a psychotherapeutic standpoint, the author was able not only to help the burn patients with hypnosis, but also to give them emotional support, help them in a crisis intervention sense, explore (but probably not interpret) accident proneness, and become somewhat involved in problem solving with them. It is estimated that over a third of the patients had contributed to their own accidents, making accident-proneness a valid assumption. In some cases it was obvious that the patients were attempting to solve problems they were having, especially in their marriages. It is also probable that some patients who did not set up their own thermal injuries, did at times utilize the situation for manipulating spouses or others.

All the patients showed deep appreciation for the relief given them by hypnosis. This is probably one of the most valid uses for hypnosis in traumatic medicine; the relief of constant, repetitive, painful situations arising from the dressing changes, debridement, multiple operations, intravenous feeding, and so forth. Due to the structure of the project no attempt was made to give anesthesia, via hypnosis, for the surgical procedures themselves. However, both before and after skin grafting and for actual debridement and dressing changes, hypnosis was very helpful for the releif of pain. The patients were also very appreciative of the interest, support, and underlying psychiatric help that they received.

Because of the excellent physical care available to the patients, including reverse precautionary measures, no contagion was evident. Specifically, neither wound infections, dehydration, anorexia, nor any other complications were noted. Although the hypnosis was not life-saving it was so startlingly successful that it led to optimism and the anticipation of a positive outcome on the part of patients and staff. It also allowed for an increased understanding of these patients by the staff as well as a chance for ego supportive measures to be instituted. This climate of affirmation and hope resulted in positive transference, and fine rapport among the author, the staff, and the patients, all of whom seemed to benefit psychologically from the pervasive emotional support.

Because the protocol allowed for only two hours per week on the ward, hypnosis was not used for the purpose of achieving anaesthesia for the surgical procedures, nor to promote healing directly. It is hoped, however, that these areas will be studied in the future.

REFERENCES

Bernstein, N.R. Observations on the use of hypnosis with burned children on a pediatric ward. International Journal of Clinical and Experimental Hypnosis, 1965, 13, 1-10.

Crasilneck, H.B., Stirman, J.A., Wilson, B.J., McCranie, E.J., & Fogelman, M.J. Use of hypnosis in the management of patients with burns. Journal of the American Medical Association, 1955, 158, 103-106.

Dahinterová, J. Some experience with the use of hypnosis in the treatment of burns. International Journal of Clinical and Experimental Hypnosis, 1967, 15, 49-53.

Schafer, D.W. Hypnosis use on a burn unit. International Journal of Clinical and Experimental Hypnosis, 1975, 23, 1-14.

IV: Clinical Studies

MIGRAINE AND HYPNOTHERAPY

Maurice A. Basker

Leigh-on-Sea, Essex, England

John A. D. Anderson and Rosemary Dalton

Guy's Hospital Medical School, London, England

Abstract: The prophylactic treatment of migraine is difficult to assess, whether by chemotherapy or autohypnosis. This is due to the intermittency of the disease and the subjective nature of the disabling symptoms. A method for investigating the value of autohypnosis in migraine by means of a controlled comparison with prochlorperazine is described.

Random allocation was made of 47 patients to one or other prophylactic measure. This was followed by monthly assessments and independent evaluation of one year of continuous care. Criteria of improvement were the number of attacks per month, the number who had Grade 4 attacks, and the number who had complete remission. Results showed that the number of attacks and the number who suffered blinding attacks were significantly lower for the group receiving hypnotherapy than for the group receiving prochlorperazine. For the hypnotherapy group these two measures were significantly lower when receiving hypnotherapy than when on previous treatment. 10 out of 23 patients receiving hypnotherapy achieved complete remission during the last three months of the trial as opposed to only 3 out of 24 patients on prochlorperazine.

Migraine is generally accepted as being caused by changes in blood flow, hormonal imbalance, and failure to adapt to emotionally stressful conditions. Drugs are ineffective in the treatment of many cases, as the insidious onset of attacks precludes their application before the symptoms have become established, and the stress factors are unresponsive to many general sedatives. However, prochlorperazine (Stemetil) has been suggested in this context.

The possibility of hypnosis and autohypnosis being of benefit is supported by the view of Citron (1968) in relation to the stressful features of asthma, and the evidence of a previous trial by Maher-Loughnan, Mason, McDonald, and Fry (1962) giving similar support.

Accordingly it was decided to compare the treatment of migraine by means of hypnosis with autohypnosis, and the drug prochlorperazine, on a random basis over a 12 month period. It was agreed that patients should be over 14 and have at least a 12 month history of migraine as defined by Whitty and Hockaday (1968), namely, that in addition to recurring, throbbing headaches they should have at least two of the following symptoms: unilateral headache, associated nausea with or without vomiting, visual or other sensory aura, cyclical vomiting in childhood, and family history of migraine.

Four grades of migraine were recognized (Sweetnam, 1965):

(1) minor severity with transient or no disability,
(2) moderate severity, where patient can maintain activity,
(3) severe, but not quite wholly incapacitating, and
(4) blinding and totally incapacitating.

METHOD

Those who were treated by hypnosis were given at least six sessions at intervals of 10-14 days. No stipulation had been made concerning either the induction or deepening techniques other than that they should suit individual patients. Simple suggestive therapy and ego strengthening suggestions as described by Hartland (1966, 1971) were given. It was thought that there would be an improved chance of complete remission of migraine if the patient was shown that his symptoms could be controlled during an actual attack. For the trial, patients were asked to practice autohypnosis daily and to give themselves ego strengthening suggestions of increased relaxation with decreased tension and anxiety. They were also taught to avert an attack of migraine when threatened, as suggested by Hartland (1966). Previous experience has shown that patients do practice autohypnosis as instructed, but find that they need to use it less and less as time goes by, with remission of the illness.

Those not to be treated by hypnosis were given prophylactic drug treatment consisting of prochlorperazine in 5 mg doses four times a day for the first month and twice a day for the remaining

11 months. Patients in this group were provided with ergotamine to be taken at the first warning of an attack of migraine.

During the course of either treatment the practitioner was asked to see the patient at monthly intervals, fill in a treatment record card, and return a monthly progress card to those monitoring the trial.

Using the therapist's monthly reports, the efficiency of the treatment was assessed in three ways during the course of the trial:

(1) the number of attacks regardless of severity, as stated by the patient to the therapist at monthly intervals;
(2) whether Grade 4 attacks were experienced, as stated by the patient at monthly intervals to the therapist; and
(3) the number of patients completely free from attacks as stated by them to the therapist at monthly intervals.

RESULTS

The trial was carried out by four practitioners on a total of 47 patients (23 receiving hypnotherapy, and 24 chemotherapy). The randomization procedure was successful in that the previous treatment of the two groups, their mean age and sex distribution, and the proportion previously suffering from Grade 4 attacks show no significant differences. The average monthly attack rate was stated by the patients at the initial interview; the median of these rates for the hypnosis group was 4.5 per month, and this is not significantly different ($p = .10$) from that of 3.3 per month for the group receiving prochlorperazine.

Ongoing assessment during the course of the trial, made in the three ways, gave the results shown in Table 1.

Number of Attacks

The group of 23 patients receiving hypnotherapy had a median rate of 4.5 attacks per month during the six months prior to the trial, 1.0 per month in the first six months of the trial, and 0.5 per month in the second six months of the trial. The number of migraine attacks per month was significantly different in these three periods for those on hypnotherapy (Friedman two-way analysis of variance by ranks, $\chi_r^2 = 39.39$, $df = 2$, $p < .005$).

For each patient the mean number of attacks per month during both six-month periods of the trial was less than that for the six months prior to the trial. Also, the number of attacks in the

TABLE 1

Treatment of Migraine by Hypnotherapy and by Prochlorperazine (Stemetil)

Outcome Criterion	Hypnotherapy N = 23	Prochlorperazine N = 24
Median number of migraine attacks per month:		
6 months prior to therapy	4.5	3.3
First 6 months of therapy	1.0	2.8
Second 6 months of therapy	0.5	2.9
Number of patients suffering Grade 4 attacks:		
6 months prior to therapy	13	10
First 6 months of therapy	4	13
Second 6 months of therapy	5	14
Patients having complete remission during the last 3 months of therapy	10 (43.5%)	3 (12.5%)

second six months was significantly less than in the first six months (Wilcoxon matched-pairs signed-ranks test, $T = 20$, $p < .01$), which perhaps suggests that those on hypnosis were becoming more proficient at averting migraine attacks using autohypnosis, whereas during at least part of the first six months they had not yet effectively learned the technique.

For the group of 24 patients receiving prochlorperazine, the median number of attacks was 3.3 per month during the six months prior to the trial, 2.8 during the first six months of the trial, and 2.9 during the second six months. The number of attacks did not vary significantly during these three periods (Friedman two-way analysis of variance, $\chi_r^2 = 2.69$, $df = 2$, $p < .30$), and thus it would seem that prochlorperazine is as effective at preventing attacks as the treatments which the patients had been receiving prior to the trial.

Prior to the trial the attack rates were not significantly different, although those who were to receive hypnotherapy had a slightly higher median attack rate. During the second six months of the trial those on hypnotherapy had a significantly lower attack rate than those on prochlorperazine (Mann-Whitney test, $z = 2.80$, $p = .005$). Thus, the improvement with hypnosis is in spite of, and not just due to, the higher attack rates in the hypnotherapy group prior to the trial.

During the first six months, the difference was only significant at the 6% level (Mann-Whitney test, $z = 1.88$, $p = .06$). These results suggest that once patients learn to use autohypnosis effectively this treatment is significantly better than prochlorperazine.

Grade 4 Blinding Attacks

For the group of 23 patients receiving hypnotherapy, 13 had Grade 4 attacks in the six months prior to therapy, 4 had Grade 4 attacks in the first six months of therapy, and 5 had Grade 4 attacks in the second six months of therapy.

For the group of 24 patients receiving prochlorperazine, 10 had Grade 4 attacks in the six months prior to therapy, 13 had Grade 4 attacks in the first six months of the therapy, and 14 had Grade 4 attacks in the second six months of therapy.

The number suffering from Grade 4 attacks varied significantly for the hypnotherapy group (Cochran Q test, $Q = 13.27$, $df = 2$, $p < .005$), and this was due to the lower numbers in the two treatment periods compared with the number prior to the trial. For the prochlorperazine group, however, the number suffering Grade 4 attacks did not vary significantly (Cochran Q test, $Q = 3.71$, $df = 2$,

$p < .20$), and thus it would appear that prochlorperazine may be about as effective as the previous treatment in averting Grade 4 attacks.

It should be noticed that prior to the trial, the number suffering Grade 4 attacks was 13 in the hypnotherapy group and 10 in the prochlorperazine group. These are not significantly different, but the fact that the hypnotherapy group was worse to start with may have caused the apparent superiority of hypnotherapy, without the number suffering such attacks being significantly lower in the hypnotherapy group as compared with the prochlorperazine group after 6 to 12 months of treatment. In fact, significantly fewer of the hypnotherapy group suffered such attacks compared to the prochlorperazine group during both six-month periods (Fisher exact test, two-tailed; first six months, $p = .019$, second six months, $p = .0226$). Thus it would appear that hypnotherapy was beneficial in reducing the number who suffered Grade 4 attacks, either because of its actual action or because of its effect as a 'New Method.'

Thirteen patients subsequently treated with hypnotherapy had had Grade 4 attacks in the six months before the trial started. Of these, nine suffered no such attacks during the trial year, three suffered such attacks during both six-month periods of the year, and one suffered Grade 4 attacks only during six months of the trial. There was one additional patient who, although free from Grade 4 attacks in the month before starting on hypnotherapy, suffered from this type of attack in both halves of the trial period.

Ten patients subsequently treated with prochlorperazine had Grade 4 attacks in the six month period before the trial started. All of these had at least one such attack during the trial period, although two did not have a Grade 4 attack during the first six months. There were, however, an additional five patients in the prochlorperazine group who, having had no Grade 4 attacks in the six months prior to the trial, had at least one attack during the first six months, and four of these had at least one attack during the second six months as well.

Complete Remission

Ten (43.5%) of the 23 patients treated with hypnotherapy were completely free from any attack of migraine during the last three months of the trial, whereas only three (12.5%) of the 24 treated with prochlorperazine were improved to this extent. This difference is statistically significant (Fisher exact test, $p = .039$). All the patients had had migraine before the trial, and this improvement for the hypnotherapy group is statistically significant, but that for the prochlorperazine group may well be a chance effect.

Independent Assessment

The original design of the trial included a follow-up interview to be conducted as soon as practicable after the end of treatment by a practitioner who had no knowledge of the therapy involved. Unfortunately the untimely death of one of the participating doctors at the end of the trial period meant that independent assessment was applied to only 37 patients (18 of whom received hypnotherapy and 19 prochlorperazine). The history recorded by the therapists was essentially similiar to that recorded by the independent assessor. However, both were liable to a common source of error in that they were based on histories given by the patients.

REFERENCES

Citron, K.M. (Chairman). Hypnosis for asthma - a controlled trial: A report to the Research Committee of the British Tuberculosis Association (G.P. Maher-Loughnan, Co-Ordinator). British Medical Journal, 1968, 4, 71-76.

Hartland, J.C. Medical and dental hypnosis. London: Balliere, 1966.

Hartland, J.C. Further observations on the use of "ego strengthening" techniques. American Journal of Clinical Hypnosis, 1971, 14, 1-8.

Maher-Loughnan, G.P., Mason, A.A., Macdonald, N., & Fry, L. Controlled trial of hypnosis in the symptomatic treatment of asthma. British Medical Journal, 1962, 2, 371-376.

Sweetnam, M.T. A new look at migraine. Journal of the College of General Practitioners, 1965, 10, 223-229.

Whitty, C.W.M., & Hockaday, J.M. Migraine: A follow-up study of 92 patients. British Medical Journal, 1968, 1, 735-736.

HYPNOSIS IN THE MANAGEMENT OF AIRPLANE PHOBIAS

Graham D. Burrows

University of Melbourne, Australia

Abstract: Over recent years there has been an increase in the number of patients presenting with marked anxiety related to travelling in airplanes. These can be divided into two major groups: the first consists of patients with multiple phobias of which air travel is only one - agoraphobia is common in these patients; the second major group consists of patients with one specific phobia - "airplane phobia."

During a period of 3 years, 43 patients presented to a Psychiatric Clinic with symptoms of difficulty in airplane travel. Following initial psychiatric assessment and psychological testing, they received treatment with hypnosis.

This paper presents psychological and clinical details of these patients. The treatment approach and results of this ongoing study, with particular reference to the role of hypnosis, is discussed.

Flying is a relatively new and potentially dangerous skill for man. Since World War I, when high psychiatric casualty rates were recorded among military air crew, a considerable amount of research has been focused on psychiatric problems associated with aviation. Psychiatric reactions to flying were first studied in detail during World War II, when psychiatrists were assigned to medical support units of operational squadrons. From their wider experience came a better understanding of gross stress reactions, psychophysiological reactions, and short-term psychotherapeutic techniques. Anxiety reactions with phobic and somatic manifestations were found to be related to the stress of military flying. The fear of flying syndrome also occurred among previously adjusted flying personnel. Symptomatology varied from neurotic, psychosomatic and behavioral disturbances to frank psychotic reactions. Psychosomatic symptoms were the most common (Sours, Ehrlich, & Phillips, 1964).

Fear of flying can be compared with "depression," in that it can descriptively mean a syndrome, a nosological entity, or a symptom. In an epidemiological study of phobias in the Greater Burlington area, Vermont, Agras, Sylvester, and Oliveau (1969) reported fear of flying as intense in 10% of the population and mild in 20%. With the greater numbers of people travelling by air, the incidence of airplane phobia is probably increasing.

Treatment of flying phobias originated with the attempt to return to flying, experienced air crew who had become psychiatrically "grounded." This occurred even with fully confident air crew who developed anxiety about a particular aspect of flying. A specific traumatic experience usually marked the onset of the illness, from which point increasing anxiety developed. By the time these men were forced to ask for medical help, the localized fear had become deeply rooted as a phobic state.

Goorney (1970) in a retrospective survey of the effectiveness of therapy found the most successful technique to be that of Wells and Anderson (Anderson, 1919). They introduced their patients to flying through a series of graded steps, assisted by a flying instructor. Their method, which they called "slow recovery," had much in common with the routine techniques of flying training. The success of this treatment of graded re-exposure to flying has been followed recently by the application of systematic desensitization to flying phobia. Gelder, Marks, and Wolff (1967) demonstrated the method of Wolpe (1958) to be the most effective treatment currently available for phobias specific to certain situations. A hierarchical list of the patient's fears is compiled. He is trained to relax and to remain relaxed while he visualizes in imagination the progression of anxiety-provoking situations. Marks (1969) pointed out that the addition of practical to ideational desensitization enhanced improvement as did modelling and social reinforcement.

An investigation by Daly, Aitken, and Rosenthal (1970) into the phenomenology of flying phobia in trained air crew concluded in psychoanalytic terms that "a variety of insults led to regression to an earlier stage of adjustment, such as before their flying training had achieved adaptation to unusual somatic sensation." Psychosocial stress and other factors may have lowered the threshold to development of anxiety and so started a vicious circle, whereby re-exposure to the situation was accompanied by recall of the previous episode.

Studies of the fear of flying in civilians are few. They include a short communication by Meldman and Hatch (1969). These authors used methoxyflurane ("Penthrane") as an adjunct to the behavioral therapy approach of reciprocal inhibition. Two case histories were given and both patients succeeded in resuming normal unaccompanied flights. This resulted in enhanced self-esteem, as well as the possibility of resuming business interests otherwise restricted by inability to undertake air travel.

Scrignar, Swanson, and Bloom (1973) presented a typical fear of flying hierarchy, developed from a "Fear Survey Schedule" and "Air Flying Survey" filled in by the patient.

Solyom, Shugar, Bryntwick, and Solyom (1973) investigated the effects of three different behavior techniques (systematic desensitization, aversion relief, or habituation) and group therapy on air travel phobia, and outcomes of the therapies were compared. The three behavior therapy techniques seemed equally effective in reducing air travel phobia. The authors suggested that since different techniques achieved the same result, possibly the repeated experience of sights and sounds in a safe environment and exposure to fear in small controllable amounts, with the option of interrupting the experience at will, reduces the anxiety of the flying experience.

METHOD

This clinical paper briefly reports 43 patients treated for airplane phobia, with hypnosis as an adjunct to their therapy. All patients were referred by physicians or psychiatrists to the Department of Psychiatry, University of Melbourne, over a period of 36 months.

They were rated on an analogue anxiety and depression scale (Aitken, 1969), the Hamilton Anxiety Scale (1959), Hamilton Depression Scale (1960), the Eysenck Personality Inventory (1964) and a Rapid Symptom Check List.

Following the initial psychiatric interview of approximately 40 minutes, the patients were instructed in relaxation techniques at the second session. It was suggested that the phobic problem was maintained by the tendency to avoid the anxiety of airplane travel, or even the thought of, or looking at, airplanes. They were told the phobia could be overcome if avoidance was prevented. Most patients understood this, but sometimes doubted whether they could tolerate the anxiety of even thinking of airplane travel. A ten-minute audio-cassette tape recording of relaxation was made at the second interview for each patient. This was made specifically for the individual patient and was not a standard tape. Patients were instructed to play this tape daily for ten minutes, and to think generally of airplane travel for the following five minutes.

At the third interview a hypnotic trance was induced with the patient sitting in an armchair. He was directed to imagine sitting inside an airplane with seatbelt fastened. Suggestions of movement of the airplane taxiing on the runway, gathering speed, and finally take-off, were given, interspersed with directions for relaxation. Further suggestions of cloud movement and finally the airplane levelling into a flight-path, were given, followed by ten minutes of "free-flight," suggestions of descent, and then touchdown with approach to the air terminal. Any observable restlessness or agitation was immediately followed by direct suggestion of relaxation. On recovery from the trance the patient was encouraged to discuss, at length, feelings in the experience. Most patients described as easy the sensation of actual flight. The time of greatest anxiety was generally immediately prior to initial take-off.

Over the next two half-hour sessions, usually one to two weeks apart, the same procedure was repeated. The sessions consisted of approximately ten minutes of discussion, ten minutes of trance, and ten minutes of further talking about feelings and the experience. Usually at the fifth or sixth session the patient was advised to go and spend some hours at the local airport watching the scene generally, and carrying out relaxation procedures. At the following session the patient was instructed to book a return airplane flight to a city one hour's flight away, and to come to the next session on the way to the airport. At the session after actual flight, and for a final one or two sessions, reinforcement in the trance state was provided.

The treatment goal was clearly delineated as the ability, actually, to fly in an airplane with no or minimal anxiety. All these patients had tried multiple treatments prior to coming to the Clinic, and 21 had been referred by psychiatrists because of previously unsuccessful therapy. All except one were considered extremely co-operative and motivated.

Following hypnotic sessions treatment was continued at home with relaxation tapes, and patients were set tasks to perform between sessions and in the natural setting of the airport. Significant family support was usually forthcoming.

Three patients were taken to the airport by the therapist, and one was accompanied on an actual flight. Self-regulation, by keeping a notebook of anxiety scores, practicing deep breathing exercises, and learning to remain in the phobic situation until anxiety had abated were strongly encouraged. Posthypnotic suggestions were given to augment behavior. It was usual practice to combine more than one therapeutic principle in the treatment regime. All patients have been followed up for at least 18 months following therapy.

RESULTS

There were 23 males and 20 females with a mean age of 41.7 years (21-69 years). The mean duration of symptoms of airplane phobia was 6.5 years (range 1-18 years). Most were of above average intelligence. The total group could be broadly subdivided into two categories. Those who had specific anxiety symptoms related to flying were considered to be suffering from a focal phobia illness (N = 24), while those in the other group (N = 19) had mixed phobia problems. Agoraphobic symptoms were common in the latter group.

Four patients were found to be suffering from moderate depressive illness (Hamilton mean score = 24) and received treatment with tricyclic antidepressant medication. Two of these responded to therapy, and when the depression resolved the airplane phobia was no longer present. For the third patient the phobia diminished in severity at the second interview, and the fourth patient failed to attend the second interview.

The mean number of flights for the total group of 43, prior to therapy, was 5.2. For the remaining 39 who received hypnotherapy, the initial scores compared with those at discharge on the phobic rating scale, the rapid symptom check list, the anxiety and depression ratings, and the Eysenck personality inventory are shown in Table 1. The mean number of sessions was 8 (6 - 14).

At follow-up of at least 18 months all of the 24 focal phobics has resumed and continued airplane travel without much difficulty or recurrence of symptoms. Of the 19 patients with mixed phobic symptoms, 15 had minimal problems with flying, although they were at times troubled by other phobias. Four patients still had major symptoms and continuing problems. Three were no longer able to travel in airplanes, and had been reluctant to admit this and resume therapy. However, they all stated that generally their anxiety levels were much lower in comparison with those experienced at the time they initially presented for therapy.

DISCUSSION

Critics might call this approach hopeless eclecticism, and dismiss the hypnosis component as irrelevant to the total behavioral psychotherapeutic practice. This was a clinical study, and double-blind methodology, or comparative approaches were not intended. From previous experience hypnosis was considered a helpful major adjunct to the total program.

The concept of exposure was important. Relief from phobia comes from the patient's repeated contact with the situation that evoked his distress. Desensitization for phobic patients generally

TABLE 1

Airplane Phobia and Hypnosis:
Rating Scales and Questionnaire (N = 39)

	Initial	Final Session
Phobic Rating (1-5)	3.9	1.0
Rapid Symptom Check List	41	10
Hamilton Depression	13	4
Depression Analogue	36	9
Hamilton Anxiety	21	6
Anxiety Analogue	82	12
EPI/N	35	
EPI/E	22	

has been shown to be superior to dynamic psychotherapy (Gillian & Rachman, 1974), but exposure in vivo even more effective (Marks, Hodgson, & Rachman, 1975).

It was not always possible to determine why some patients developed their phobia. Most, however, were intelligent, obsessive, compulsive personalities with a preoccupation with fear of loss of control, who had had a bad flight at a time of feeling more anxious than usual. Why re-exposure to a traumatic situation as occurs in therapy cures, when previously it caused the illness, is not known. Which conditions predict a traumatic or curative result must still be delineated. Some researchers claim that phobias improve with exposure treatment, but that it does not matter whether patients are relaxed, neutral or anxious during such exposure (Mathews, Johnson, Shaw, & Gelder, 1974). The concept of implosion holds that for improvement to occur, anxiety must be maximally aroused during exposure. Duration of exposure is also presumably important for people to develop self-regulatory mechanisms or to reach critical levels of habituation.

These airplane phobics were no strangers to anxiety, and had often previously used large amounts of alcohol or drugs to enable them to go anywhere near an airport or plane. First class travelling allowed for more "space" and more alcohol. They found the repeated flights during hypnosis and the following relaxation to be extremely beneficial. The self-help, the active participation program, and the beliefs of the therapist and the patients are obviously extremely important. Nevertheless, hypnosis clearly added greatly to the treatment regime.

Why there is failure in some to improve, why others treated with antidepressants have a complete remission of phobic symptoms, and why certain cues precipitate phobic illness are still unknown and basically conjectural. Further comparative studies and research would certainly be worthwhile in this rapidly growing field of behavioral psychotherapy.

REFERENCES

Agras, S., Sylvester, D., & Oliveau, D. The epidemiology of common fears and phobias. Comprehensive Psychiatry, 1969, 10, 151-156.

Aitken, R.C. A measure of feelings using visual analogue scales. Proceedings of the Royal Society of Medicine, 1969, 62, 989-996.

Anderson, H.C. The medical and surgical aspects of flying. London: Oxford Medical Publications, 1919.

Daly, R.J., Aitken, R.C.B., & Rosenthal, S.V. Treatment of flying phobia in trained aircrew. Proceedings of the Royal Society of Medicine, 1970, 63, 878-882.

Eysenck, H.J., & Eysenck, S.B.J. Manual of the Eysenck Personality Inventory. London: University of London Press, 1964.

Gelder, M.G., Marks, I.M., & Wolff, H. Desensitization and psychotherapy in the treatment of phobic states: a controlled enquiry. British Journal of Psychiatry, 1967, 113, 53-73.

Gillian, P., & Rachman, S. An experimental investigation of desensitization in phobic patients. British Journal of Psychiatry, 1974, 124, 392-401.

Goorney, A.B. Treatment of aviation phobias by behavior therapy. British Journal of Psychiatry, 1970, 117, 535-544.

Hamilton, M. The assessment of anxiety states by rating. British Journal of Medical Psychology, 1959, 32, 50-59.

Hamilton, M. A rating scale for depression. Journal of Neurology, Neurosurgery, and Psychiatry, 1960, 23, 56-62.

Marks, I.M. Fears and phobias. London: Heinemann Medical Books, 1969.

Marks, I.M., Hodgson, R., & Rachman, S. Treatment of chronic obsessive-compulsive neurosis by in-vivo exposure: a two-year follow-up and issues in treatment. British Journal of Psychiatry, 1975, 127, 349-364.

Mathews, A.M., Johnson, D.W., Shaw, P.M., & Gelder, M.G. Process variables and the prediction of outcome in behavior therapy. British Journal of Psychiatry, 1974, 125, 256-264.

Meldman, M., & Hatch, B. In-vivo desensitization of an airplane phobia with penthranization. Behavior Research and Therapy, 1969, 7, 213-214.

Scrignar, C.B., Swanson, W.C., & Bloom, W.A. Use of systematic desensitization in the treatment of airplane phobic patients. Behavior Research and Therapy, 1973, 11, 129-131.

Solyom, L., Shugar, R., Bryntwick, S., & Solyom, C. Treatment of fear of flying. American Journal of Psychiatry, 1973, 130, 423-427.

Sours, J.E., Ehrlich, R.E., & Phillips, P.B. The fear of flying syndrome: a re-appraisal. Aerospace Medicine, 1964, 35, 156-165.

Wolpe, J. Psychotherapy by reciprocal inhibition. Stanford, California: Stanford University Press, 1958.

HYPNOTIC TREATMENT OF 100 CASES OF MIGRAINE

Claes Cedercreutz

Hamina Hospital, Finland

Abstract: One hundred cases of migraine were treated under hypnosis with a variety of procedures that included symptomatic suggestions, suggestions related to blood circulation in the head, ego-strengthening suggestions, and situation-specific suggestions. Results of a follow-up, at an average of 11 months, are presented and related to depth of hypnosis during treatment.

In 1893, Hirsch described in detail the treatment of migraine with hypnosis. Since then, the migraine problem has been touched upon briefly in most textbooks (Crasilneck & Hall, 1975; Hartland, 1966; Magonet, 1959; Stokvis, 1955). In 1965, Harding described the treatment of 74 patients. He achieved complete relief in 38% of his cases and a reduction of frequency, duration and intensity of migraine episodes in 32%. In a study by Anderson, Basker and Dalton (1975), 10 of 23 hypnotic patients achieved remission of migraine as compared with 3 of 24 patients who were treated with medication.

Since the beginning of 1974, the author has treated 100 migraine patients with hypnosis. Each patient was hypnotized an average of 3.4 times over a period of from one to two months. Those who benefited from the treatment were kept under observation for an average of 11 months. On the basis of experiences during the course of the treatments, the suggestions were standardized in the summer of 1975, giving each patient four different kinds of suggestions:

(1) Symptomatic suggestions.
"Each hypnotic experience is a step forward. Each time, you sink into a deeper trance. Each time, all symptoms disappear, and if they reoccur, it is after a longer and longer interval; they are lighter and lighter, and their duration is shorter and shorter until they disappear completely after three to five treatments, never to return."

(2) Physiological suggestions.
"The reason for an attack of migraine is the dilation of the artery in your right or left temple. When a blood vessel is dilated the amount of blood passing through the vessel is multiplied many times. If the diameter of the blood vessel is doubled, the quantity of blood is quadrupled. Each time your heart beats, this large volume of blood is pressed up through the blood vessels in your head. The blood vessels that have to sluice the blood cannot cope with this large quantity of blood. The blood vessels are stretched by each heartbeat and it is this stretching that causes the throbbing pain. Finally when the walls of the blood vessels are stretched thin as paper, the serum starts trickling through the walls out into the brain substance. An oedema appears and the brain substance swells, and it is this swelling that causes the nausea and vomiting.

"Your whole body is full of blood vessels alternately contracting and expanding. The blood vessels in the lungs and in the heart expand during daytime when you are in motion but contract during the night when you rest. The blood vessels in the stomach dilate when you eat but, as soon as the stomach is empty, they contract again. The blood vessels of the liver and the spleen dilate during the night when they serve as a reservoir for all the blood that is withdrawn from other parts of the body. Who looks after all these blood vessels? It is your subconscious that regulates them. Since your subconscious is able to attend to all these blood vessels, surely it can also look after the arteries in your temples. Every time the arteries in your temples dilate your subconscious will contract them. To begin with, this process will take half a second, or at the outside, a second and a half; but gradually, it will happen so quickly that you will not even notice it. Naturally, you will neither feel nausea or vomit."

These suggestions are effective. Many patients have said: "Doctor, last week I had a typical attack of migraine. I felt it coming - but before I could feel it, it was gone."

(3) Ego-strengthening suggestions.
"For ten years you have had an attack of migraine every fortnight. You have gotten used to expecting the attack. Every time you decided to do something special, you thought, 'If only I did not get an attack of migraine,' and this thought provoked the attack precisely on the least suitable day for you. Once a thought can provoke an attack it can also prevent it. You have said that an attack is due within a week. It will not come. When a week has passed without an attack you will think, 'If I can be without an attack for a week surely I can be without one for two weeks.' When two weeks have passed without any headache, you will feel certain that you can be without one for a whole month. When a month has passed you will feel certain you can stay well for two months. After two months, you will be convinced that you can stay well for four months. After four months you will feel certain that you are completely cured. Every day you will feel a greater feeling of personal well-being. A greater feeling of personal safety and security. Every day you will become - and you will remain - more and more relaxed. You will develop more and more confidence in yourself now that you do not suffer from migraine any longer. Confidence in your ability to do not only what you have to do but also what you ought to do and everything you would like to do. When someone suggests something agreeable and asks you to join a trip, an excursion, or a visit to a movie, you can immediately make a decision without being afraid that you might get an attack of migraine like before."

(4) Special suggestions regarding smells and situations which act as triggers to provoke the attacks.

Every patient that could be induced into a deep trance (spontaneous amnesia) or into a medium trance (reaction to a suggestion of a stinging mosquito) has, since the summer of 1975, received a tape with appropriate suggestions. The patient was requested to listen to the tape once a week for one month and then less and less frequently.*

---

* When recording a tape for the treatment of migraine, suggestions for removing acute pain must be added or else the patient must be given an additional tape for this purpose. Patients state that they can usually terminate an attack by listening to the tape, unless the attack has lasted so long that they have already begun to suffer from nausea.

The early results, about three months after termination of treatment were quite good: 40% of the patients were symptom free and 18% were ameliorated. A later follow-up, at an average of 11 months after termination of treatment, showed, however, that relapses were frequent. (See Table 1). There was a strong relationship between depth of hypnosis and therapeutic outcome. All who entered a deep trance were either symptom free or ameliorated. Of those who entered a light trance, on the other hand, only one patient got some lasting benefit. Of the 32 ameliorated cases, 6 were symptom free for more than one year, a finding that suggests that a more prolonged treatment might have produced a permanent cure. Of the 28 patients who received a tape, 11 were symptom free and 12 were ameliorated. Only 5 received no benefit from the tape.

Of the 100 patients, 29 came initially for therapy during an acute migraine attack. They were immediately hypnotized and received suggestions against pain and nausea. In 26 cases, the symptoms disappeared in 15 minutes. At the follow-up, 8 were symptom free and 15 were ameliorated.

TABLE 1

Results of Follow-up an Average of 11 Months after Termination of Treatment

Depth of hypnosis	Number of cases	Symptom free	Ameliorated	No effect
Deep	18	13	5	0
Medium	53	10	26	17
Light	16	0	1	15
No effect	13	0	0	13
Totals	100	23	32	45

REFERENCES

Anderson, J.A., Basker, M.A., & Dalton, R. Migraine and hypnotherapy. _International Journal of Clinical and Experimental Hypnosis_, 1975, _23_, 48-58.

Crasilneck, H.B., & Hall, J.A. _Clinical hypnosis_. New York: Grune and Stratton, 1975.

Harding, C.H. Hypnosis in the treatment of migraine. In J. Lassner (editor), _Hypnosis and psychosomatic medicine: Proceedings of the International Congress for Hypnosis and Psychosomatic Medicine, Paris, 1965_. Berlin: Springer-Verlag, 1967. Pp. 131-134.

Hartland, J.C. _Medical and dental hypnosis_. London: Baillière, 1966.

Hirsch, M. _Suggestion und hypnose_. Leipzig: Verlag von Ambr. Abel, 1893.

Magonet, A.P. _The healing voice_. London: Heinemann, 1959.

Stokvis, B. _Hypnose in der ärztlichen praxis_. Basel: S. Karger, 1955

HYPNOTHERAPY IN ASTHMATIC PATIENTS AND THE IMPORTANCE OF TRANCE DEPTH*

David R. Collison

Chatswood, New South Wales, Australia

Abstract: Certain patients with bronchial asthma can benefit, often greatly, from hypnotherapy. This paper presents a retrospective analysis of 121 asthmatic patients treated by hypnotherapy.

All 121 patients were ambulant and non-hospitalized, requiring regular drug therapy (including continuous steroids in 54 cases) and were referred for hypnotherapy. There were 68 males and 53 females with a mean age and range respectively of 27 (8 to 69) and 35 (8 to 73) years.

The individual result was classified as excellent when completely free from asthma with no drug therapy, good if there was 50% or more improvement as assessed by the decrease in frequency and severity of the attacks and drug usage, poor if there was less than 50% improvement, and nil if there was no change.

Twenty-five patients (21%, 19 under 20 years of age) had an excellent response and remained asymptomatic during the period of follow-up (greater than one year in all but two cases). Forty (35%) had a good response, 27

---

* Tables and figure reproduced by permission of the Medical Journal of Australia.

(22%) had a poor response, and the remaining 29 (24%) experienced no change. Twenty-nine (52%) of the 56 with a poor or nil response had subjective improvement in general well-being.

It can thus be seen that hypnotherapy appears to have a definite place in the management of asthma. In order to try and determine which of a variety of factors was most responsible for the improvement, the results were subjected to multiple factor analysis. Six factors were analyzed: age, sex, result, trance depth, psychological factors, and steroid usage (15 variables). The product-moment correlations among all the variables measured were calculated. This matrix was factor analyzed to see whether a simple economical solution could be found for the pattern of correlation, i.e., a hypothetical or conceivable explanation in terms of the small number of causal factors. The matrix was factor analyzed by the centroid method, the highest correlations being placed in the diagonal cells. This statistical evaluation confirmed the clinical impression that the ability to go into a deep trance (closely associated with youthfulness) gives the best possibility of improvement, especially when there are significant etiological psychological factors present and the asthma is not severe. Subjective improvement in well-being and outlook is a potential outcome at all age levels, independent of severity of the illness or entranceability of the patient.

INTRODUCTION

Asthma has been treated effectively by hypnotherapy and although much of the published evidence is anecdotal some controlled trials have been published (Smith & Burns, 1960; Mayer-Loughnan, MacDonald, Mason, & Fry, 1962; British Tuberculosis Association, 1968). The present study confirms that some benefit is to be expected for asthmatic patients treated by hypnotherapy. This report is a retrospective analysis of 121 patients with bronchial asthma who were treated in that manner.

The 121 patients were ambulant and non-hospitalized, and all were receiving medication to control frequent attacks of asthma they had been experiencing up to the time of hypnotherapy. All were referred to the author for this therapy by the supervising physician either on the decision of the doctor or at the patient's request; they were, therefore, a selected group. It is a sequential series over a period of ten years, all patients having been treated by the author by means of hypnotherapy. No preselection on the basis of hypnotizability or suggestibility took place. However, two patients were rejected from treatment by hypnosis, one having severe endogenous depression and the other being schizophrenic; they are not included in the series.

Although all patients were asthmatic, and hypnotherapy was considered a possible means of help for all, there were, in a broad sense, two main groups of patients who were referred. In the first group, referral occurred because it was thought there were significant underlying psychological problems responsible for the asthma; the second group was made up of those taking steroids continuously to control the severe asthma so that giving hypnotherapy was considered a possible way of enabling them either to decrease the dosage or to stop taking the steroids altogether.

A complete history was taken at the first visit with special reference to the psychological aspects and interpersonal relationships. In some cases specific psychological tests were undertaken to assist in arriving at the final psychological assessment of the patient. These included the Sixteen Personality Factor Test (Cattell, 1957), Self Analysis Form, Minnesota Multiphasic Personality Inventory (Hathaway & McKinley, 1943), Fear and Willoughby Questionnaires (Willoughby, 1934), and the Neuroticism Scale Questionnaire and Eysenck Personality Inventory (Eysenck & Eysenck, 1964).

Serial respiratory function measurements (peak expiratory flow, forced expiratory volume in one second, and vital capacity) were carried out.

THE HYPNOTIC TECHNIQUES AND TREATMENT PROCEDURE

The treatment procedure has been described in detail (Collison, 1975). After an explanation of the nature of hypnotherapy, the state of hypnosis was induced and the trance deepened using a variety of techniques. The actual wording of suggestions given in the trance state varied greatly, but in all cases was directed toward obtaining both physical and mental relaxation. Suggestions were aimed at improving the patient's ability to cope with his environment, or, for example, suggestions were given to help the patient overcome his inferiority feelings; i.e., psychotherapy carried out in the hypnotic state using the various phenomena of the trance such as age regression to facilitate such therapy, was routine in all cases. Post hypnotic suggestions of continued relaxation and ability to cope with the various situations in life were given in all instances. Care was taken not to practice symptom removal, i.e., to suggest to the patient that he was not wheezing when obviously he had significant asthma.

Autohypnosis was taught to enable the patient to reinforce the positive ego-boosting suggestions given in the therapeutic session, and to remain in or selectively achieve a relaxed state of calm and ease.

ANALYSIS OF DATA

The individual result was put into one of four classifications:

(1) "excellent" was scored when there was complete freedom from asthmatic attacks with cessation of all therapy during the period of follow-up, during which time the patient was fully active with normal exercise tolerance and respiratory function studies giving results within normal limits;

(2) "good" was scored when there was marked improvement, with either continued attacks which were less severe and less frequent, or with the necessity to continue therapy, but reduced, to keep the patient free from asthma. The separation of this group from the third group was determined by the history of the patient with regard to subjective and objective improvement. Those with 50% to 100% improvement were included under this classification;

(3) "poor" was scored when there was less than 50% improvement determined as above; and

(4) "nil" was the classification when there was no alteration from the pretreatment assessment.

The hypnotic state was divided into three levels: 1) "light," including hypnoidal states; 2) "medium;" 3) "deep" including the somnambulistic state.

In the assessment of the role of psychological factors in the genesis of the asthma, three gradings were used. The first group ("nil") was made up of those in whom it seemed that emotional factors were not relevant to the development and continuance of the asthma. In "Grade 1" there were significant psychological factors but to a degree where the link with asthma was less clear-cut. The "Grade 2" group had clear-cut psychological factors linked to the genesis of the asthma.

The possible role of allergy and a positive family history of allergy was considered. For allergy to be considered present, skin testing with a positive result, or a clear-cut history of allergic reaction to repeated exposure to identified allergen was needed. Steroid usage and dosage were taken as a measure of the severity of the asthma, continuous steroid therapy of high dosage indicating the most severely afflicted.

TABLE 1

Age and Sex Factors in Results of Hypnotherapy

Number of Subjects

Age (Years)	Sex		Result			
	Male	Female	Excellent	Good	Poor	Nil
0 - 10	4	2	1	3	-	2
11 - 20	29	10	18	14	5	3
21 - 30	14	10	2	10	7	4
31 - 40	7	7	3	6	3	2
41 - 50	2	6	1	3	1	3
51 - 60	11	14	-	4	10	11
61 - 70	1	3	-	-	1	3
71 - 80	-	1	-	-	-	1
	68 (56%)	53 (44%)	25 (21%)	40 (33%)	27 (22%)	29 (24%)

n = 121

TABLE 2

Depth of Trance in Relation to Result of Hypnotherapy

		Number of Subjects			
		(n = 121)	Excellent Result (n = 25)	Good Result (n = 40)	Poor/Nil Result (n = 56)
Sex:	Male	68 (56%) (a)	20 (80%)	26 (65%)	22 (39%)
	Female	53 (44%)	5 (20%)	14 (35%)	34 (61%)
Trance Depth:	Deep	43 (35%)	19 (76%)	17 (43%)	7 (12%)
	Medium	47 (39%)	6 (24%)	21 (52%)	20 (36%)
	Light	31 (26%)	0 (0%)	2 (5%)	29 (52%)
Psychological Factors:	Grade 2	65 (54%)	21 (84%)	26 (65%)	18 (32%)
	Grade 1	44 (36%)	4 (16%)	14 (35%)	26 (46%)
	Nil	12 (10%)	0 (0%)	0 (0%)	12 (22%)
Steroids:	Continuous	54 (45%)	1 (4%)	9 (23%)	44 (79%)
	(Dosage in mg of prednisone)		(5)	(2.5 - 10, 5)	(2.5 - 40, 13)
	Intermittent	21 (17%)	2 (8%)	10 (25%)	9 (16%)
	Nil	46 (38%)	22 (88%)	21 (52%)	3 (5%)

(a) Percentages relate to the total in each result group

RESULTS

A retrospective analysis has limitations. Routine recorded data only can be used. However, all the patients had been interviewed by the same person who also did the actual therapy and other investigations (psychological assessment and respiratory function studies).

It was not a controlled trial. All the patients had been referred specifically for hypnotherapy and, except for the exclusion of two patients (one schizophrenic and one depressive), no further preselection took place. Hypnotherapy was never a first-line therapy, but was generally considered either as a possible "cure" or as a means of trying to enable the patient to stop taking steroids, when other methods had failed. It is thus unlikely that the group represents a continuous spectrum of asthma.

The representation of sexes was approximately equal (68 males, 53 females) but with a greater number of young males and a slight dominance of the older females (see Table 1). This could in part explain the excellent results in the males (20 of 25), although overall the younger asthmatics (under 30 years) responded best to hypnotherapy. Fewer of this younger group were taking steroids and were thus less severe asthmatics.

Trance depth and good improvement appear closely related. Of the 65 subjects with an excellent or good result (17 over 30 years of age), only two could not be taken beyond a light trance (see Table 2). This contrasts to the poor/nil group of 56, in which only 27 went into a medium or deep trance, more than 50% going no deeper than the light trance. The average age of this light trance group (with a poor/nil response) was about 50 years, and this is in keeping with the fact that the older age group goes less deeply into the hypnotic state. Peak hypnotizability is reached between nine and 12 years of age, with a gradual decline thereafter (Morgan & Hilgard, 1973), and this could explain the poor response in the older group. However, 17 of those with subjective improvement achieved this from the light trance state and were also mainly older patients.

The role of psychological factors or emotional stress in the genesis of asthma is complex. In practically every patient with asthma there are psychological problems; it is often difficult to ascertain whether these led to the asthma, or have resulted from the asthma. There are wide variations of opinion as to the importance of the role of emotional factors in asthma. It is impossible adequately to measure the former, and the latter, by definition, is a fluctuationg condition, so that the evidence of a relationship between the two can only be circumstantial. Hypnotherapy not only gives phsycial and mental relaxation, but the state of hypnosis and the use of attendant phenomena (e.g. age regression) can be used

TABLE 3

Results of Hypnotherapy in Relation to Family and Presence of Other Allergic Conditions

Result	Number of Subjects				
				Family History	
	Nil	Allergy	Hay Fever Eczema	Asthma	Hay Fever Eczema
Excellent (25)	4 (16%) (a)	20 (80%)	15 (60%)	10 (40%)	8 (32%)
Good (40)	1 (2.5%)	33 (83%)	24 (60%)	22 (55%)	14 (35%)
Poor/Nil (56)	10 (18%)	34 (61%)	25 (45%)	27 (48%)	12 (21%)

(a) Percentages relate to the total number of patients in each result group.

TABLE 4

Intercorrelations Between Variables

Parameter	Age	Sex	Result	Depth of Trance	Psychological Factors	Severity
Age	-	-	-	-	-	-
Sex	+29 (a)	-	-	-	-	-
Result	+50	+31	-	-	-	-
Depth	-66	-35	-60	-	-	-
Psychological Factors	+43	+11	+46	-43	-	-
Severity (steroids)	-48	-38	-70	+52	-43	-

(a) Decimal points omitted

to facilitate psychotherapy. It is therefore not surprising that 84% (21) of those with an excellent response and 65% (26) with a good response showed Grade 2 (that is, significant) psychological factors in contrast to 32% (18) of those with a poor/nil response.

The presence of allergy or the ability to develop hyperactivity as shown by a positive family history of asthma, hay fever, or eczema determines the oversensitivity of the respiratory tract, an integral part of the asthma attack (which is the exaggerated response of an over-sensitive respiratory tract to irritation by an allergen, infection, or other irritant, or emotional stress). It is on this sensitized respiratory tract that emotional stress can act as an irritant (Luparello, Lyons, Bleeker, & McFadden, 1968). A positive family history of allergy, hay fever, or eczema appears to be unrelated to the response to hypnotherapy in this series (see Table 3).

From these clinical data it is apparent that certain asthmatic patients can respond, often very successfully, to hypnotherapy. The younger patient with psychological problems able to enter a deep trance seems to be the most likely to benefit from hypnotherapy, but we cannot be sure about which of the variables is the most relevant to a successful outcome. For example, it appears that both age and depth of trance favorably affect the success of hypnotherapy in asthmatic patients. But depth and age may be linked and the apparent effect of age may then be entirely attributable to depth.

To give some clarification to this problem, the results were subjected to multiple factor analysis. Six factors were analyzed: age, sex, result, trance depth, psychological factors, and steroid usage (15 variables). Product-moment correlations amongst all the variables measured were calculated. This matrix was factorized to see whether a simple and economical solution (that is, a hypothetical or conceivable explanation in terms of a small number as causal factors) could be found for the pattern of correlations. The matrix was factorized by the centroid method, the highest correlations being placed in the diagonal cells (Thurstone, 1947).

The correlations between the six variables (age, sex, depth of trance, psychological factors and steroid therapy or severity) are shown in Table 4. These figures are correct to two decimal places and the decimal points have been omitted. For example: result-depth correlation (r) = -0.604; age-psychological factor correlation = 0.428. These are shown as -60 and +43.

Table 5 and Figure 1 demonstrate what may be two causal influences responsible for the whole pattern of correlation. The first (I') may be interpreted as a factor of trance depth which is closely associated with youthfulness and which is also associated with a considerable amount of psychological causation of the illness. A less severe illness goes along with this factor to some extent as

TABLE 5

Unrotated Factor Solution

Parameter	I	II
Youth	73 (a)	-29
Maleness	44	23
Success of Treatment	80	15
Depth of trance	78	-20
High psychological factors	56	-21
Mild disease	78	29

(a) Decimal points omitted

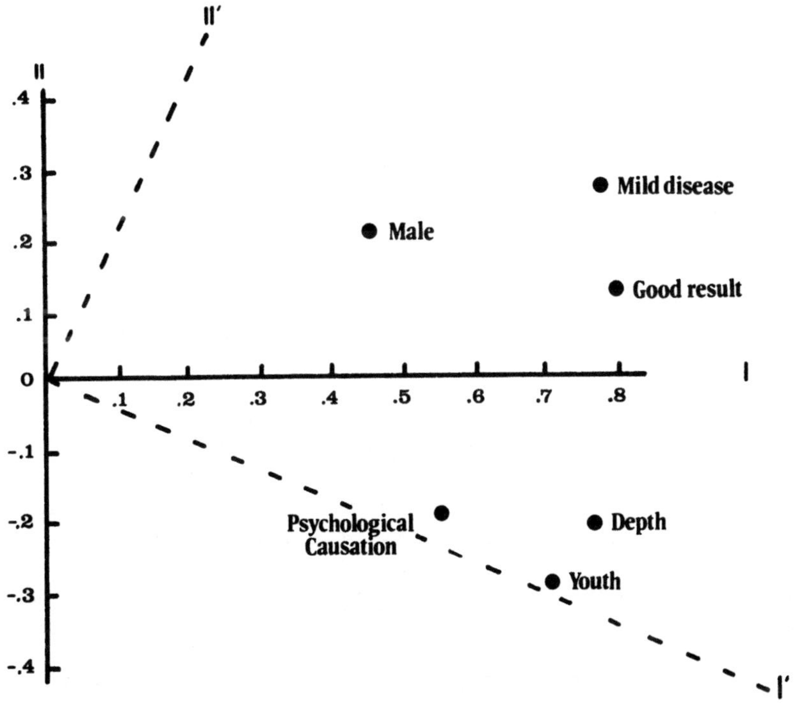

Fig. 1

does the probability of a good outcome to treatment. The second factor (II') is more difficult to interpret. It may be one of "Maleness" as against "Femaleness." It is to be noted that less severe illness and the probability of recovery with treatment are associated. All patients in the study were preselected by referral. Not only were the younger males more common in the series by chance, but it is quite likely that the females happened to be for accidental reasons more severely ill, and presumably as a result, more difficult to cure.

CONCLUSION

It appears that the ability to go into a deep trance, which is closely associated with youthfulness, gives the best possibility of improvement in asthma, expecially if there are significant etiological psychological factors present and the disease is not severe (that is, the patients are not steroid-dependent). Subjective improvement in well-being and outlook without alteration in the asthma is a potential outcome at all age levels independently of severity of the illness or the entranceability of the patient.

The use of these facts to assist in better patient selection for hypnotherapy in the management of asthma has been used in an on-going way by the author with even better results than those reported.

REFERENCES

British Tuberculosis Association. Hypnosis for asthma - a controlled trial. British Medical Journal, 1968, 4, 71-76.

Cattell, R.B. Sixteen Personality Factor Questionnaire. Champaign, Illinois: The Institute for Personality and Ability Testing, 1957.

Collison, D.R. Which asthmatic patients should be treated by hypnotherapy? Medical Journal of Australia, 1975, 1, 776-781.

Eysenck, H.J., & Eysenck, S.B.G. Manual of the Eysenck Personality Inventory. London: University of London Press, 1964.

Hathaway, S.R., & McKinley, J.C. Minnesota Multiphasic Personality Inventory Manual. New York: Psychological Corporation, 1943.

Luparello, T., Lyons, H.A., Bleeker, E.R., & McFadden, E.R. Influences of suggestion on airways reactivity in asthmatic subjects. Psychosomatic Medicine, 1968, 30, 819-825.

Mayer-Loughnan, G.P., MacDonald, N., Mason, A.A., & Fry, L. Controlled trial of hypnosis in symptomatic treatment of asthma. British Medical Journal, 1962, 2, 371-376.

Morgan, A.H., & Hilgard, E.R. Age differences in susceptibility to hypnosis. International Journal of Clinical and Experimental Hypnosis, 1973, 21, 78-85.

Smith, J.M., & Burns, C.L.C. The treatment of asthmatic children by hypnotic suggestion. British Journal of Diseases of the Chest, 1960, 54, 78-82.

Thurstone, L.L. Multiple Factor Analysis. Chicago: University of Chicago, 1947.

Willoughby, R. Norms for the Clarke-Thurstone Inventory. Journal of Social Psychology, 1934, 5, 91-95.

HYPNO-DESENSITIZATION THERAPY OF VAGINISMUS

Karl Fuchs and Zvi Hoch

Rambam Medical Center, Technion, Aba Khoushy School of Medicine, Israel

Moris Kleinhaus

Tel-Aviv University, Israel

Abstract: Fear and anxiety are most important in the production and maintenance of a symptom. Vaginismus, a reaction of avoidance of an anxiety-producing situation, is readily amenable to treatment by systematic desensitization. This may proceed in either of two main ways: "in vitro" or "in vivo." In order to strengthen and accelerate the desensitization process, a hypnotic technique was combined with the above-mentioned methods.

The "in vitro" treatment proceeds with the imagery, under hypnosis, of an "anxiety hierarchy" of increasingly erotic and sexually intimate situations, which are then reproduced at home with the partner. In the "in vivo" method, in self-hypnosis, the patient inserts into her vagina first her finger, then Hegar dilators of gradually increasing size. First the physician, then the patient, and then her partner, members of the therapeutic team, are successively involved in the insertion of the dilators. This continues until the "female superior position" practiced first with the largest dilator is reproduced by the couple at home in intercourse.

With these techniques from 1965 to 1974, complete success was obtained in 68 of 71 patients suffering from severe vaginismus. Follow-up of the 68 patients showed that these couples were leading a normal sexual life with no symptom substitution.

Several authors (Malleson, 1942; Frank, 1948; Masters & Johnson, 1970; Dawkins & Taylor, 1961; Beigel, 1971) interpret the etiology of vaginismus in different ways. As defined by Masters and Johnson (1970), "Vaginismus is a psycho-physiological syndrome affecting woman's freedom of sexual response by severely or totally impeding coital function." Anatomically this clinical entity involves all components of the pelvic musculature investing the perineum and outer third of the vagina. Physiologically these muscle groups contract spastically as opposed to their rhythmic contractual response in orgasmic experience. This spastic contraction of the vaginal outlet is a completely involuntary reflex, stimulated by imagined, anticipated, or real attempts at vaginal penetration.

The treatments most commonly used are: 1) surgical correction under general anesthesia, which was obviously unsuccessful in the majority of cases. We believe that these patients (Graber, Barber, & O'Rourke, 1969) in addition to a perineo-vaginal scar, received an even more pronounced psychological one; 2) psychoanalysis and other insight oriented psychotherapy (very time-consuming); and 3) vaginal dilators of increasing size, with controversial results depending on the context of the procedure.

The authors believe that vaginismus constitutes a medical emergency and should be treated as such. If not secondary to organic dyspareunia, vaginismus is a symptom of faulty psychosexual development which generates a phobic process: phobia to the penetration of a foreign body into the vagina. As Wolpe (1969) pointed out, fear and anxiety are tremendously important in the production and maintenance of a symptom. Vaginismus, being a reaction of avoidance of an anxiety producing situation is readily amenable to treatment by systematic desensitization. We use systematic desensitization under hypnosis as used by Beigel (1971) in male impotence. Systematic desensitization may proceed in either of two main ways: "in vivo" or "in vitro." In both methods we use a basic state of relaxation and feeling of safety in order to prepare the patient for a gradually increasing hierarchy of anxiety provoking stimuli. Item after item is presented and repeated until eventually even the strongest of the anxiety provoking stimuli fails to produce any stir of anxiety in the patient. In the "in vitro" technique the stimuli are presented to the imagination of the patient. In the "in vivo" method real stimuli take the place of the imaginary ones.

In order to stengthen and accelerate the desensitization process we use hypnosis; it is an easy and smooth method of achieving a deep state of relaxation, and visualization of suggested content is much more vivid and plastic under hypnosis. In some cases hallucinations of the suggested scenes and situations can be produced.

MATERIAL AND METHOD

During a ten year period, 1965-1974, we treated 71 women suffering from severe vaginismus. Most of these patients had been suffering for more than two years, and a few for five to seven years. All had been treated previously by gynecologists and psychiatrists for long periods of time without results. A large proportion had undergone surgical dilatation of the hymen and vagina, and several had undergone plastic surgery.

As reported in our previous articles (Fuchs, Hoch, Paldi, Peretz, & Kleinhaus, 1972; Fuchs, Hoch, Paldi, Abramovici, Brandes, & Timor-Tritsch, 1973; Kleinhaus, Hoch, Brandes, Timor-Tritsch, & Fuchs, 1972) the first one or two sessions with the couple are identical for both methods. A careful history is taken in conjoint and individual sessions. Myths and fallacies about sexuality and hypnosis are dispelled. The real involuntary nature of vaginismus is explained with the use of pelvic models and diagrams. Hypnosis and self-hypnosis are discussed as a learning process, and systematic desensitization is explained by describing the analogy of a child afraid of water being taught to swim. The doctor-couple relationship which is established now will have great importance during actual therapy sessions. The couple is asked to refrain from any attempt at intercourse until otherwise instructed. From here on, the approach is different for the "in vitro" and "in vivo" methods, except for the fact that the hypnotized patient will communicate her feelings of relaxation by lifting her right arm, and her feelings of anxiety by lifting her left arm.

The "in vitro" technique, after the first one or two sessions devoted to history taking and forming an adequate relationahip with the couple, proceeds by inducing a deep trance and if possible, hallucinations. An "anxiety hierarchy" is presented to the imagination. A typical stimulus-hierarchy under hypnosis could commence as follows: we ask the patient to imagine herself at the beach or mountain in the company of her husband, in a pleasant and relaxing situation; she is then asked to imagine herself returning home, resting and having a pleasant chat, after which they both feel tired and go to sleep. At the next session, after repeating the initial scenes from the previous session, we start presenting gradually increasingly erotic scenes: "Imagine yourself stroking and kissing your husband"..."Imagine caressing and fondling each other over the whole body while completely undressed"..."Imagine you and your husband undressing and caressing while both of you clearly decide to do just that, without proceeding to intercourse ... you feel good, relaxed and able to enjoy it." Between suggestions it is important to allow the patient enough time to imagine herself, vividly, in the suggested situations. At the next session the previous scenes are repeated and continued; erotic stimuli are increased as they are in the following sessions until the patient is able to imagine full penetration of the vagina by the penis, without fear or anxiety. The patient is asked to reproduce in reality, at home between sessions, the situations with her husband that she imagined during the preceding session. Thus her achievements are continually reinforced in a practical situation. Her self-esteem and self-confidence continually increase. The husband's full cooperation is essential. Intercourse, generally successful at the end of such a hierarchy (8-10 sessions) will continue in the female superior position for the first weeks.

The patient treated by the "in vivo" method is generally hypnotized first with a class of pregnant women learning self-hypnosis for natural childbirth. She is then instructed to practice autohypnosis at home, and while in our office every other day. She is told that gynecological examination will have to be performed during one of the future sessions in order to rule out any organic causes for her dysfunction. This is purposefully delayed until a better relationship with her physician has been established. She generally asks for the examination, and this takes place with the use of a special technique. The patient on the examining table proceeds to self-hypnosis, after which bimanual examination is done with one hand on her lower abdomen and the other only pressing against her vulva without actually penetrating the vagina. After one to two minutes she is informed that "the examination is over," and she is then asked to insert her own finger into the vagina, which she readily does. She is then shown a set of prelubricated Hegar dilators and asked to choose the one comparable with the width of her finger for insertion into the vagina. The physician then asks for her permission to insert it a number of times and in doing so, manages to switch to a larger dilator without the patient's being aware of the switch. She is then asked to check again and again the depth to which she can penetrate the vagina; she is asked to check the depth rather than the width of the instrument. The couple are given the largest Hegar used in this particular session for further "homework;" both will successively carry out the vaginal insertion after the wife's self-hypnosis. Involving the husband as an active participant in therapy provides an important means of deepening their relationship, and of positively conditioning the wife for the early achievement of post-treatment, pleasurable (even orgasmic) coital union. Within 8-10 sessions the patient is able to insert a Hegar dilator 28 with ease, and is asked to insert it in a female-superior position, first in the office and then at home. Following this, she is informed that she may proceed to actual penile-vaginal penetration in the same female superior position, by inserting her husband's penis as she did the largest

Hegar dilator. The husband is asked to be passive and to allow his wife to assume the active role. This generally succeeds and the couple is instructed to continue intercourse in the same position for the coming 2-3 weeks. Being active, the wife automatically prevents the previously dreaded image of an "attacking husband." The self-esteem and self-confidence gained during therapy will be thus further reinforced by successful intercourse. The practical differences between the two techniques are:

(1) deep trance is not necessary for the patient treated by the "in vivo" method; for the "in vitro" technique more rapid results are obtained by a deeper trance, with hallucinations if possible;
(2) in the "in vivo" method self-hypnosis is taught; in the "in vitro" method this is not necessary; and
(3) the husband has an active role - almost a co-therapist's role (team work situation) in the "in vivo" method, being only a willing and collaborative partner in the "in vitro" situation.

RESULTS

By the "in vitro" systematic desensitization method under hypnosis, we were able to deal successfully with 16 of the 18 patients in a relatively short time. One patient who did not achieve full penetration was referred to a gynecologist for further treatment by the "in vivo" technique. Of the 17 patients treated by the "in vitro" technique, we followed up 16 patients for a period of two to three years.

In our series of 54 patients treated by the "in vivo" technique, 53 were successfully treated, and one discontinued treatment after the first few sessions. Of the 53 patients treated by this technique, it was possible to do a follow-up on 49 for a period of two to five years.

On follow-up, all successfully treated patients (in terms of both the "in vitro" and "in vivo" techniques) maintained a normal sexual adjustment, and none showed evidence of symptom substitution. Sixty five patients reported having orgasm in most of their sexual intercourse.

COMMENTS

We believe that hypno-desensitization is the treatment of choice in women suffering from vaginismus; every physician trained in medical hypnosis is capable of achieving good results in this most distressing marital situation. The therapist must decide which of the two methods he feels is the more suitable.

REFERENCES

Beigel, H.G. The hypnotherapeutic approach to male impotence. Journal of Sex Research, 1971, 7, 168-176.

Dawkins, S., & Taylor, R. Non-consummation of marriage. Lancet, 1961, 280, 1029-1033.

Frank, R.T. Dyspareunia: A problem for the general practitioner. Journal of the American Medical Association, 1948, 136, 361-365.

Fuchs, K., Hoch, Z., Paldi, E., Peretz, B.A., & Kleinhaus, M. Hypno-behavioral approach for the non-consummated marriage. Part I "in vivo" method. Journal of the American Society of Psychosomatic Dentistry and Medicine, 1972, 19, 77-82.

Fuchs, K., Hoch, Z., Paldi, E., Abramovici, H., Brandes, J.M., Timor-Tritsch, I., & Kleinhaus, M. Hypno-desensitization therapy of vaginismus. Part I "in vitro" method. Part II "in vivo" method. International Journal of Clinical and Experimental Hypnosis, 1973, 21, 144-156.

Graber, E.A., Barber, H.K., & O'Rourke, J.K. Newlywed apareunia. Obstetrics and Gynecology, 1969, 33, 418-421.

Kleinhaus,M., Hoch, Z., Brandes, J.M., Timor-Tritsch,I., & Fuchs, K. Hypno-behavioral approach for the non-consummated marriage. "In-vitro" method. Journal of the American Society of Psychosomatic Dentistry and Medicine, 1972, 19, 129-135.

Malleson, J. Vaginismus: its management and psychogenesis. British Medical Journal, 1942, 2, 213-216.

Masters, W.H., & Johnson, V.E. Human sexual inadequacy. Boston: Little, Brown and Company, 1970, p. 250.

Wolpe, J. Basic principles and practices of behavior therapy of neurosis. American Journal of Psychiatry, 1969, 125, 1242-1247.

TREATMENT OF ANXIETY AND PAIN IN CHILDHOOD CANCER THROUGH HYPNOSIS

Josephine R. Hilgard and Arlene H. Morgan*

Stanford University, U.S.A.

Abstract: Data from consecutive referrals of 34 patients ranging in age from 4 to 19 years are summarized. Sixteen patients were referred for pain and anxiety in bone marrow aspirations and lumbar punctures, five patients for reduction of pain in short procedures such as intravenous injections and changing bandages, three for relief of continuous pain, and ten for ancillary symptoms such as anxiety. All patients were tested on the Stanford Hypnotic Clinical Scale for Children. For young children aged four to six years, it is usually inappropriate to rely upon formal hypnotic procedures. They respond to a kind of protohypnosis where the fantasy is part of the external situation. Anxiety can be reduced by the use of relaxation and distraction; reduction in anxiety is minimally correlated with hypnotic responsiveness. Once anxiety is reduced, the patient is better able to experience hypnotic analgesia.

After a number of years during which the reduction of pain through hypnosis was studied in the laboratory, with a modest amount of clinical application (Hilgard & Hilgard, 1975) it was determined to extend the investigation to a more controlled clinical setting. A grant from the National Cancer Institute,** made possible a three

---

* The authors wish to thank David Gettinger for his valuable assistance on the project during part of this period.
** This research is supported by a grant from the National Cancer Institute, CA 18325.

year study of the treatment of children with cancer through the help of hypnosis. All research has been conducted at Children's Hospital at Stanford where the full cooperation of the Oncology Unit was obtained. Consecutive referrals of children aged 4 to 20 were accepted, whether the referrals came from doctors, parents, or the children as they heard of the work from others at the hospital.

From the beginning it was clear that the scope of the clinical problems was complex. A child coming to the hospital for the treatment of cancer suffers far more than pain. While the primary interest was in reducing pain, it was evident that several questions beyond the basic one of studying a possible correlation of pain reduction with hypnotic responsiveness had to be addressed.

Anxiety as well as pain is present when a child is in the midst of a disease that holds the threat of death. This was true not only for the patient but for the family members. In addition, anxiety reactions were accentuated by painful treatment procedures that were repeatedly experienced. There seldom were any referrals of a child who had not previously been exposed to such procedures for diagnostic or treatment reasons. Thus it was necessary to use methods of anxiety reduction prior to an approach to pain.

Because of the wide age range of the patients, uniform hypnotic procedures were inapplicable. The usual scales of hypnotic susceptibility are not very useful below the age of seven. It happened that more children ages four to six were referred for pain relief than children of older ages.

For those who are not familiar with the medical procedures in the diagnosis and treatment of childhood cancer, a brief summary is in order.

The most frequent diagnostic procedures include bone marrow aspirations and lumbar punctures. Few children have had experiences which enable them to tolerate the continued invasiveness of needles. Bone marrow aspirations in leukemia, depending on the stage of the disease, may be repeated every six weeks for a long period. Preceding the bone marrow aspiration, a local analgesic is usually injected. The child feels both the needle going through the skin and the brief sting of the analgesic itself. A large needle then penetrates the bone at the crest of the ilium and the bone marrow is sucked out through this needle. Although the skin and surrounding tissues have been rendered insensitive by the local anesthetic, no anesthetic, short of a general one, would be apt to relieve the total pain. In the lumbar punctures, an analgesic is injected first. The puncture itself should not be very painful, but the operation is out of the child's line of vision and for some children this produces more anxiety than the bone marrow aspiration. A frequent treatment procedure is an intravenous injection of medication. Not only may the repeated punctures be painful and frightening to the child, but the material injected may produce burning sensations along the course of the blood vessel.

In addition to these primary occasions for anxiety and pain there are ancillary symptoms associated with the progressive disease, the repeated treatments, and a recognition on the part of the child of the possible outcome. These ancillary symptoms include depression, insomnia, nausea, and the like. There are also wounds to be treated, and bandages to be removed from injured areas. It is evident that the uniformity of controls that are preferred in the laboratory are not possible in a complicated setting of this kind.

PATIENT POPULATION

There have been a total of 44 referrals, with some of the individual children in treatment for several months. Of these 44, three were not appropriate to the project for various reasons set up in advance for exclusion, such as drug addiction and age limitations; in seven cases the child, having been referred by parent or doctor, refused hypnosis. The remaining 34 cases can be classified into four general categories, as follows:

(1) first, 16 of the patients were referred for control of pain and anxiety over bone marrow aspirations and lumbar punctures. Of these, ten were aged four to six, and the remaining six were aged 7 to 13;
(2) a second group numbering five patients was referred for reduction of pain and anxiety in short procedures such as intravenous injections and changing of bandages. They were all in the age range of 9 to 16;
(3) the third group referred for relief of continuous pain consisted of three patients aged 13 to 19;
(4) finally there was a group consisting of 10 patients, 14 to 19, referred for the relief of ancillary symptoms such as diffuse anxiety reactions, depression, insomnia, nausea, and high blood pressure.

CLINICAL PROGRESS

It is evident that one cannot use the same methods with all of these, and it would be inappropriate to use the same criteria for success of treatment, or even to assign the role for success to hypnosis alone when other psychotherapeutic processes are involved.

As the first group, referred for control of pain and anxiety over bone marrow aspirations and lumbar punctures will be discussed in more detail, a few remarks about the other groups will be presented first.

The continuous pain group which would seem particularly appropriate for hypnotic treatment, consisted of but three patients. One was completely refractory to hypnosis and was unable to benefit from it. The other two were highly hypnotizable and able to reduce pain completely within hypnosis, but could sustain this relief after hypnosis was terminated neither through posthypnotic suggestion nor self-hypnosis. One of these had severe ulcers of the mouth and was in the final stage of the disease, a factor which may have influenced the effectiveness of hypnosis; the other had back pain as a result of a tumor pressing on spinal nerves.

The group of 10 with ancillary symptoms, not primarily pain related, were most successfully helped. Of these seven made excellent progress, one substantial progress, and only two were not helped. The relationship to hypnotic responsiveness as measured by the short Stanford Hypnotic Clinical Scale for Children was probabilistic only, with all of those scoring medium or high in hypnosis showing excellent or substantial improvement. The two who failed to improve were in the low scorer group although two other low scorers showed excellent results, one reducing blood pressure, the other learning to relax.

Five patients were referred for help during short procedures not involving bone marrows or lumbar punctures, four for intravenous injections, and one for bandage removal. All were satisfactorily hypnotizable on the scale, and all reduced their anxiety; four of the five obtained substantial to excellent reduction of pain. The bandage removal case illustrates what we have come to expect when hypnosis is fully successful. A high scorer on the Stanford Hypnotic Clinical Scale, this 16-year-old boy found bandage removal a very painful process. He was hypnotized with his eyes closed. The nurse removed the bandage and exposed the open wound on his arm. Presently he asked, "Well, when are you going to do it?" He was incredulous when the nurse replied, "It's already off." He opened his eyes and said, "I don't believe it. Hypnosis <u>really</u> works." He added that he had felt nothing. He had followed the procedure of turning off the switch to the bandaged arm and had been at home comfortably watching a television program.

Now we return to the group of 16 referred for bone marrow aspirations and spinal punctures. There was less success with these cases. Of the two factors operating, age was the first. Among the 16 cases, 10 were aged four to six where standard hypnotic procedures are less applicable. This was shown by the relatively low scores on the measurement scales, a common finding in this age in a population of well children. The second factor overriding all other considerations was the high degree of anxiety prior to the referral. Without exception, these patients were referred after developing severe anxiety as a consequence of previous diagnostic and treatment procedures.*

The youngest children were extremely anxious, least responsive to hypnotic procedures, and with less understanding of what they were experiencing. Their anxiety was evidenced by crying, screaming, and struggling. While there were no outstanding successes with any of them from a hypnotic standpoint, the best clinical result was with one who had proved highly responsive on the clinical scale.

Of the remaining six older children in the group of 16 referred for the bone marrow and lumbar puncture procedures, hypnosis proved feasible for use with four. All scored high on the scale; all came with considerable anxiety, some with a very severe degree.

An example is a 10 year old non-communicative boy, Tony, who had had to be restrained by three or four adults during prior procedures. It was possible to help him by using reassurance and non-hypnotic distraction techniques such as diversion of attention through story telling. He soon was able to tolerate the procedures without restraint, but always maintained a vigilant attitude. He subsequently accepted a hypnotic condition during treatment with consequent pain reduction, first in an intravenous injection, and then in a lumbar puncture. When sufficient rapport had been established to allow testing a month before this successful hypnotic intervention, he scored at the top of the hypnotic scale. Although he was able to use hypnosis in the practice sessions for pain relief, it was necessary for the hypnotist to continue his participation in imaginative activities during the actual bone marrow aspirations.

A number of the patients in this older group are progressing, but it is too early to report on their final result.

PRINCIPLES OF PRACTICE

It is important to specify what was actually done. The standard procedure is as follows. The reason for referral, i.e., the type and degree of discomfort, is discussed with both child and parent, followed by a discussion of hypnosis and the signing of a consent form. After becoming acquainted with the child through attention to his special

---

* These patients were those most severely upset by treatment procedures or they would not have been referred. Thus the sample is skewed in the direction of extreme reactors.

interests and activities such as favorite games, sports, television programs, reading, and fantasies, the short Stanford Hypnotic Clinical Scale for Children (Morgan and Hilgard, 1977) is administered. It is important to give the child a feeling of success no matter what he does, though the older children who fail the tests are apt to realize that they are not having an experience of full participation. This initial determination of hypnotic responsiveness is essential because of the research goals, whether or not it would be useful in the usual clinical practices. Only with its help is it possible to relate the outcome to hypnotic responsiveness, and make some important distinctions between the relief of anxiety and the control of sensory pain.

For those who are referred specifically for pain reduction, but not those referred for ancillary problems such as insomnia, we begin by playing with the child, and training in analgesia is gradually introduced using the "switches in the brain" technique through which sensitivity can be turned off, a technique already successfully used by Karen Olness at Children's Hospital in Minneapolis (1975), and Jane Porter Roark at the University Hospital in Little Rock, Arkansas (1975).

After practicing a couple of times the child is encouraged to use the technique in the bone marrow and lumbar puncture procedures, or at the time of the intravenous injection. When the child is able to use self-hypnotic procedures there are advantages to him, and, of course, to those who are responsible for his care and treatment.

In reflecting on the results so far, these points emerge:

First, for the young child, approximately the age group of four to six, with as always a few exceptions, it is inappropriate to rely upon formal hypnotic procedures. These procedures involve two major elements: (a) the implied difference between voluntary and involuntary action, and (b) the expectation of distraction through self-controlled fantasy. Instead, this group is more responsive to a kind of <u>protohypnosis</u>, in which the distraction has at first been set up in the external situation. That is, the very young child is better able to be distracted by listening to a story or by participating in a verbal game with a friendly adult than by removing himself from the scene through his own fantasy or through reliving an earlier game or experience on his own. Gradually the content of the external stimulation can be altered in such a way that the child achieves the control. From the beginning, the primary goal is to give the control to the child. This technique of distraction works with children who are unable to use formal hypnosis; such a group also includes some of the older children.

Second, and this follows more or less from the first, anxiety can be reduced very successfully by the use of relaxation and distraction methods without any formal involvement in hypnosis. Hence these results will be minimally correlated with hypnotic responsiveness. One reason why some clinicians believe that everyone is hypnotizable, may be because many can be helped to some extent through relaxation alone.

Third, once anxiety is reduced, whether or not by hypnotic methods, the patient is better able to reduce felt pain through hypnotic analgesia.

This is an initial progress report. The results indicate the need for careful research in order to know more precisely what is actually done when hypnosis is used with patients. Others are working in the same field, e.g., LaBaw, Holton, Eccles, and Tewell (1975) and Gardner (1976). Hypnosis is of evident benefit to some fraction of the children, but to avoid disillusionment it is important not to promise too much.

REFERENCES

Gardner, G.G. Childhood, death and human dignity: Hypnotherapy for David. International Journal of Clinical and Experimental Hypnosis, 1976, 24, 122-139.

Hilgard, E.R., & Hilgard, J.R. Hypnosis in the relief of pain. Los Altos, California: William Kaufmann, Inc., 1975.

LaBaw. W., Holton, C., Eccles, D., & Tewell, K. Use of self-hypnosis by children with cancer. American Journal of Clinical Hypnosis, 1975, 17, 233-238.

Morgan, A.H., & Hilgard, J.R. Standardization of the Stanford Hypnotic Clinical Scale for Children. Paper presented at the Annual Convention of the Society for Clinical and Experimental Hypnosis, Los Angeles, October 15, 1977.

Olness, K. Discussions with J.R. Hilgard on the use of hypnosis in children with cancer, November, 1975. Children's Health Center, Minnesota Children's Hospital, Minneapolis, Minnesota.

Roark, J.R. Discussion with J.R. Hilgard on the use of hypnosis in children with cancer, November, 1975. University of Arkansas, Medical Science, Department of Pediatrics, Division of Hematology and Oncology.

THE USE OF AUDITORY DISTRACTION AND MUSIC HALLUCINATIONS IN DENTAL PRACTICE

Per-Olof Wikström

Stockholm, Sweden

Abstract: Not very much is known about auditory stimuli and their importance within the clinical application of hypnosis in dental practice. Yet we do know that stimuli which mean danger (e.g., the sound of the dentist's drill) are factors of great importance when we try to keep the dental patient, who is suffering from fear, calm and relaxed. Sounds are important to psychosomatic pain control and the pain perception threshold. Methods to gain control are discussed in this paper.

Ear-phones built into the dental chair - invisible and unknown to the patient - and delivering a "white sound" have been used by the author. When the patient enters the dental situation, the pleasant sound is switched on and is gradually increased to that level where the fearful noises from the drill and the dental instruments are erased. A study is described which involves one group of patients exposed only to the auditory distraction, and another exposed to auditory distraction in combination with suggestions of relaxation given in hypnosis. The experiences of the patients in the experimental situation are compared with a control situation.

Because many patients are interested in music, this, too, can be used in hallucinatory strategy. Entering deeper trance they can imagine music they love and thereby exclude fearful negative sounds.

The story of this paper begins very long ago. In fact it started when the author first became interested in music and the emotional effects of music on people. Not only do music lovers enter a special altered state of consciousness; almost everybody will more or less be influenced by music and rhythmical sound. Recent studies have found that even hospitalized chronic schizophrenics showed positive changes when they received taped hypnotic treatment with music (Ihalainen & Rosberg, 1976).

Induction is the very "art" of hypnosis. There are probably as many varieties of induction techniques as there are hypnotists and as many sub-varieties as there are subjects. From the days of Mesmer, techniques using rhythmicity, monotony and repetition have been widely accepted, and verbal formulae based on such principles can be found in most textbooks. Yet not much is known about auditive stimulus and its importance in the clinical application of hypnodontics.

We know that sounds which mean danger to the patient, for example the sound of the drill, are factors of great importance when handling a patient who suffers from dental fear. Sounds are important in psychosomatic pain control and the pain threshold. However, there are different kinds of sounds. Most hypnodontists will agree that the roaring traffic outside will not disturb their patient's trance, while sharp sounds from the assistant-nurse handling instruments which mean danger can evoke reactions. The most important sound, however, is that which we produce ourselves - in other words, our voices. Many hypnotists are of the opinion that monotonous wording is the most effective way of inducing hypnosis. The author disagrees. Consider how an actor uses his voice in the creation of a fantasy, and to achieve rapport with his public. It is rarely monotonous. Similarly in hypnosis the inflection, intervals, and tone of voice exert an influence on the results. In the author's opinion what we say is not as important as the way we say it, the tone we use and the music of the speech. Those hypnotists who recognize their inability to paint with words can facilitate their task of bringing about a favorable mind-set in the patient by using music (Gabai, 1968, 1969, 1971).

Both deafness and hyperacuity can be suggested to a hypnotized subject. As he can be trained to hear a sound as uninteresting as a needle dropped on the floor at the opposite end of the room, we might anticipate a more impressive response when combining the hyperacuity with music. Music fascinates many, is loved by others, and seldom leaves anyone uninvolved. For those who cannot enjoy music an apparatus producing distractive sound is useful. Audioanalgesia alone or combined with nitrous-oxide anesthesia was in vogue some years ago, but the use of a tape-recorder and earphones was never very popular in Sweden. A technique was described (Cherry

& Pollin, 1948) in which music was played to the patient while nitrous gas was being administered.

Many patients dislike the syringe but take it to escape pain while accepting dental treatment. One seldom meets anyone who likes the sound of the drill. Even after an anesthetic injection the sound creates a fear for many, because the nature of the drilling conveys information about depth and closeness to the nerve. The result is a tense patient. Freedom from pain and a noiseless environment will provide the ideal setting for dental treatment.

I. AUDITORY DISTRACTION

Method

A new and improved type of equipment for auditory distraction has been studied. It can be described as an acoustic shell with one-way speech communication. A pilot study was carried out with 54 randomly selected patients in two groups, who underwent dental treatment. Earphones distributing "white sound" were built into the head-cushions of the dental chair. Audio-analgesia was achieved with this sound composed of all frequencies within the audiospectrum. This principle was recognized and discussed by others elsewhere (Rothbauer, 1972) but earlier equipment had disadvantages such as fixed uncomfortable earphones, delays because of the time needed for the application of the equipment and instruction, and not permitting the patient to hear the doctor.

This equipment (Figure 1) works differently. The earphones in the head-cushions are connected to an Auditive Distraction Unit which distributes the white sound. When the patient is seated he notices nothing. He believes the large cushions hiding the earphones are meant for comfort. At the beginning of the treatment the white sound is switched on and slowly increased. The doctor uses these few minutes for conversation and for distracting the patient. Without knowing it the patient becomes accustomed to the sound. Thus the acoustic shell is built up around his head by the white sound to a level where the noise from the drill cannot penetrate it. Only the doctor can interrupt it with the help of a small microphone built into the cushion.

The microphone is modulated to the normal frequency of the doctor's voice. An indicator-glow-lamp tells him when it is open. When the operator drops his voice below normal frequencies the microphone will be off. Thus instructions can be given to the nurse without communicating them to the patient. If deeper analgesia is wanted, the white sound can be increased. We believe that the degree of analgesia is related to the pain-threshold which in turn is affected by the fear created by the drilling noise.

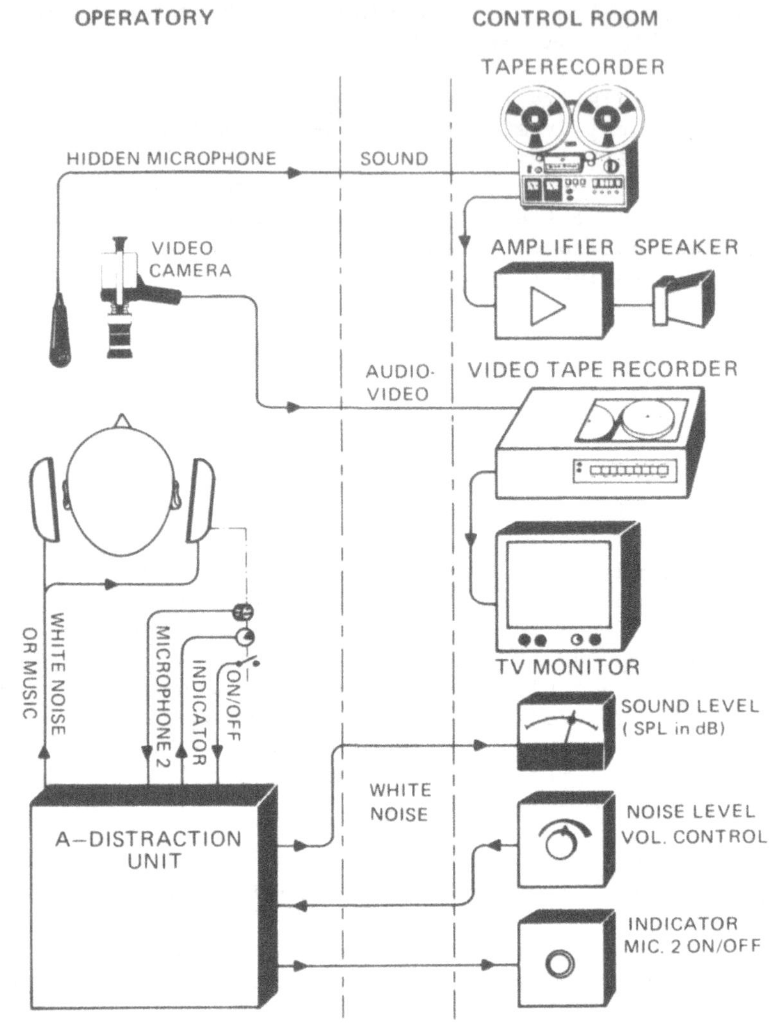

Fig. 1. Scheme of auditive distraction.

When the treatment is almost completed the knob is switched to "off." With variation in the susceptibility of the different patients to sounds, that is, in the limits of comfort, the normal level was found to be 110 decibels. The most sensitive patient did not accept more than 90 decibels. The most suitable length of time for building up the sound to levels of comfort for most patients was determined. It is easy, however, to adjust the apparatus for sound limits, spectral mixture, and microphone sensitivity for communication from dentist-to-patient.

Treatment. From a studio next to the operatory, the technicians with the help of a hidden television camera and videotape could follow and register the reactions of the patients. Answers to questions as well as spontaneous comments from the patients were recorded.

The two groups of patients formed their own control groups. Procedures as alike as possible (e.g. a mesial-occlusal) were carried out on both groups. Those in Group I were first treated with the A.D. equipment only, then without it as a control. This latter is the kind of treatment usually given in a dentist's chair. Patients in Group II were treated first with the A.D. equipment in combination with suggestions of relaxation given in hypnosis, then as a control without A.D. and hypnosis. The hypnotic reactions of the patients ranged from hypnoidal to deeper trance states.

Results

The results are presented in Table 1. After treatment all subjects were asked to compare their experiences regarding pressure, drilling noise, vibrations, and pain in both the experimental and control conditions. "Positive response" means no sensation felt or less sensation felt in the experimental situation than in the control. "Negative response" means no decrease in sensation, or doubtful responses. Two subjects were not evaluated because of technical reasons. No patients in either group were informed of the two parts of the investigation before the treatment started. Under "No comment" in Group II, patients with full or partial amnesia are reported. It can be supposed that this reflects a positive result.

II. MUSIC HALLUCINATIONS

When hypnotized, a patient can be instructed to listen to hallucinated music of his own selection. Even without hypnosis many of us use music to distract the patient and create a favorable mood. The author has tried various ways of combining different sounds, music, and hypnosis. The induction technique found most helpful is Halker's Rapid Induction Technique (RIT) (1975) combined with Ebrahim's Secluded-Room Technique (SRT).

A music-hallucination may require a trance of medium depth. The patient signals with his finger when the sound-hallucination is perceived. Clinically the depth is rather unimportant. Most dentists have their patients trained to enter trance by means of a posthypnotic signal. The sound of flowing water in the cuspidor in the dentist's office is used as a background to the suggestions given, and helps create the music-hallucination.

TABLE I

Evaluation of Dental Treatment with Auditive Distraction, and with Hypnosis plus Auditive Distraction.

	Group I Patients treated with auditive distraction.		Group II Patients treated with hypnosis plus auditive distraction.		
Heard or felt less:	Patients with positive response	Patients with negative response	Patients with positive response	Patients with negative response	Patients with no response
Drilling	20	6	23	3	2
Vibration	26	0	27	0	1
Pressure	26	0	26	0	2
Pain	22	4	26	0	2

The suggested "secluded mental room" will serve as a music box. The following description of the technique is included for those not familiar with Ebrahim's SRT.

> Now when I tell you, but not before, I want you to take a deep breath, and then, when you exhale, hear yourself within you say the word CALM. And feel and see in front of you this CALM will rise like a glass wall. And so - next deep breath, exhale, another wall of CALM to your right. And so - next deep breath, exhale, another wall of CALM to your left. At last let the fourth wall of CALM be created behind you. Thus a room of CALM filled with SECURITY is created around you. You proceed then to exhale with CALM, building your walls thicker and thicker, so that ultimately nothing can break through them to disturb you. You will pay attention only to my voice and what I tell you.

The suggestions are repeated, and when the patient has completed the assignment the dentist proceeds:

> Now concentrate on the purling sound next to you. Listen.

In this way he conditions the patient while he waits. After a while the following suggestions are given:

> If you listen closely, among all the sounds in the purling water you can recognize fragments of music that you love, which will increase more and more, becoming louder and louder until everything has disappeared except the sound of your music and my voice.

The cuspidor has an extra faucet to regulate the waterflow, which can be operated by the dentist. The purling from this facilitates the hallucination of waves when patients choose to imagine a sunny shore or the deck of a sailboat.

The handling of the fear of the drilling noise now begins. It is important not to mention what they are expected "not to hear," such as: "You won't hear the sound of the drill etc." Instead, the wording should be: "You will hear nothing but the music from the water. You will be so involved with the music, so surrounded by it, that nothing can disturb you. Your right finger will rise by itself when you hear your music." When the patient hears the music, he can often be trained to use his finger as the volume-control. This makes it possible for him to increase the music-hallucination until the mental-room is filled with music.

The capacity of the patient to select sounds, that is, not to hear what he does not wish to hear, can be tested by knocking a metal object on a hard surface. If the finger-signalling persists it can be assumed that the suggestions have been effective. Evidently the number of patients with dental fear for whom the noise of the drill is an important factor is great. During the last two years Ebrahim's technique has been tried successfully by the author in more than one hundred cases.

The music selected by the patients is very different, sometimes surprising. The choices in a month cover everything from Gregorian church music to Jimmy Hendrix in Concert. Included among them are Greek dance music, an Air by Bach, two piano concertos by Mozart, Beethoven's 4th Symphony, the Barber of Seville, and Ravel's Bolero. A lover of Chopin produced a couple of waltzes. One patient visualized himself in the town of Ronda in Spain. He loved bullfighting and experienced the colors, the folkloric scenes, the atmosphere, and most importantly the music. Throughout the treatment he was there, all the fearful sound in the dental office obscured by the fiery marches and paso dobles. This was his favorite place, although far from calm and peace.

Comments

Experiencing auditory hallucinations is regarded as somewhat difficult; more difficult than, for example, gustatory and olfactory hallucinations. Consequently rather deep trance would seem to be necessary. However, according to Erickson (Haley, 1967) phenomena of deep hypnosis can often be developed in light and medium trance. The author has therefore attempted to work rather frequently with music hallucinations to combat dental fear.

A couple of patients reported that the sound of the drill penetrated the music barrier. The observation was then made that other sounds, for example a buzzer or an amalgamizer, could not be heard at all even though both were loud and noisy. It seemed that anticipated sounds such as heavy drilling, to be expected from the procedure for a deep filling, were more likely to be noticed than unexpected or new sounds for which patients were still deaf. In keeping with this, the method of testing the patient's response with the noise of a metal object on a hard surface had to be altered. Initially the patient was informed of the knocking test about to take place. Some subjects rather than becoming more deaf would then hear the knocking. This altered when the noise occurred unexpectedly.

Another observation made was that the music barrier was also broken when the grinding or drilling was prolonged over a couple of minutes. This is apparently due to a summation process. However, as the operator can avoid extensive drilling by pausing occasionally, this might not be a problem.

A report of Aldous Huxley (Haley, 1967) is reminiscent of a musical hallucination experienced by a patient some years ago. Huxley noted that it was at first difficult for him to develop auditory hallucinations, and that the attempt to do so made his trance lighter. However, by means of combining various sensory experiences - by attaching so to say an easier one to a more difficult one - he succeeded. His method was to hallucinate rhythmical movements of his body, to create a rhythm, and then to attach an auditory hallucination to it. Some years ago a patient, a young woman who was a good hypnotic subject, was encouraged to concentrate on the faint purling sound of the cuspidor which would keep her steadily relaxed. She was left in the office for a couple of minutes. On my return she was found waving her hands rhythmically, and exclaimed: "No, doctor, let's have a rest." After arousal she reported that she had felt the beat of a monotonous rhythm, that she had seen herself dancing on a Mexican patio to the music of an orchestra, and that the one she had danced with was her doctor. The visual-rhythmical experience stopped when, exhausted, she pleaded loudly for a rest. Without knowing it she had combined ideosensory and ideomotor activity. Evoking the one with the other, she enhanced the effect of each, as Huxley had done.

The importance and power of music has been known since the very beginning of man's cultural development. It is also often used as therapy. A deep experience of music can be described as an altered state of consciousness. This paper demonstrates how we can use music to advantage by combining it with our usual hypnotic techniques for the benefit and enjoyment of our patients.

REFERENCES

Cherry, H., & Pollin, I.M. Music as a supplement in dental nitrous oxide analgesia. Dental Digest, 1948, 54, 455-457.

Gabai, M. Psychosophrologie et musique. Information Dentaire, 1968, 50, 862-864.

Gabai, M. Thérapie par les sons et sophrologie. Information Dentaire, 1969, 51, 2443-2455.

Gabai, M. La détente psycho-musicale. Revue Française d'Odonto-Stomatologie, 1971, 18, 961-967.

Haley, J. Advanced techniques of hypnosis and therapy. Selected papers of Milton Erickson, M.D. Grune and Stratton, New York, 1967.

Halker's Rapid Induction Technique. A syllabus on clinical hypnosis. Swedish SCEH - Investodont, 1975, 18-21.

Ihalainen, O., & Rosberg, G. Relaxing and encouraging suggestions given to hospitalized chronic schizophrenics. International Journal of Clinical and Experimental Hypnosis, 1976, 24, 228-235.

Rothbauer, G. Audio-analgesie. Zahnärtzliche Praxis, 1972, 23, 262-263.

CONTRIBUTORS

John A. D. Anderson, M.D., F.F.C.M., D.P.H.
Guy's Hospital Medical School
London, England

Maurice A. Basker, M.R.C.S., L.R.C.P., M.R.C.G.P.
Leigh-on-Sea, Essex, England

Ronald W. Botto, Ph.D.
School of Dental Medicine
Southern Illinois University at Edwardsville
Edwardsville, Illinois, U.S.A.

Kenneth S. Bowers, Ph.D.
University of Waterloo
Waterloo, Ontario, Canada

Andrée Brisson, M.A.
Hôpital des Laurentides
L'Annonciation, Québec, Canada

Graham D. Burrows, M.D., Ch.B., B.Sc., D.P.M., F.A.N.Z.C.P., M.R.C.P.
University of Melbourne
Parkville, Victoria, Australia

Giancarlo Carli, M.D., Ph.D.
Istituto di Fisiologia Umana Dell 'Universita' di Siena
Siena, Italy

Claes Cedercreutz, D.M.
Hamina Hospital
Hamina, Finland

David R. Collison, M.B., B.S., F.R.A.C.P.
Chatswood, New South Wales, Australia

Rosemary Dalton, B.Sc.
Guy's Hospital Medical School
London, England

Edward Dengrove, M.D.
West Allenhurst, New Jersey, U.S.A.

A. D. Diment
Sydney University
Sydney, Australia

Dabney M. Ewin, M.D.
Tulane Medical School
New Orleans, Louisiana, U.S.A.

Seymour Fisher, Ph.D.
Boston University School of Medicine
Boston, Massachusetts, U.S.A.

Karl Fuchs, M.D.
Rambam Government Hospital
Technion
Aba Khoushy School of Medicine
Haifa, Israel

Ruben C. Gur, Ph.D.
University of Pennsylvania
Philadelphia, Pennsylvania, U.S.A.

A. Gordon Hammer, M.A.
Macquarie University
North Ryde, New South Wales, Australia

H. Clagett Harding, M.D.
Portland, Oregon, U.S.A.

Ernest R. Hilgard, Ph.D.
Stanford University
Stanford, California, U.S.A.

Josephine R. Hilgard, M.D., Ph.D.
Stanford University
Stanford, California, U.S.A.

Reijo Hirvenoja
University of Oulu
Oulu, Finland

Zvi Hoch, M.D.
Rambam Government Hospital
Technion
Aba Khoushy School of Medicine
Haifa, Israel

Beata Jencks, Ph.D.
Murray, Utah, U.S.A.

Reima Kampman, M.D.
University of Oulu
Oulu, Finland

Robert A. Karlin, Ph.D.
Rutgers University
New Brunswick, New Jersey, U.S.A.

Moris Kleinhaus, M.D.
Tel-Aviv University
Tel-Aviv, Israel

Milton V. Kline, Ed.D.
The Institute for Research in Hypnosis
New York, New York, U.S.A.
and
Florida Institute of Technology
Melbourne, Florida, U.S.A.

V. Jane Knox, Ph.D.
Queen's University
Kingston, Ontario, Canada

William S. Kroger, M.D.
University of California at Los Angeles School of Medicine
Los Angles, California, U.S.A.

Germain Lavoie, Ph.D.
Hôpital Louis-H. Lafontaine
and
Université de Montréal
Montréal, Québec, Canada

Arnold A. Lazarus, Ph.D.
Graduate School of Applied and Professional Psychology
Rutgers University
New Brunswick, New Jersey, U.S.A.

John Lieberman, M.A.
Université de Montréal
Montréal, Québec, Canada

Deborah McLaughlin
Queen's University
Kingston, Ontario, Canada

Arlene Morgan, Ph.D.
University of Queensland
St. Lucia, Queensland, Australia

William Nuland, M.D.
Scarsdale, New York, U.S.A.

Campbell Perry, Ph.D.
Concordia University
Montréal, Québec, Canada

V. E. Rozhnov
Central Institute of Postgraduate Medical Training
Moscow, U.S.S.R.

John C. Ruch, Ph.D.
Mills College
Oakland, California, U.S.A.

Michel Sabourin, Ph.D.
Université de Montréal
Montréal, Québec, Canada

Donald W. Schafer, M.D.
University of California, Irvine
Orange, California, U.S.A.

Kit Shum, M.D.
Queen's University
Kingston, Ontario, Canada

Wendy-Louise Walker
Sydney University
Sydney, Australia

André M. Weitzenhoffer, Ph.D.
Veterans Administration Hospital
Oklahoma City, Oklahoma, U.S.A.

Per-Olof Wikström, D.D.S.
Stockholm, Sweden

INDEX

GPSR Compliance

The European Union's (EU) General Product Safety Regulation (GPSR) is a set of rules that requires consumer products to be safe and our obligations to ensure this.

If you have any concerns about our products, you can contact us on ProductSafety@springernature.com

In case Publisher is established outside the EU, the EU authorized representative is:

Springer Nature Customer Service Center GmbH
Europaplatz 3
69115 Heidelberg, Germany

Batch number: 10854269

Printed by Printforce, the Netherlands